Doing Your Social Science Dissertation

Doing Your Social Science Dissertation

Judith Burnett

Los Angeles | London | New Delhi
Singapore | Washington DC

SAGE Publications Ltd
1 Oliver's Yard
55 City Road
London EC1Y 1SP

SAGE Publications Inc.
2455 Teller Road
Thousand Oaks, California 91320

SAGE Publications India Pvt Ltd
B 1/I 1 Mohan Cooperative Industrial Area
Mathura Road, New Delhi 110 044

SAGE Publications Asia-Pacific Pte Ltd
33 Pekin Street #02-01
Far East Square
Singapore 048763

Library of Congress Control Number: 2008936557

British Library Cataloguing in Publication data

A catalogue record for this book is available from the British Library

ISBN 978-1-4129-3112-0
ISBN 978-1-4129-3113-7 (pbk)

Typeset by C&M Digitals (P) Ltd, Chennai, India
Printed by MPG Books Group, Bodmin, Cornwall
Printed on paper from sustainable resources

Contents

List of Boxes, Figures, Tables and Tasks

Boxes

Figures

Tables

Tasks

Introduction: Why Do a Dissertation in the Social Sciences?

Overview

Why do a dissertation?

To have or to be? Your dissertation experience

What does the dissertation mean to you?

- The love of learning
- Career moves
- Broadening your horizons

The benefits of research for undergraduates

How to use this book

- An overview of the book
- Boxes, tables, figures
- Tasks
- Chapter structures
- Overviews
- Summaries
- Discussion points
- Further Reading

Doing a dissertation in the social sciences can be a rewarding end to your degree, rounding off studies with the opportunity to explore more or less anything you want to. A dissertation is all your own work. From the original idea to the final product which is an independently conducted, fresh piece of inquiry, it will be you, and you alone, who will ultimately make all the creative, academic, and editorial decisions. You are the designer, the board room executive, the professor and the D.J. all rolled in to one!

Even so, you might walk away from your first dissertation class feeling a little apprehensive as well as excited. A dissertation is a challenge. After all, by the end of it you will be able to reel off books and ideas as well as the best data sources, who's who in your field of study, and will have your own anecdotes about doing research. Finally, you will have written up your work, submitting a beautifully presented document in its own binding, with a title page, a table of contents, a literature review, a methods debate, data, findings, conclusion and appendices. You will have produced tables and charts, built up quite a long bibliography, and will have had experience of discussing your research and of giving and receiving constructive feedback. Phew! Yes, it's a lot of work, and even the most competent and hard working students will know that the dissertation will find your weak spots as well as allowing you to shine. But don't have preconceptions about how the dissertation will go for you or your classmates. You might be surprised by some of the outcomes, your colleagues' ingenious solutions and great ideas. In turn, you might surprise some of them.

This book is for everyone doing a dissertation. It has been written in the knowledge of the challenges you face, and the aim is to be both supportive and encouraging, as well as pushing you a little. Dissertations are curiously personal documents: no two are the same. They often represent the first real opportunity which you have had to discover something about your own and unique voice as a researcher, and is a chance to mark the intellectual landscape with your footprint. This is at once an exciting and daunting prospect. The aim of this book is to guide you through the process of the dissertation so that you can make the most of the journey rather than become stressed and bored.

Like most things in life, the dissertation is what you make of it. The first thing you have to decide is what you want from your dissertation. What is your attitude towards your dissertation? To decide this, read on.

Research: To Have or To Be?

This book assumes a readership of mixed experience – not mixed ability. Everyone reading this book can do a dissertation. The question is – how well can you do the dissertation, and will you enjoy the journey? Your attitude towards your dissertation will make quite a difference to your experience of doing it.

Erich Fromm, in his book *To Have or To Be?* (2005), argues that people operate largely in one of two modes of self:

1) The having mode: a mode of self which is acquiring, possessing, conquering. In turn this gives rise to other basic feelings and motivations, for example, being jealous (of others' possessions); becoming violent (to achieve having);

2) The being mode: a mode of self which is loving, generous, open, critical and reflexive.

In his book *Successful Study for Degrees*, Rob Barnes (1992) connects Fromm's thinking to studying for a degree. He argues that students' approaches to their studies in the 'having' mode leads them to strive to acquire knowledge. In other words studying is focused on the object (the degree), rather than the experience, so the goal becomes an instrumental one, i.e. to have or acquire your degree becomes more important than living, and learning from, it. The consequences are a different set of attitudes towards doing a degree, and a different approach. On the one hand, there is the process of jumping hurdles and ticking boxes in which the experience never touches the sides. On the other hand, there is a learning mode, in which students become open, honest, critical, well informed, reasoning and engaged. Of course, in practice we should expect that you will engage to some extent with both modes. After all, doing a dissertation is usually a requirement of honours degrees programmes, and it is important to realise that if you are serious about your degree, then doing a dissertation is an essential part of the task of doing your degree. However, in order to do a good dissertation, you will need to develop your interests and should aim to become critically engaged with your line of inquiry.

Doing a dissertation is an opportunity to develop competentcies as a researcher and thinker. Don't assume that you won't produce anything of interest to the academic community. Every year, some undergraduate students do go on to get work published in academic journals. At the time of writing, there are many more outlets for work, including journals and networks specifically for undergraduate research. See Box 0.1 for some suggestions.

Box 0.1   Browse: Undergraduate Research Online

Universitas 21 is a small network of international research intensive universities which provide some opportunities for undergraduates to publish
www.universitas21.com

Geoverse journal publishes undergraduate research in geography at Oxford Brookes University
www.brookes.ac.uk/schools/social/geoverse

The Reinvention Centre at Warwick University publishes an undergraduate research journal
www.warwick.ac.uk

The University of Lancashire has launched a new undergraduate research journal, *Diffusion*, (at time of going to press)
www.uclan.ac.uk

Approaching the Dissertation: What does the Dissertation Mean to You?

'Interesting', 'boring', 'exciting', 'difficult', 'fun', 'an awful experience', 'wouldn't have missed it for the world' are some of the descriptions of doing a dissertation used by students. Before you get stuck into the practicalities, take a moment to reflect upon what doing the dissertation means to you.

You will find that there are many different attitudes, expectations, and feelings towards it amongst your class. For example, the possibilities include:

1) The 'love of learning'

   The likeable aspect of doing a dissertation is that you get to study something of interest to you. You can study it purely because you want to. This is a common reason given by students in the social sciences for doing their dissertation. Student surveys show that students give the subject of study as the number one reason for their degree choice. It seems that most students embark on their studies expecting to enjoy at least some aspects of the experience, and being able to pursue something in depth and develop an independent view is a marker of this. While recognising some of the challenges which lie ahead and possibly feeling trepidation about some aspects of them, many people regard doing the dissertation as an intrinsically rewarding experience.

2) To prepare for career moves

   Employers are keen to find graduates with transferable skills, and many of the skills developed by independent research are precisely those which are sought. These skills include being able to take a line of inquiry and shape a project through to a successful conclusion, on time. Others include being able to find appropriate sources, developing good working relationships with people and organisations, and being able to make a logical argument. Sue Duncan, the first Government Chief Social Researcher, was in charge of social research in the civil service for many years. As part of her role, she developed a graduate recruitment and training scheme, and was actively involved in the selection and interview process. She commented that graduates do not always see the benefits of their degree experience including their dissertation experience. See what she said about this in Box 0.2.

Box 0.2   Sue Duncan on Talking About Your Dissertation

'Employers are looking for evidence of potential; in a competitive job market, applicants need to draw fully on their experience to make their application stand out. Graduates tend to cite disserations purely in terms of the subject matter; if the subject is relevant to the job, they mention it. But a successfully completed dissertation also provides evidence of a number of key competencies, such as critical analysis, written communication, project management and the ability to work on your own initiative. These competencies are key to a wide range of jobs...'

Sue Duncan, first Government Chief Social Researcher and independent consultant

You may be able to use the dissertation to develop an area of present or future professional interest, for example, by developing your awareness of, and insight into an area, problem, policy, organisation, particular social or client group, or, a social issue dear to your heart. It is also an opportunity to apply some of the principles which you have been learning about in the real world.

The research design may necessitate making links with people and organisations and learning about their work and the issues that they face. One aspect of this presented by students who recognise the value of linking their dissertation with their future career moves is the opportunities it provides for developing your own working relationships outside of the university, and being able to find ways of connecting these back up with your learning at university. You might be able to do research which a client group or organisation will be pleased to know about, and you might find that you can make a difference, however small.

If you are already an established employee, then completing your dissertation demonstrates academic ability as well as personal characteristics such as determination and good organisational and time management skills. As a new graduate, you may wish to use your degree study to ask for promotion or to access different kinds of development opportunities at work which perhaps are only open to graduates. You could consider identifying a research project which is of interest to your employer. Alternatively, you might not wish to pursue those ends, but may still find that you have a sympathetic manager who is willing to agree to providing some support towards your studies particularly when you get to the final stages. For example, your workplace might be able to help you to access potential interview subjects (for example, via a staff newsletter or e-bulletin) or might give you some leeway with time off to complete some empirical work (as long as this is not abused).

3) Broadening your horizons and rising to the challenge

Doing a research project allows you to broaden your horizons in academic, personal, and professional terms. There is a balance to be struck between defining your research project so that you can successfully complete it, and ensuring that you build into the project a sufficient degree of challenge, interest, and opportunity.

Dissertations in every subject are demanding. Moving away from being prisoners of the work ethic, we can see that dissertations can still be demanding in a good way, or simply demanding! For most of you, doing a dissertation is an opportunity to take some risks and learn about yourself as well as the world at large. Enlist your tutor's help in setting the bar so that you attempt a manageable project, but bear in mind that reaching for something and stretching yourself is ultimately more enriching than doing yourself a disservice, missing the opportunity and muddling through at the lower end. The idea that what you get out of something is related to what you put into it seems true when thinking about dissertations. See Box 0.3 for some further ideas about the benefits of doing a dissertation.

Box 0.3   What Are the Benefits of Doing a Dissertation?

Deepening and extending your knowledge of your chosen field of study	Developing networks and contacts which broaden horizons	Finding out your strengths and weakness in doing large and complex projects
Thinking on your feet and solving problems with confidence and style!	Developing your career interest and employability	Seeing the world differently; developing your own unique view of the world and the judgements and values which you hold about it
Applying things which you have learnt in your course to the real world	Learning to talk about your own work with confidence; exchanging feedback; learning to take on board feedback	Relating to staff and students in a different way than in taught courses

---

Task 0.1

Discussion Point: Why Are You Doing a Dissertation?

What does doing a dissertation mean to you?

Make a bullet point list arranged in priority order from the reasons which are most important to you to the least important.

How do you think the dissertation will go for you? What do you think will be the highs and lows?

Compare your thoughts with your colleagues'.

How to Use This Book

This book is written in a series of chapters which break down the dissertation into a process consisting of a series of tasks. The chapters broadly tackle these in chronological order. Each chapter starts with an Overview, has a main body, a Summary and a Further Reading section. Chapters contain tables and charts, and there are a few tasks to complete.

To explain further, here is an overview of the structure of the book:

Ready to Research?

This chapter takes you through a reflection upon your preparedness to research, helping you to think through your attitudes to study at this stage in your degree programme. In practical terms, the chapter emphasises:

- Getting organised
- Brushing up the study skills you will need for the dissertation
- Your dissertation team: getting your people behind you

You are asked to identify what actions you need to take in order to make sure that you are ready to research.

Great Expectations

This chapter will help you to see how doing a dissertation fits into your degree programme. Doing social research is valued as part of doing a degree in the social sciences. Learning how to do it, how to talk about it, and how to write it up, are all invaluable skills and rewarding experiences in their own right.

The chapter also provides a debriefing on dissertations, beginning with a typical dissertation structure and its main sections. This will allow you to develop an overview of the project and what's involved in the production process.

Next, the chapter considers what makes a good dissertation in the examiners' eyes, and explores a marking scheme. Finally, the chapter looks at the relationship between you and your supervisor.

Defining the Research Question

This chapter takes you through the process of selecting a theme or topic, and turning this into a focused, manageable, and clearly defined research question.

The chapter begins by considering ways of generating possible research topics using mind maps and brainstorming, and then moves to consider how to choose between them.

You are then asked to consider the difference between a *theme* or topic area, and a research *question*. This is followed by a tips list of common pitfalls in defining a question.

What Kind of Researcher Are You?

This chapter considers the possible answers which you could give to the question: what kind of researcher are you? The question relates to your view of truth and knowledge; ways of thinking about what they are and how they might be established.

The chapter considers the place of empirical research and positivism, inductive and deductive approaches, and considers different perspectives on the scientific method. The chapter next considers how this translates into the personal stances of researchers, giving some examples of how academics of different kinds have thought about their role, and what thinking and writing means to them.

The chapter isn't a comprehensive guide to this complex, philosophical area. Rather, the aim is to provide some signposts which you should investigate under your own steam, according to your needs and interests.

Writing the Research Proposal

This chapter takes you through the process of writing the research proposal. You should draft a proposal, however roughly, as part of reading this chapter. It is suggested that designing, proposing and writing the research project is a process of going back and forth between the different parts of the proposal. Most proposals benefit from an investment of time being spent on them.

Finding Resources and Doing the Literature Review

This chapter turns to preparing a literature review. The chapter explores the purpose of the literature review and gives some tips on producing a good one. This includes working with a range of sources and different ways of finding and accessing them, such as via online gateways and sources. The chapter encourages you to critically evaluate the usefulness and reliability of sources. Next, the chapter turns to consider how to build up the literature review, providing some tips on linkages, giving the review some pace, and referring you to Chapter 12, for further thoughts about grammar and English for academic purposes.

Research Design

In this chapter, we consider research design and how this can help you to achieve your project, beginning with some common pitfalls and then moving on to consider key concepts such as validity, reliability, generalising and triangulation. Next, the chapter identifies the characteristics of a good research design before examining the diversity of possible approaches to doing a research project. These are: Case Studies; Surveys; Grounded Theory; Narrative Research; Ethnographies; Action Research; Theoretical Explorations; and Comparative Approaches. After this, we refresh our memories about qualitative and quantitative methods, both their strengths and weaknesses and their vexed relationship. Qualitative and quantitative methods: combination or separation? The big debate!

Collecting Data: Quantitative Methods

This chapter focuses on quantitative methods. The larger part of the chapter deals with surveys, and includes using secondary sources and doing your own surveys and the different kinds of sampling techniques available. There is a discussion about how the different mechanisms for administering surveys, such as by post or phone, will affect the sample as an example of the more general problem of bias. Following this, we move on to designing questionnaires, including a detailed section on setting questions and some tips on making your questionnaire attractive and easy to use. Finally, other quantitative methods are considered, particularly tally or score sheets, which are a quick and easy way to collect data in an unobtrusive way.

Collecting Data: Qualitative Methods

This chapter focuses on mainstream qualitative techniques, based on a framework of biographical inquiry and lived experience. Suggestions of good examples are made under each section which explore in turn, using documents: life histories; oral history; and data collection for these by interviews. Guidance on doing both one-to-one and group interviews is provided alongside discussions about structured, semi-structured and focused techniques. Another form of data collection is considered, that of time budgets, logs, and diaries which allow for detailed record-keeping, often by the research participants themselves. Finally, the chapter considers visual methods.

This chapter, like Chapter 8, explores a rich area, and does not seek to be comprehensive. There are suggestions throughout of possible avenues for further exploration and more detailed texts, as well as additional suggestions under Further Reading at the end of the chapter.

Carrying Out the Research

This chapter considers the nuts and bolts of doing research, taking you through the various stages such as actually finding your research respondents, including those hard-to-reach people, such as the disadvantaged and elites. Following this, how to manage the research relationship is examined with tips on relationship maintenance, money, gifts, and what to do about being cast in the role of expert and asked advice.

The next section looks at safety and the researcher, with some suggested *Do's and Don'ts*, before moving on to consider how best to manage the research by keeping track of it as a project. Without needing to do anything overly complex, keeping a running log of completed and outstanding tasks is recommended.

Finally, the chapter raises the issue of doing research in real life, and foregrounds the need to stay flexible, go with the flow, make adjustments, and keep it real.

What Do I Do with All the Data?

This chapter begins by considering when it is time to stop collecting data, and the next steps to take in response to that frequently asked question: What do I do with all this data?! The chapter will briefly survey the coding of both quantitative and qualitative data and making an analysis, including a brief overview of the main principles of making sense of quantitative data by bringing variables together using statistical techniques. Examples of interpretations of qualitative data are also given. The section that follows briefly refers to using software for quantitative and qualitative data analysis, before moving on to consider negative evidence i.e. the significance of omissions in data, before finally turning to the question of the relationship between qualitative research and numbers.

Drawing Conclusions and Writing Up

In this chapter, we finally turn to writing up. A core task is to work towards drawing conclusions which are based on the preceding dissertation. In this chapter we look at what goes where in a dissertation; what a good conclusion looks like; and how to produce a dissertation draft which is interconnected, moves at a pace, and covers all the bases. Specific issues in writing up include guidance on managing the process; some tips on making the material read well; on good grammar and using English for academic purposes; avoiding plagiarism; and finally, 'knowing when to stop'.

Troubleshooting

This is less of a 'chapter' than a quick reference guide, the theme of which is 'what to do when things go wrong'. This troubleshooting section looks at issues such as word counts which are the wrong length; adjusting your research design to scale up or down; problems of access and so on.

Appendices

- Appendix 1
  This is a listing of online sources mentioned in this book, to inspire your successful browsing.

- Appendix 2
  This consists of a readability index, a fun and insightful guide to the readability of texts, useful in the contexts of populations who do not read as easily as might be expected.

- Appendix 3
  This is an example of a template for a consent form, showing the items typically found in one.

Glossary

This is a quick reference guide to definitions of many of the key concepts used in doing a research project.

Guide to Study Aids

Here is a guide to the study aids in each chapter:

- Boxes, tables, figures

  These present useful summaries, checklists, and signposts to potentially useful sources.

- Remembers

  'Remembers' are a few lines or short paragraphs which repeat a vital point.

- Tasks

  The optional tasks for completion present you with the opportunity to check your understandings and reflect a little. Some provide discussion points, some are geared towards working on your own and others towards working in pairs.

- Overview

  Each chapter begins with an Overview which gives a brief rundown of the chapter's contents.

- Summary

  The Summary appears at the end of the chapter and repeats the main points made.

- Further Reading

This is the last section of every chapter. Suggestions made under Further Reading are in addition to those made in the main body of the chapter. They are a mixture of introductory level material, survey texts and more specialised, in-depth texts.

Summary

- You will find that students in your class do dissertations for a variety of reasons in addition to needing to meet course requirements. Common ones tend to be for the love of learning; to further career opportunities; and to broaden their horizons. Task 0.1 will have revealed many more

- Independent research has a special place in the undergraduate curriculum, providing opportunities to synthesise your learning across your degree programme and allowing you to delve into areas of interest in greater depth

- Attempting the dissertation provides many challenges and most students find it a worthwhile experience in the sense of learning something from doing it. There are also clearly defined benefits which you could familiarise yourself with, and remember when the going gets tough!

Further Reading

Barnes, R. (1992) *Successful Study for Degrees*. London: Routledge.

Levin, P. (2005) *Excellent Dissertations!* (Student-Friendly Guides series). Maidenhead: Open University Press.

Rudestam, K.E. and Newton, R.R. (2001) (2nd edn.) *Surviving Your Dissertation: A Comprehensive Guide to Content and Process*. London: Sage.

Slibergh, D.M. (2001) *Doing Dissertations in Politics: A Student Guide*. London: Routledge.

Chapter 1

Ready to Research?

Overview

Know what you are aiming for: track down previous students' dissertations and have a good look at them

Getting organised:

- Filing
- A place to work
- Making a project plan
- Managing by objectives: smarter planning
- Bibliography: start early

Working practices discussion

Study skills

Procrastination

Skill sets and skill set boosters:

- Academic writing skills
- Methods and methodology
- ICTs and typing
- Numeracy and statistics

The dissertation team and working as part of a group

Ready to Research?

This chapter takes you through a process of reflection upon your preparedness to research, helping you to think through your attitudes to study at this stage in your degree programme, and getting organised. The main purpose of the chapter is to provide you with lots of ideas and checklists which you can use or ignore at your discretion. The aim is to raise your awareness of what is involved in doing a dissertation, and to provide some concrete suggestions for things to do and think about which will support your efforts as you go along.

In practical terms, the chapter emphasises:

- Getting organised

- Brushing up the study skills you will need for the dissertation

- Your dissertation team: getting your people behind you

You are asked to identify what actions you need to take in order to make sure that you are ready to research.

The first and most important thing to do is to look at previous students' dissertations and develop a clear idea of what you are aiming at as detailed in Task 1.1

Task 1.1

Look at Previous Students' Dissertations

Ask to look through some undergraduate dissertations. If you are lucky, you will find some out on open shelves in the library that you can browse at your leisure. However, you may find that previous dissertations are kept by your department or tutor. In any case, ask your tutor for suggestions about good ones to study.

Look at the physical layout and presentation of the dissertation. Feel the quality of the binding; observe the layout including the title page and the abstract, and check out the table of contents. Understand the overall size or weight of the dissertation; look at the tightness of the referencing in the text and the length of the bibliography at the end; and check for examples of how data has been presented, example, tables and interview extracts. Do take time to read a few sections to develop a sense of the density of the text.

What makes a good dissertation good? List its best features.

Remember three things:

1) This is the final product – this is what you are aiming to produce.
2) This is what a good dissertation looks like.
3) Your dissertation will one day sit alongside the others.

Managing Your Dissertation

Dissertations flow from personal choices and individuals' original work and ideas. However, in order to successfully carry it off, you will need to get organised. Start as you mean to go on, and develop good working practices which will allow you to complete your dissertation to the best of your ability.

Getting organised is an essential first step – staying organised is the second! Being well organised will substantially impact the quality of the research that you are able to do.

The benefits of being well organised throughout your project are:

- The time saved (for example, from searching for lost items) and the quality time which can be carved out from your busy life as a result (for example, having the time to sit down with the data and work with it in a calm and collected manner)

- Having time to think about and bring the project together, for example to synthesise data, or juxtapose different aspects of your work in ways which had not originally occurred to you

- Keeping good records, including bibliographies, from early on will allow you to complete the otherwise endless and time-consuming tasks of checking quickly and easily and will reduce your risk of losing easy marks through errors and omissions

- It will enable you to execute your data collection in a systematic and effective way. It will prevent developing bad working practices, such as having to repeat the steps of carrying out the research

- Last but not least, being well organised allows you to relax into your project and get the most from the experience. Students sometimes say that they find the academic work challenging but enjoyable. But this enjoyment is spoiled by arriving somewhere late and flustered, finding that you have left your things at home, and with only a few vague questions lined up to ask your smiling participant with you realising that you have missed a great opportunity

---

Figure 1.1 **Get Organised!**

Task 1.2

Getting Organised – Essentials Checklist

Make sure that you have at least some if not most of these in place (you might need to keep some of these things in hard copy form as well as on your PC):

- A project file – keep all of the materials you need to manage the project in this. Don't use this file for the content of your project. It should contain a list of the tasks which you have completed and what you have left to do. It should also contain other information such as contact details, including a specific section for your respondents

- The unit or module guide prepared by your tutors

- The regulations and requirements of the dissertation, including word length, presentational style etc.

- The marking scheme

- Your research project proposal, i.e. the document setting out your research question, rationale, methods, first initial reading, bibliography

- Your research project plan, i.e. a paper version of the timetable and the major landmarks of the project. Note: if you have used spreadsheets for this, prepare an easy to read 1–2 sides of A4 which give a snapshot of the project in its entirety with key dates highlighted

- A spare copy of the consent form

- Leaflets and print-outs from websites of interest, such as library, museum or archive details including opening hours; online reservation details

- A listing of books and papers reserved or ordered, tick them off once obtained

- A file or two for handwritten notes from papers and books

- A separate file for each kind of data collected from subjects, e.g. one file for survey data, another for interview data

- Keep a bibliography as you go along – do not wait until the end of writing up to construct one. You might want to do it the old-fashioned way using a card index and box or software such as EndNote

Box 1.1   Tips: Time and Space

- Identify a key place in which you are going to work on your dissertation. If possible, find a table on which you can leave papers and books undisturbed between work sessions so that you can pick up tasks without having to get everything out each time. Clear a shelf and cupboard space specifically for storing things to do with your dissertation

- Find a quiet corner in the library which you can commandeer at key times. You may also find that locating an anonymous café away from other students will give you some space to read or think while eating

- Try not to work in a mess; clean up after a work session, and make your environment one which is pleasant to return to. A friendly muddle is different from a mess

- Make sure that you have adequate light, both natural light from a window and room lighting including a table lamp

- Consider in advance whether you would benefit from staying elsewhere for a few days during your dissertation write-up, for example, with friends or family. Beware that you may need to access library and other sources including a tutor, however, and that staying with other people can be demanding! So you will need to carefully plan your sojourn, but this might be a possibility to think about

Understanding the Dissertation Task: Making a Project Plan

Dissertations typically go through a series of stages. It is strongly advised that you develop your own project plan. Clearly identify each task involved and allocate some time to it. Doing this will allow you to develop an overview of the dissertation in terms of:

- The scale of the task

- The steps which you will go through

- A rough chronological order

Here is a list of the typical tasks which you might encounter:

- Analyse project; decide on primary purpose and audience; choose topic

- Whittle away at the topic so that it becomes a more narrowly focused research question rather than a broad issue or topic area

- Set aside library time; develop searches on your theme

- Send for materials needed from Interlibrary Loan

- Do background research, narrow topic further or rework question in the light of your searches

- Decide on research questions and a tentative hypothesis

- Start working on bibliography; begin tracking down sources in a purposeful manner, following leads found in the bibliographies of the texts which you are reading

- Begin to develop a research proposal: make a template document for each of its constituent parts

- Begin reading some methods texts: decide on an approach to your project and begin to develop a critical view of your project

- Consider the need for statistical data: gather or develop graphs and any other visuals needed

- Develop working thesis and rough outline of a research design

- Work up your research proposal, checking carefully for its internal consistency: will it give you the data which you need? Is it a manageable project given the constraints of time that you have?

- Data collection: as necessary, conduct interviews, make observations, or distribute and collect questionnaires

- Data coding, analysis and interpretation

- Read and evaluate further sources

- Draft explicit thesis and outline

- Prepare first draft of the dissertation, including visuals

- Obtain and evaluate critical responses to your draft

- Revise draft

- Prepare and check your bibliography

- Edit and revise draft; craft the text; use spellchecker

- Prepare final draft, including all of its components such as title page, abstract and so on

- Do final proofreading

Your final project plan would normally be structured chronologically in the phases and thus tasks of the project. You can choose how detailed a project plan you want – some people prefer to make very detailed ones indeed, as shown for example in Table 1.1, Example of an Entry from a Detailed Project Plan: this is more like a series of 'To Do' lists.

Table 1.1 **Example of an Excerpt from a Detailed Project Plan**

Phase	Tasks	Sub-tasks	Time
Identify research problem	Generate ideas	Brainstorm with peers	2 hours
		Use internet	2 x 2.5 hours
		Go through old files and notes from courses done so far	3 hours
	Research initial topics	Using internet database, identify some recent articles	1 hour
		Read and take notes from articles	4 hours
		Start bibliography	15 minutes
	Turn topics into research problems	Mind maps	2 hours
		Discuss in class	Class session
		Draft some rough questions	1 hour
		Discuss with supervisor	30 minutes
		Present to class	Class session

There is nothing wrong with the approach shown in Table 1.1, although it isn't for everyone. The advantages of this are that it splits tasks down into manageable bite sizes. However, many people will make the size of the unit larger; for example, they might have 'Brainstorm ideas' as one task, and 'Turn idea into a research question' as a different task. This is fine too. However, be careful of making the tasks too big. For example, defining a task as 'Doing the literature review' is too big a task; it needs to be broken down a little more.

In effect you are using your project plan to set goals. In terms of effective goal-setting, it is often suggested that good goals are much easier to reach if they are split down and made manageable. Based on Drucker's (1954) ideas of Management By Objectives (MBO), the mnemonic SMART (which more recently has been amended to SMARTER) (see Figure 1.2) is a useful way to check that the goals, or dissertation tasks, which you have set yourself are achievable in a reasonable time limit. You might learn that you consistently overestimate how difficult something will be but underestimate how long it will take you which will give you a clue in working out how long something will take you in the future.

S Specific, fixed
M Measurable
A Achievable, do-able, manageable
R Relevant or realistic
T A set time – with a clear beginning and end
E Evaluated, exciting
R Recorded and reviewed

Figure 1.2   **Mnemonics: Management by Objectives (based on Drucker, 1954)**

Task 1.3

Draft a Project Plan

List the tasks which you need to do over the next few weeks. Break them down into manageable sizes, bearing in mind the amount of work involved and how easy or difficult it will be for you to do it. Check your tasks, treating them as objectives: are they SMARTER?

The Bibliography: Start It As Soon As You Can

A common but unfortunate pitfall is to leave the bibliography until the end. However, you need to start your bibliography as soon as you can, and maintain it throughout the project. Students doing their dissertation often underestimate the importance of doing this. One of the reasons is making the assumption that you can wait until you are writing up before compiling the bibliography – rather as you would when writing up an essay or case study.

But bibliographies for dissertations are much longer and more complex, and you will do the project over a much longer period of time than you spend on an essay. Waiting until late in the day will turn preparing the bibliography into quite a task, possibly quite a difficult one. You will find that you don't want to take on that task the night before the submission deadline. It will be difficult to compile your bibliography in one attempt; you will find that you will need to check some things, however careful you have been in keeping your bibliographic details.

Bibliographies are usually maintained in two ways:

1) in hard copy form, using a card index system;

2) using software which will capture your referencing.

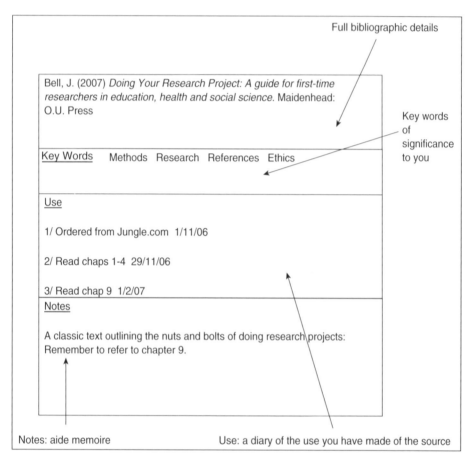

Figure 1.3   Example of a Card Index for Bibliographies

In both cases keep a list which can be printed out from time to time for checking and don't be surprised if you find things falling off the list, however carefully you work with software or cards. Figure 1.3 sets out the details which you need to keep. Do check which referencing system you will be working with (e.g. Harvard) and make sure that you know how to use it!

Task 1.4

Begin Your Bibliography

- Decide whether you are going to use card indexes or software
- Decide on the information which you are going to record and how and when (for example, the frequency with which you will do this)

- Make a couple of entries, so that you can say that you have truly started
- Don't forget to maintain the bibliography as you go along. Don't wait until the end of the dissertation before trying to construct one

Review Your Working Practices

Starting out on your dissertation gives you an opportunity to reflect upon the working practices you have developed as a student. Useful or painful? Only you know!

At this stage, it is worth taking a moment to reflect upon your approach to tasks, especially relatively large or complex ones. You will already have a sense of how you work, for example, whether you tend to hurry or prevaricate, but it is often interesting to ask other people (whose judgement you trust) what their perceptions are. Stella Cottrell's CREAM strategy offers five planks to cling to in the sea of imponderables which surround this kind of reflection. You can use these planks as jumping off points to focus your attention. See Figure 1.4 for a brief description of each element. Consider whether this applies to you as you read through them.

Study Skills As Working Practices

Many students get along quite well until their final years. However, the final year can bring an additional loading which presents a challenge, especially if by this point you are striving for a good degree or are concerned about your underachievement. Strategies which until then have worked well become less effective. A classic method is the 'all-nighter', a tactic of many a student in assessment systems which require a combination of sustained effort and last minute cribbing. This is an effective way of working quicky and can help you avoid distractions. On the other hand, many students arrive at the final year having never done all-nighters, preferring to stick to a 9–5 model. This is an effective way of sustaining your effort over time. In the final year, you might find that you need to change your behaviour and do a bit of the opposite approach. Night owls might find that they have to travel to libraries in the daytime, while the Fordist day workers might benefit from going the extra mile of an evening. You may need to be prepared to experiment with whichever approach you don't normally do.

Try the 'True or False' questions in Table 1.2 to reflect upon how your skill set is coming along. Use the final column to work out how important this is to you to deal with. What top few issues would it be helpful for you to address? The reasons for your selection will be personal and specific to your previous experiences and current circumstances.

C Creative

By this, Cottrell means be creative in how you approach your work, don't worry about doing things your way – and developing your way of doing things.

R Reflective

By this, Cottrell means being able to learn from your experience by carefully considering what happened and why, and evaluating what you learned and how you might be able to apply it in the future.

E Effective

By this, Cottrell means getting ready to work both mentally and physically, so that you can sit down and get on with it. Rather like cooking a meal, you need to make sure that you have all the ingredients to hand before you start and have set aside enough time to do the task.

A Active

By this, Cottrell means getting and staying engaged. Be interested in what you do and go the extra mile to feed your interest.

M Motivated

By this, Cottrell is asking you to work out how you are going to keep going. Be clear within your own mind about what you are trying to achieve, and your own reasons for doing it. Irrespective of whether you are racing along or have hit heavy water, remember to look up and hold on to your objectives and dreams.

Figure 1.4   **The CREAM Strategy**

Source: Based on Cottrell (1999: 49)

Skill Set Booster: Academic Writing and Critical Thinking skills

It is never too late to boost your academic reading and writing skills. They should be pretty good by the time you have reached dissertation level, and you might find some basic texts and exercises *too* basic. Even so, it is likely that there will be:

- Areas for improvement: speed, facility, finesse

- Gaps of knowledge: you know most things about most things but not everything about everything

There are some suggestions about academic reasoning and writing books under Further Reading at the end of this chapter which you might like to peruse.

Table 1.2   **Your Skill Set: True or False?**

Question	True	False	Priority
I can type reasonably quicky			
I am confident when using I.C.T.s			
I can connect material I learned on one course to material I learned on other courses			
I know how to introduce and discuss academic ideas and other people's writing			
I regularly read the broadsheet press and a few key magazines and am reasonably well informed about current affairs, the arts, and sciences			
I am purposeful in my reading and writing			
I am familiar with academic conventions and manage academic reading and writing fairly quickly and easily			
I have a clear idea of why I am doing a dissertation and what I will get out of it			
I work well with people as part of a group			
I have reliable study habits: I know what works for me and can manage blocks of work effectively			
I can evaluate the strengths and weaknesses of various sources			
I can source and sift information appropriate to my line of inquiry			
I am comfortable with statistics. For example, I can manipulate and present data using a range of techniques			
I have strong spelling and grammar, and an excellent vocabulary			
I work out the order of work according to the priority of each task			
I check what is required of assessments of every kind, including the dissertation			
I am reasonably competent with my university's systems, for example the inter-library loan system			

Box 1.2   Academic Writing Skills and Finding a Good Book

The key to good writing for most people is reading. Read as much as you can, and as broadly as you can. However, see Chapter 6, *Finding Sources and Doing the Literature Review* and Chapter 12, *Drawing Conclusions* and *Writing Up* for tips on specifically improving your writing skills, and remember that writing for academic purposes is a particular kind of writing.

   Meanwhile, here are some ideas for finding a good book, which might be related to your studies or read just for interest:

The American Indian Resource Directory includes short oral stories which have been written down
www.indians.org/Resource/natlit/natlit.html

The Bartleby site contains all manner of on-line books
www.bartleby.com

The Commonwealth Writers' Prize: the annual prize for short-listed books from Africa, Europe and South Asia, the Caribbean, Canada, South East Asia and the South Pacific. Look under Culture and Diversity for listings, links, and reviews
www.commonwealthfoundation.com/

The Internet Public Library
www.ipl.org

The Man Booker Prize website contains listings and reviews of books
www.themanbookerprize.com/

The Nobel Prize for Literature which is awarded for work of an 'idealistic' nature, The website contains all past winners with links to their books
nobelprize.org/nobel_prizes/literature/

The Orange Prize for Fiction website contains listings and reviews
www.orangeprize.co.uk/home

The TIME Magazine best 100 English language novels since 1923 website provides listings and reviews
www.time.com/time/2005/100books/the_complete_list.html

The 'whichbook' website will draw on its database of 20m books to recommend a book based on your requirements.
www.whichbook.net/

Doing a dissertation is an excellent opportunity to develop your skills in critical thinking, reasoning, and argument as well as to take more interest in philosophical problems such as morals and ethics. These are life-enriching competencies and sensibilities, and many students find that it is through doing a dissertation that they move up a rung in their thinking.

There are some suggestions about critical thinking under Further Reading at the end of this chapter which you might like to pursue.

Skill Set Booster: Methods and Methodology

There are a number of excellent texts to guide you on methods, ranging from overviews of social research to more in-depth texts which examine particular techniques. We will refer to many of these throughout the remainder of the book. For now, some good suggestions are Bell (2007); Denscombe (2003); and Bryman (2008).

It is also possible to take short courses in all aspects of methods, including for example, survey techniques. This can be very useful to do if you lack confidence or experience in doing surveys and have the time and money, but hopefully most undergraduates will not need such opportunities.

However, if you do have the time and money or are considering continuing with your educational career to postgraduate level, or perhaps are looking for jobs which involve a lot of research and report writing, then you can do much worse than to consider an investment in a short course to boost your skills.

Some suggestions for reliable places to check out for short courses, workshops, and events (which range from 1–2 days to a few weeks; and may be in person and via e-learning), include:

- The National Centre for Social Research

- The Essex University Summer School in Social Science Data Analysis and Collection

- The Social Research Association

- The Market Research Society

- Your own and other local universities

Skill Set Booster: ICTs, Typing and Managing Long Documents

It is one thing to be able to create and manage a simple document using text and a few headings which you manually create (all that is needed for an average essay), but the dissertation is a good opportunity to do a bit more.

Doing a dissertation in the social sciences typically involves long hours hammering away at a keyboard with additional time spent working on internet sources and searching. Apparently 'un-academic' and dare we say 'boring' skills like learning to type can seem a bit more useful than it first seems when it is midnight and you are still trying to get your document sorted out.

A possible approach to take is that you would be aiming to upgrade your hitherto 'gets-me-along' level of skill to the 'I-can-do-anything I-want-quickly-and-easily' level of skill. The skills you could develop include:

- Using *all* of the various functions on offer in standard word processing software and using them *well*, including headers, footers, automatic table of contents generation and heading levels, track changes, file importing, drawing tools etc.

- Creating and manipulating data in spreadsheets

- Working effectively with digital images

- Developing skills with PowerPoint and other presentational software

- Being able to produce labelled and titled graphs, charts, tables and diagrams, and being able to change them and move them around, quickly and easily

- Using book marking, tagging and other networking tools to develop your own rich bank of resources and engage with on-line communities

A Word on Typing

Many people learn to type in a two-or three-fingered 'search and attack' style. This is not necessarily a problem in the short- to mid-term and many people become very fast typing in this way. However, using ICTs will be part of many readers' working and social lives for the foreseeable future.

This need not take very long: dedicated students with some time on their hands could manage to touch type in under a month, although most people will take a couple of months to get speedy. Most people can get the basic hang of it in around 20–30 hours.

You could also consider improving your general facility or comfort with technology. For those readers who already have a high level of ICT skill, you too might consider whether there are further activities which you could usefully do at this stage which would boost your skill set and your CV.

There are a range of ways in which you can brush up your skills. These include:

- Taking a short course at a local college or private sector provider

- Exploring independent learning tutorials and software which may be provided by your university

- Buying a study book, for example – one of the numerous 'How To' guides on the market, and/or CD Roms, DVDs etc

Here are some specific suggestions:

- Mavis Beacon Touch Typing: a well known provider of typing tutorials which is very successful in the USA and sells internationally. The claim is that you can learn to type well in a fortnight

- Pitman-training.com: the Pitman Institute offers a range of certification which can be added to your CV including for typing, ICT skills, presentation and web design, book-keeping and accounts, spreadsheets, and software use; they also provide opportunities for taking business seminars and diplomas. Many local centres are available in the UK

- The European or International Computer Driving Licence (ECDL/ICDL): You can undertake testing at a test centre local to you and will be able to include this on your CV

Skill Set Booster: Numeracy and Statistics

Of all the areas in which many students lack confidence or in truth, have never really developed familiarity, statistics remains one of the major ones.

Specific issues arise when students choose methods and refer to sources with which they feel comfortable, rather than methods and sources appropriate to the line of inquiry. This is a tactic to avoid quantitative methods. This 'anti-numerical' approach will mean that your project suffers: it may well produce fuzziness in your understanding and could lead you to make blunders.

Yet developing your numeric skills will allow you to:

- Create good literature reviews which can refer to patterns such as expenditure, social trends, and the relative importance of this versus that, with confidence

- Make good selection decisions for samples, and be able to handle the data which you collect

- Improve your general grasp of mathematical concepts and reasoning, and improve your general knowledge

- Boost your reasoning and logic skills with data, theories, and 'facts' of all kinds

- Understand your data; both qualitative and quantitative data require you to draw reasoned conclusions about their meanings, including the inter-relationships between variables, and connections between meanings

- Make the most of your data by good presentation: it is always easier when you know what you are talking about and can choose how to present it

- Talk about research with confidence

Some sources of help include:

- Statsoft on-line contains a useful glossary and hints on techniques across a full range of statistical techniques which you are likely to encounter as an undergraduate on a social sciences/humanities programme (see www.statsoft.com/textbook/stathome.html)

- *Statistics Every Writer Should Know: A Simple Guide to Understanding Statistics, for Journalists and Other Writers Who Might Not Know Math* is the accessible guide by Robert Niles to what to look for in discussions and texts which rely on numbers to prove a point, i.e. to make truth claims (see www.robertniles.com/stats/)

- See under Further Reading in Chapter 8

Task 1.5

Working Practices: An Action List

What actions will you commit to? Identify one or two things to do in a few of the following areas, according to your priorities:

- Getting organised
- Tackling procrastination or improving your time management (see Figure 1.5 overleaf)
- Pick 1–2 items inspired by Table 1.3, Your Skill Set: True or False?
- Skill Set Boosters

The Dissertation Team

Your dissertation is, and has to be, all your own work. However, students at the writing up stage, or later at graduation ceremonies, often feel the need to acknowledge the help they received from others. Likewise, students also note some of the difficulties which arose with their network over the course of doing the dissertation. Finding help and anticipating difficulties will assist you in the long run.

Why do people procrastinate?

Fear of failure and perfectionism – rather than try and fail it is better to put it off, or make a start but never complete it. Write it down first, and worry about it later.

Don't know what to do – unclear about expectations and don't know if doing the right thing. Solution: find out what to do. Ask someone who knows what they are talking about. If you don't understand their explanation, don't give up and go away until you have understood the explanation.

Competency issue – really cannot do it, lack the skills and/or experience to successfully attempt the task. Solution: recognise that it isn't so much cannot do it, as don't know how to do it. The answer is to find out how to do it first, and then attempt it, then think about how you would do it next time.

Stressed – too much going on. Being under some pressure is widely regarded as healthy but too much pressure can trigger anxiety. The behaviour which results might feel personal and special to you, but it is rather more common than that. Examples include flitting between tasks, making excuses to put them off, becoming overwhelmed and staring into space, finding other things to do. Solution: choose one task, and forget about the rest. Choose something small and simple. Do it, and then choose the next one.

What to do about procrastination:

Avoid aimlessness: set up specific study periods and allocate particular tasks or goals to them. When you have finished them, get up and walk away.

Stay healthy and relax. All the boring things can really help: eat and sleep well, take regular exercise, see people and get out, go easy on drink and drugs.

Consider the True and False questions below: can you boost your skills so that you zip through work?

Inspiration: Make a list of things which have gone well for you and put it up; collect memorable quotations and read inspirational stories; make plans for the future.

Motivation: Identify some treats to have lined up along the way

Figure 1.5   **Procrastination**

Task 1.6

Your Dissertation Team

This task asks you to identify the key people in your network, those people who will be important in terms of your dissertation experience, and are in effect part of your study team.

In particular, you could consider forewarning your employer and workmates if you have them, that you are doing your dissertation. If you are going to need time off or wish to work flexible hours, you should consider how best to approach the subject, and give them plenty of time to make alternative arrangements if they are agreeable.

A special word on children and other dependents. Many students today have families, both young and old, and others whom they care for. Most of the degree programme to date will have presented challenges in terms of time and your focus, but the dissertation and achieving those vital marks in your other courses at the end of the year presents a special challenge. Enlist the support of those who can give it, and be prepared to share your plans well in advance. Ask for suggestions, you might be surprised by their good ideas. Talk things over with the important people in your life, including any children you may have. As far as you can, handle the situation: don't let it handle you.

Who are the key people in your dissertation team? What, if anything, do you need to talk to them about?

Table 1.3   Your Dissertation Team

Team member	What, if anything, do you need to discuss with them?
Partner, spouse, boy or girlfriend, ex-partner	
Workplace: boss	
Workplace: colleagues and peers	
Parents	
Children	
Other students	
Flatmates	
Tutor	
Medic	
Librarian	

(Continued)

Table 1.3   (Continued)

Team member	What, if anything, do you need to discuss with them?
Bank manager	
Counsellor	
Community or faith organisation; sports or arts organisation; volunteering body	
Others	

Working as Part of a Group

Much dissertation work necessarily involves working on your own. Even the most disciplined and motivated person may nonetheless feel that it would be nice to share mutual congratulations and commiserations from time to time. A way to systematise informal meetings is to set up a study group. Working as part of a study group can be a very successful approach. While you may find that tutors will assign you to groups through the dissertation classes, you might find that you will benefit from a group of your own choosing.

Membership

- Consider a mixture of peers including one or two who are not from the same course as you. Remember: all final year students attempt an independent project of some kind. You may find a lot more in common with other students than you initially think
- Invite slightly more people than you initially need, in order to cope with drop-outs, and the (almost inevitable) emergence of preferred pairings or trios
- Draw up a list of contact details for members of the group

Ground Rules

- As with all new groups, set the ground rules at the first meeting. These should cover how often, how long, and where you will meet, as well as deciding who will lead the group (check that members are happy for you to do it if you wish to and suggest rotation)
- A second set of ground rules relate to conduct, for example, you might wish to propose that what is said in the group is confidential. You might also think about how you will give and receive constructive criticism, help or advice

Keeping the Group Going

- Each group member should be active. This means turning up on time and staying until the end of the meeting; responding to emails and phone calls; and making sure that everyone gets the chance to contribute in each session
- Be flexible with how each member wants to work with the group: some may bring a draft of their work and ask for specific advice, while others will want to talk and might not welcome any advice at all
- Try to set a balance between negatives and positives. A supportive group will look for opportunities to celebrate achievements however small, as well as sharing problems. Both of those activities are different from a more general moan and groan session about tutors, money, being a student etc.
- End each group with some actions agreed. In other words, each member of the group leaves with one thing that they promise to do before you meet next time

The End of the Group

- Inevitably, the group will come to its end. You might find that you need to force the issue, or alternatively it will fizzle out naturally. Don't despair either way. Just remember that even the Beatles split up!

Figure 1.6   **Setting Up Your Own Study Group**

Summary

- Get a sense of the dissertation as a final product
  Begin by tracking down previous students' dissertations and have a good look at them. Look at their structure as well as content, and become aware of the amount and quality of work involved

- Get organised
  Do this early on, it will save a lot of time and aggravation later. In particular, make sure that you have got a good filing system going and that you can anticipate where the bottlenecks might be. Taking basic steps such as making sure that you have got a place and some time to work undisturbed could be quite important

- Don't leave things to chance
  Draft a project plan, and break down each major task into smaller, bite-sized pieces which you can work through

- Manage by objectives

Tasks are manageable when they are:

o   Specific, fixed
o   Measurable
o   Achievable
o   Relevant or realistic
o   Time-bound
o   Evaluated, exciting
o   Recorded so you know how far you have come and what is left

- Bibliography
  Start early! Even if you use software (over the now old-fashioned, although still functional, card index), you still need to record all of the information – and maintain your bibliography as you go along. You must check it before submitting your dissertation

- Reflect on your working practices
  Are you?

  o   Creative
  o   Reflective
  o   Effective
  o   Active
  o   Motivated

- Study skills
  It is never too late to learn

- Procrastination: a student's best friend?
  Tackle it. Get down to work and don't be put off by there being other things to do. They are not other things to do – they are distractions

- Skill sets
  Consider whether or not it would help you to brush up your basic skills including 'boring' ones such as typing. Certainly consider other skills: academic writing, argument and reasoning are all key to doing a dissertation, and are life-enriching; getting to grips with methods if you haven't yet done so is now essential. Don't rule out reading a good book for pleasure

- The dissertation team
  Get your people behind you early on. Tell them what you are going to do and enlist their help

- Group working
  Remember the possibility of working as part of a self-selected group is a strategy for study which many students find useful although it is not for everyone

Further Reading

Bailey, S. (2006) *Academic Writing: A Handbook for International Students*. London: Routledge.

Bowell, T. and Kemp, G. (2005) (2nd edn.) *Critical Thinking: A Concise Guide*. London: Routledge.

Jones-Devitt, S. and Smith, L. (2007) *Critical Thinking in Health and Social Care*. London: Sage.

Oshima, A. and Hoque, A. (2005) *Writing Academic English*. London: Pearson.

Phelan, P. and Reynolds, P. (1995) *Argument and Evidence: Critical Thinking for the Social Sciences*. London: Routledge.

Tracy, B. (2004) *Eat That Frog! Get More of the Important Things Done, Today!* San Francisco: Berrett-Koehler Publications.

Chapter 2

Great Expectations: What You Need to Do for Your Dissertation

Overview

Doing a dissertation: why do you have to do one as part of your under-graduate programme?

Graduateness and subject benchmarks

The dissertation requirements

The structure of the dissertation: typical models

The importance of marking schemes

The supervisor and you

This chapter will help you to see how doing a dissertation fits into your degree programme. Doing social research is valued as part of doing a degree in the social sciences. Learning how to do it, how to talk about it, and how to write it up, are all competencies of graduateness as well as invaluable skills and rewarding experiences in their own right.

This chapter also provides information about what is expected of you in doing a dissertation, setting out what makes a good dissertation in the examiners' eyes and for example by exploring a marking scheme. Finally, the chapter looks at the relationship between you and your supervisor.

Understanding Dissertations as Part of Your Undergraduate Programme

Doing a dissertation has several meanings. It is an opportunity to:

- Bring together work which you have done across your undergraduate programme
- Develop an area of interest
- Work independently, and follow your star. Freedom!
- Develop a range of skills, including analytical, critical thinking, creative, interpersonal, and presentation skills

In general, the dissertation rounds off degree programmes, allowing students to develop graduateness, i.e. the level of educational competencies which characterise graduates. Secondly, doing the dissertation allows students to fully graduate in a specific academic area of study. As such, the Quality Assurance Agency for Higher Education (QAA) provides subject benchmark statements which define the role of independent research and attempt to define what it means to graduate in each particular subject. Every subject has got a benchmark statement which:

> ...describe the attributes, skills and capabilities that a graduate with an honours degree in a specific subject might be expected to have. Each statement has been written by a group of academics and other specialists (such as representatives from professional bodies, industry and commerce) from the subject area.
>
> *Source*: Understanding Courses: benchmark statements and programme specifications, on the QAA website, qaa.ac.uk/students/guides/understandcourses.asp

These statements attempt to define the major characteristics of each discipline. They set out the knowledge and understanding of the subject and any specific skills which someone studying the subject should develop. They also set out other expectations relating to learning, teaching and assessment. The benchmark statements are not a national curriculum but provide a framework within which all universities must operate. The degree programme which you are taking will have been approved as meeting its subject benchmark.

The QAA benchmarks relating to the social sciences and cognate subjects typically include statements about developing research skills. This is thought of as being vitally important since it will allow you to become a competent researcher and an independent, critically engaged, and creative thinker in your specific discipline.

The extract in Figure 2.1, from the Subject Benchmark Statement for an undergraduate honours degree in health studies, provides a good example of the main areas of study expected and illustrates 'The central place of research activity in the development of the subject'. (Source: Subject knowledge and understanding on, the QAA website www.qaa.ac.uk/academic infrastructure/benchmark/honours/healthstudies.asp)

The example in Figure 2.2, drawn from the Subject Benchmark Statement for Criminology, sets research into the wider context of the subject as a whole, showing its connections to theoretical developments and to policy formulation.

3.1 The single honours health studies graduate will demonstrate
   knowledge and understanding of:

- health as a contested concept
- the multidisciplinary nature of health studies
- the central place of research activity in the development of the
  subject
- the diverse determinants of health and well-being
- the contemporary issues at the forefront of the subject
- the range of theories of causality relating to health
- social policy approaches and potential influences upon health and
  well-being
- the theoretical and professional rationales concerning health
  interventions
- the role of individual differences in affecting health status
- the diversity of the experience of health and well-being
- the diversity of values associated with health and well-being
- comparisons within and between healthcare systems and modes
  of delivery
- cultural diversity within health and well-being
- the central theoretical arguments and paradigms in health
  research
- the use and application of information technology to
  communication and analysis within the discipline.

Figure 2.1   **Extract from the QAA's Subject Benchmark Statement for
Health Studies**

Source: aa.ac.uk/academicinfrastructure/benchmark/statements/
healthstudies/08/PDF

The extract shows the equal importance attached to both empirical investigation and theoretical developments, as well as criminology's intimate
connections to policy and the criminal justice system. The statement claims
that the lifeblood of the discipline depends upon good empirical research
and the effective use of this as an evidence base in policy making. These
statements can be quite useful to you when you come to think about how
you will talk about your degree and what you learned to the outside world.

Finally, the extract in Figure 2.3 (see p. 40), from the Subject Benchmark
Statement for Anthropology, shows the range of assessments by which
such learning outcomes might be assessed. Note that this specifically
includes doing dissertation and other projects which give students the
opportunity to carry out a 'sustained piece of research'.

As can be seen, there is a full range of possible approaches to assessment and different things, including the capacity to conduct independent
thought and work, are picked up as a focus for assessment. Note too, that
in the discussion of dissertations the project is viewed as a positive opportunity for students to develop an area specifically of interest to them.

3.2   Criminology is both a theoretical and an empirical discipline.

3.3   At the heart of criminology are theoretical debates about a wide range of perspectives. Criminology emphasises the importance both of theoretical work and of a firm evidence base for its theories. It also engages in formal and critical evaluation of crime prevention, security and crime control policies, as well as of other responses to crime and deviance. However, in furthering these values, it needs to nurture a lively debate and dialogue between a range of theoretical and methodological perspectives, employing both quantitative and qualitative data. It must guard against attempts to foreclose this dialogue with the premature creation of theoretical or methodological protocols favouring particular sub-discipline fields, whether endorsed by state officials, by the mass media, or by fashions of academic thought.

3.4   Empirically, criminology is concerned with:

- processes of criminalisation and victimisation
- the causes and organisation of crime and deviance
- processes of preventing and managing crime and victimisation
- official and unofficial responses to crime, deviance and social harm
- representations of crime, offenders, victims and agents and agencies of control.

3.5   Given its strong policy orientation and close relationship with the criminal justice professions, many of criminology's most significant theoretical advances have been made through empirical studies. Criminology also contributes to and benefits from continuous theoretical debates within the social sciences. The vitality of the discipline also requires a continuous interchange between theory and analytic and evaluative research, and attention to increasingly salient ethical debates about crime, security, and human rights at international, national, regional and local levels.

3.6   Criminology is intrinsically a reflexive discipline, involving an understanding of contested values in the constitution and application of criminological knowledge.

Figure 2.2   **Extract from the QAA's Subject Benchmark Statement for Criminology**

Source: qaa.ac.uk/academicinfrastructure/benchmark/statements/ Criminology07.asp

Generally, all final year undergraduates in the UK attempting an independent research project will produce a piece of work which has many similarities. The generic features are:

- Producing a unique piece of work which flows from formulating an original research question

Assessment in anthropology is intended to test knowledge and understanding of the theory, content and methods of anthropology. According to the combinations of subjects comprising any particular anthropology programme, assessment will be made up of an appropriate mix of some or all of the following:

- unseen and seen timed, written examinations, which are designed to test students' knowledge and understanding of a module or course's subject matter
- essays, to allow the opportunity for students to develop a more discursive account or argument, which is supported by reference to primary or secondary literature, and completed within a prescribed word limit
- seminar presentations, to encourage students to present an argument or a point of view to a peer audience and offer clarification and a reasoned defence, if necessary
- dissertations or extended essays, to give students the opportunity to identify a topic and carry out a sustained piece of research (based upon library sources, original or secondary data) within a prescribed word length and under the supervision of a member of staff
- oral examinations, for example, of dissertations, which allow students to defend and discuss their work in detail with examiners
- demonstrations, displays and posters, involving work being prepared in specified ways that demand, for example, presentational, graphical or performance skills
- other writing exercises, including project reports, notebooks and fieldwork reports, which are designed to test students' observational and recording skills
- where programmes have a material culture element, students may be required to produce museum and gallery displays
- where programmes have an element of biological anthropology, student performance in laboratory-based or other project work will often be assessed.

Figure 2.3   Extract from the QAA's Subject Benchmark Statement for Anthropology

Source: www.qaa.ac.uk/academicinfrastructure/benchmark/statements/Anthropology07.asp

- Sustaining a study in much greater depth than coursework

- There will be an element of live research, whether this is collecting empirical data (for example, conducting a survey or running a focus group) or using secondary sources (for example, working with a specialist archive or a library-based investigation), which produces an evidence base

- Operationalising a theoretical framework, bringing this together with an evidence base to make an argument or exploration of some kind

- Synthesising and evaluating contradictory literature and evidence; this includes both the substantive area of inquiry and the literature relating to methodology

- Drawing a reasoned conclusion based upon the study which has been conducted

- Developing an understanding of the ethical issues raised by the research and adjusting working practices to take account of these.

Remember: If you are interested in finding the benchmark statement for your subject, either visit the QAA website directly, or Google on 'Benchmark + your subject'.

The Dissertation Requirements: Great Expectations

Getting ready to attempt and follow through the dissertation requires each student to develop their understanding of what is required. In the Introduction we considered your expectations of the project. If you haven't yet read the Introduction, turn to it now.

In addition, all students are advised to set aside some time in order to read, and make notes from, any instructions, tips and suggestions that your tutors make available to you as well as engaging with study guides, sites (see Box 2.1), and books such as this one which are designed to support you in doing the dissertation. See also under Further Reading at the end of this chapter for other suggestions.

Box 2.1   A Companion for Undergraduate Dissertations

www.socscidiss.bham.ac.uk/s2.html

This website is a Companion learning resource designed to support students through the dissertation process. The site was put together by academic and support staff in a grant-aided project funded by the Centre for Sociology, Anthropology, and Politics (C-SAP) at Birmingham University.

Task 2.1

Reminder! Find Some Dissertations and Have a Good Look at Them

Task 1.1 of Chapter 1 was to find dissertations and have a good look at your department or school's previous work. If you haven't done this yet – do it now!

Typical Dissertation Structures

The length of the dissertation in the social sciences and cognate disciplines varies, typically falling between 6,000–10,000 words, although there are variations, for example, where health studies dissertations may contain a clinical component, or a media studies dissertation may contain a production element.

Structures also vary, although the core elements are usually:

- An introduction

- A literature review

- A chapter on methodology

- A findings chapter

- A discussions chapter

- And a conclusion

Even if your structure differs from this, you will probably find that the final document must *cover* each of those areas. You may wish to use or submit different kinds of media and materials including electronic ones as well as objects of different sorts. In this event, you should always consult with your tutors before proceeding.

Every department, school and faculty does things slightly differently. You should make sure that you get hold of a copy of the requirements which you must fulfil in order for your dissertation to be seen as a worthy attempt. In the example shown in Figure 2.4 below, taken from the field of Childhood, Education and Culture at the University of Leeds, you should note the following fairly typical requirements:

- The requirement of a title page

- The requirement for an abstract. Abstracts are read by fellow researchers. This short summary of the dissertation should provide them with everything that they need to know in order to judge whether or not to obtain and read the dissertation in depth. While short, it is important that the abstract is produced and does the dissertation justice

- The requirements of the conclusion which ask the researcher to consider the implications of their research findings, and to signal further areas of research which may lead out of this one

- The use of appendices – in preparing your dissertation you may well find that data and its representation interrupts the flow of text in the main body, and that you will need to use appendices

---

3.8 Structuring, Writing and Presenting Your Dissertation

The dissertation should be typed or word-processed, double-spaced, on one side of the paper only. The following is a *suggested* structure.

1. **Title Page**: title of study, name, date and supervisor.
2. **Acknowledgements**: of anyone to whom you owe particular thanks.
3. **Contents Page**.
4. **Abstract**: maximum 250 words.

   This should briefly describe the focus of your study; your research questions, methodology and main findings. It should be kept separate from the dissertation and attached to the undergraduate assignment sheet on submission for second markers, external examiner.

5. **Introduction**:

   This should:

   - state the aims and purpose of the dissertation making reference where appropriate to any contextual factors (e.g. historical, social, political factors etc.)
   - give a brief overview of content;
   - make very brief reference to the methods used to gather information/data.

6. **Review of the Literature:**

   This should:

   - provide a historical, social or political context for the study where this is relevant;
   - provide a review of literature in the field which outlines the current state of knowledge/research evidence in the area;
   - identify and consider theoretical perspectives relevant to the focus of the dissertation;
   - present contrasting views where appropriate;
   - identify issues and raise questions in relation to the study.

7. **Methodology:**

   This should:

   - reiterate the central aims and purpose of the study;
   - identify key research questions;

(Continued)

(Continued)

- describe and justify the research methods used, making reference to literature in the field where appropriate;
- describe the context and subjects of the research;
- describe how and when the research was carried out;
- describe how the data was organised and analysed;
- discuss any methodological issues.

8. **Presentation of Findings:**

This is different to analysing and discussing your findings. This should present your findings as tables or figures but only when you have data that lends itself to this, i.e. quantitative data, if your data is qualitative then you wouldn't present your findings in this way.

9. **Analysis and Discussion of Findings:**

This should:

- present key findings in relation to your original research questions;
- discuss how your findings compare with what other researchers in the field have found;
- make reference to literature in the field where appropriate;
- reflect upon the impact (if any) that your research methods might have had upon your findings.

10. **Conclusion. This should summarise the study by:**

- reiterating key findings in relation to the research questions;
- identifying issues;
- discussing the implications for this area of knowledge;
- identifying areas for further research.

3.9   Academic Referencing:

Please see the advice on referencing given in the Undergraduate Handbook and follow this carefully.

3.10   Appendices:

Students should take careful advice from their supervisor about what to include in Appendices e.g. copies of questionnaires, interview schedules, transcript extracts, document extracts.

Figure 2.4   **Example of Structure of Undergraduate Dissertation: in the field of Childhood, Education and Culture, University of Leeds**

Source: Taylor, D. (2008: 8)

Remember: Vital to your success: you need to develop your understanding of what is expected of your particular degree programme by your particular department, faculty or School and thus your university.

For further discussions of the various sections of the dissertation, see Chapter 12 under 'What Goes Where'.

The Importance of Marking Schemes

It is important to develop your understanding of:

- What you need to do to score minimum marks to pass

- What you need to do to score good or the best marks

- The holistic nature of the project – you need to hit the target in each and every area: not in some but not in others

Again, the exact marking schemes in use may differ slightly depending for example on subject-specific requirements. Again, it is very helpful to you to make sure that you have obtained a copy of the marking scheme which will be used to assess your dissertation. The extract from the School of Social Sciences at Southampton in Table 2.1 shows just three elements from a much more comprehensive list found in a well laid out marking scheme.

To score well in the dissertation, you need to ensure that you have covered all the bases. To achieve a good mark you need to have performed strongly across *all* areas.The different components of a dissertation are linked. A weakness in the foundations will produce weaker results downstream. On the other hand, doing most of the project well and then failing to draw conclusions means that you throw away valuable marks. You should generally be seeking consistency, rather than producing one outstanding element and scraping by elsewhere.

Furthermore, you will probably find that there are different kinds of requirements in the dissertation guidelines or marking schemes, for example:

- Whether a particular kind of binding is specified

- The font type and size

- There may be information about the use of particular kinds of phrases, for example, how to write out numbers (in words or numbers), dates, American spelling, double line spacing and so on

- Some departments may split marks between the final dissertation and linked project work or other requirement, for example, working with a supervisor, or may not split marks but stipulate that providing evidence of engagement with the supervisor is necessary in order to pass the dissertation

- There may be specific rules about seeking ethical clearance and submitting evidence of your engagement with ethics (for example, forms)

- The kind of referencing system you should use

- The date of submission – and whether there is a set time

Again, do ensure that you have obtained and understood all of the different tasks which you need to do in order to achieve maximum marks.

Table 2.1 Extract from the Marking Scheme Used by the School of Social Sciences at the University of Southampton

Area	1st (70–100)	2.1 (60–69)	2.2 (50–59)	3rd (40–49)	Fail (0–39)
Identification of research area and formulation of research question	Introduction identifies an important research area and formulates a well-defined research question	Introduction identifies research area and formulates defined research question	Introduction may either identify a research area without necessarily formulating a clear research question, or may formulate a research question without making much attempt to explain its importance	Weak introduction, which fails to justify the research area or identify a clearly-defined question	Very weak introduction, which fails to justify the research area or identify a clearly-defined question
Research methodology	Provides clear statement of methods used to obtain information, and shows a good understanding of the strengths and weaknesses of chosen methodology	Identifies methods used to obtain information and makes some attempt to evaluate their strengths and weaknesses	Identifies methods used to obtain information, but may apply these uncritically	Little attempt to explain methods used to obtain information, with little discussion of their strengths or weaknesses	Little or no attempt to explain methods used to obtain information, and little or no attempt to evaluate them
Quality of argument and clarity of conclusions	Clear and logical argument, leading to appropriate and relevant conclusions. A first-class dissertation may also show an awareness of ways in which the topic or investigation may be extended further	Clear and logical argument, leading to appropriate and relevant conclusions	Argument may not always be clearly and logically presented; conclusions may not always be supported by evidence on which they are supposed to be based	Argument may be difficult to identify or follow	Failure to develop a clear argument

Source: Heath (2008: 17 and 18)

Remember: You need to meet the threshold of each task area in order to do well in the dissertation. It is pointless doing everything else very well, if you miss out one thing, and you risk failing if you miss out something substantive. The dissertation tests all-round competencies including the ability to keep on top of the project as a whole. Do keep a weather eye on how the dissertation is going: maintain an overview, and avoid problematic situations such as simply running out of time. In terms of typographical and presentational issues don't lose easy marks.

Task 2.2

Obtain the Marking Scheme for Your Dissertation

Make sure that you are clear about:

- The range of areas which are going to be assessed
- The standard at which you need to be working in each area
- The regulations relating to the presentation of the dissertation

The Supervisor and You

As part of the dissertation process, you will be assigned a supervisor. A dissertation supervisor is a key tutor whose job is to guide you through the process. They will develop a good understanding of your project and will be able to offer different kinds of support, including:

- Reading suggestions and pointers regarding recent research
- Good sources
- Possible contacts, suggestions of organisations to approach
- Help with shaping the research question
- Feedback on the research proposal
- Feedback on drafts
- Practical advice about priorities at different stages of the project
- A sounding board about things which are going wrong

Working with a supervisor will be a new experience for most since it is unusual to have so much one-to-one access which is focused entirely on you and your research. But it is one about which most students are positive. The relationship with your supervisor is something which you will need to work out as you go along. Generally, you will find that the onus is much more on you than you may have previously experienced in your degree programme. You and your supervisor will be expected to meet in order to discuss your work. The responsibility for setting up these meetings, especially after the first one, might rest with you. Certainly, if you don't keep the meeting, it won't happen. To get the most out of your relationship with your supervisor see Box 2.2

Box 2.2   Expectations of Supervisors and Students

- Supervisors are there to guide you. You can enjoy an informal style of learning and really benefit from your supervisor's experience
- Arrange a schedule of meetings; be clear about how often you are supposed to turn up and what preparation you are supposed to have done
- Make sure that you are prepared for your meetings
- Do ask your supervisor for specific help, e.g. with books, people, organisations, ideas
- Ask for help when it is going well as well as when it is going badly
- Share things with your supervisor. This means:

    o Sharing your aspirations: if you are looking for a good 2:1 or a First – tell them. Likewise, if you are concerned about passing – tell them
    o Talking things over when things aren't going to plan can be helpful

---

Summary

- Doing a dissertation is an opportunity to bring together work which you have done across your undergraduate programme. You can:

    o Develop an area of interest
    o Work independently, and follow your star
    o Develop a range of skills, including analytical, critical thinking, creative, interpersonal, and presentation skills

- Doing a dissertation produces a quality called 'graduateness' which is a combination of a particular level of skills and expertise in a particular subject. QAA Subject Benchmark Statements, which the QAA produce, define what both of these are for each subject. They almost all contain references to the place of research and independent inquiry, and this is usually a central place
- Make sure that you know what the dissertation requirements are in your institution, including each of its constituent parts, and whether or not you need to do empirical research

- Dissertations generally follow fairly typical models, with:

  o A title page
  o Acknowledgements
  o A table of contents
  o An abstract
  o An introduction
  o A literature review
  o A methodology
  o A presentation and discussion of findings
  o A conclusion
  o A bibliography
  o Appendices

- Make sure that you know what your department or school will look for, including the regulations which define the layout and presentation. Make sure that you follow these. Marking schemes give important information about what the examiners are looking for. This includes:

  o The range of areas and tasks being assessed
  o How well you need to do in each one

- The supervisor and you: supervision should be an informative and relaxed relationship in which you can really benefit from your tutor, who can provide one-to-one tailored help and support all the way through your dissertation. To make the most of this relationship, do make sure that you fix a schedule of meetings; prepare for them; and turn up on time!

Further Reading

Bell, J. (2007) *Doing Your Research Project: A Guide for First-Time Researchers in Education and Social Science.* Buckingham: Open University Press.

Levin, P. (2005) *Excellent Dissertations!* Maidenhead: Open University.

Rudestam, K.E. and Newton, R.R. (2001) *Surviving Your Dissertation: A Comprehensive Guide to Content and Process.* London: Sage.

Silbergh, D.M. (2001) *Doing Dissertations in Politics: A Student's Guide.* London: Routledge.

Swetnam, D. (2003) *Writing Your Dissertation.* Oxford: How To Books.

Walliman, N. (2004) *Your Undergraduate Dissertation: The Essential Guide for Success.* London: Sage.

Chapter 3
Defining the Research Question

Overview

Generating research questions

Finding a topic:

- A course or academic area
- Drawing on life experience
- In the news
- Historical importance
- Eye-witness
- Local issues
- Country or region specific
- Tutor's inspiration
- Cyber inspiration

Turning a topic into a research question: using mind maps

What makes a good research question

Common pitfalls in defining research questions

In this chapter, you will go through the process of selecting a theme or topic, and working it up into a focused manageable and research question. In essence, the issue at hand is how to formulate research problems as lines of inquiry which are possible to research.

We begin by considering ways of generating possible research topics using mind maps and brainstorming, as well as thinking about some of the usual ways in which you might find a dissertation topic. You are then asked to consider the difference between a theme and a research question, and to work more on turning a research *topic* into a research *question*. This is followed by a tips list of common pitfalls in defining a question.

Generating Research Questions: Finding a Theme

There are a number of ways in which you might go about finding a research topic. You could take the opportunity to follow up on an aspect of your course which you have found particularly interesting or intriguing. This might be something that they have already studied in some depth, so it is important to ensure that the work you do for the dissertation builds on this rather than repeats it. However, you may find inspiration from things that are of the moment, for example, burning issues of the day, or new research finding or popular frameworks of beliefs and assumptions which are in circulation which prompt you to inquire further. Alternatively there may be historical events that you would like to explore further. In any event, a starting point is to brainstorm for initial ideas. In the first task (Task 3.1), you are invited to generate a few ideas under every heading.

Good brainstorming is where you:

- Keep coming up with ideas for as long as you can

- As soon as you dry up on one point, move on to the next, and then return later

- Don't evaluate your own or others' ideas: keep moving not thinking

- Write down everything which is suggested, however crazy or irrelevent

Task 3.1

Go Fishing: Brainstorming for Good Ideas

Identify a few ideas under each of the following headings which appeal to you as potential dissertation research projects:

1) *A course you have done or academic area which you have encountered*, irrespective of in what depth, which you would like to find out more about. Think concretely about particular hooks, for example, a theory, a situation, a policy, an event etc.

2) *Something from your life experience* which raises issues that you could explore: to do with family, work, identity, state of health, finance, housing, travel, fashion, food, your life-long love of Arsenal or Madonna etc.

3) *Something in the news*: a policy problem; governance issue; corporate news; something pertaining to a particular sector

such as sport; topical subjects such as social mobility, social exclusion, British identity, the property market, oil and food prices, elections, exam results etc.

4) *Career-related subjects*: you could consider how to use the dissertation as part of your professional development or in terms of steps towards a career. This might involve making an inquiry using frameworks found in the social sciences for researching the labour market: looking at the role of professional associations; the link between education, training and occuptional status; class systems and the division of labour; ethnographic studies of workplaces; producing a history of a particular organisation; policy areas; investigating the history of a service; user groups; the role of the media (for example, in mental health or crimes); globalisation and work etc.

5) *Matters of historical significance*: new data comes to light which raises new questions about the past; are there hidden stories of individuals and communities which could be told?; how things came to be as they are today and/or how historical events affect us in the present.

6) *Being an eye-witness*: you could focus on an observation from your everyday life; something you see or have seen. This could include repetitive behaviour (people, systems, structures etc.), or some aspect of attitudes and beliefs which you have observed; it could also involve bearing witness to an extraordinary event or a specific incident (to do with yourself or somebody else).

7) *Local issues*: you might like to consider community reactions to proposed developments; the fate of a local institution, for example, the post office or football ground; what is going on with services such as schools, hospitals, shopping, car parking, transport; a local scandal; an event of importance etc.

8) *Country or region specific issues*: think of an issue arising in a particular region or state or combinations of states; supranational and global institutions (EU, NATO); agenda-setting; approaches to problems by policy makers and other actors; the behaviour of individuals, collectives, agencies, partners; media; a particular train of events or process for example, an election; environmental change; conflict; economic change.

9) *Your tutor's individual research subjects*: you may find inspiration from your academic tutor in terms of specific research areas that they pursue. Be careful that you don't ask them to choose the area or question for you – while this may seem a tempting and tidy solution to a rather tricky problem, you will find it quite difficult to map your thinking on to someone else's conceptualisation of the problem, however interesting you find it. Work with your tutor to develop your own thinking and choice of area.

Cyber Inspiration

Online sources are the bane and joy of social scientists, young and old. There is a dizzy array of materials now available online. Be inspired by the rich array of data stored in cyberspace. Well-funded and professionally maintained sites are a rich source of great ideas for your project and in due course can also be used as a source in their own right for certain kinds of data. Table 3.1 contains just a snapshot of a few on-line sources: there are many more in Appendix 1, many of which appear later in the book; see for example Chapters 8 and 9, pertaining to collecting quantitative and qualitative data and the variety of secondary sources. But don't be limited by this, think laterally and go your own way.

Table 3.1   **Online Sources: Be Inspired**

www.gettyimages.co.uk	One million images for your consideration. Can also be purchased at £39 per image
www.medphoto.wellcome.ac.uk	The library of the Wellcome Trust provides thousands of wonderful images. Current categories are: War, Wonderful, Witchcraft, Wellness, World. Collect and download for free
www.iwm.org.uk Collections.iwm.org/server. php?show=nav.oog	The Imperial War Museum in London has partially digitalised its collections. A rich database includes 160,000 personnel records, 10m photographs, 15,000 posters, and many different kinds of other record including, for example, inventories of war memorials
www.loc.gov/index.html	The Library of Congress in the USA has been digitalising its collections since 1994: browse and be happy
www.manchestergalleries.org	The museum and galleries of Manchester and the North West of England have also been busy. Manchester alone has a collection of 30,000 works online There are many smaller museums and galleries which are also well worth browsing online
www.publications.parliament.uk	The United Kingdom parliamentary publications and records office website contains Hansard; archives and records; research papers; committee papers; Commons publications; Early Day

(Continued)

Table 3.1   (Continued)

	Motions; Order Papers. Note: Portcullis is the online catalogue to the 3m historical records of Parliamentary Archives
www.ellisisland.org	The Statue of Liberty and the Ellis Island Foundation Inc, have produced an online site for the Ellis Island Immigration Museum, containing all records including narrative documents such as diaries and letters; and data sets and timelines of immigration into the USA. The website includes a passenger name-search facility
www.naa.gov.au Further hint: Google on 'national archives' to access more countries' records, each in their various stages of digitalisation; try Japan and India	The National Archives of Australia, containing records since 1901 plus many 19th century records transferred from the colonies to the Commonwealth
http://dig.lib.niu.edu/amarch/index.html	Documents of the American Revolution 1774–1776 as collected by Peter Force and published as the American Archives

Developing Your Theme into a Research Question

Generally, start with a broad theme, from which topic areas can be generated. A mind map can be drawn up identifying some possible topics, as for example in Figure 3.1.

From this mind map, a number of topic areas can be derived from the broad theme of 'housing needs for key workers':

- The need for affordable housing within walking distance of the hospital

- The need for affordable and available public transport within a three-mile radius of the school

- The way there is plenty of housing but not the right kind

- Seasonal demand for key workers creates temporary housing needs

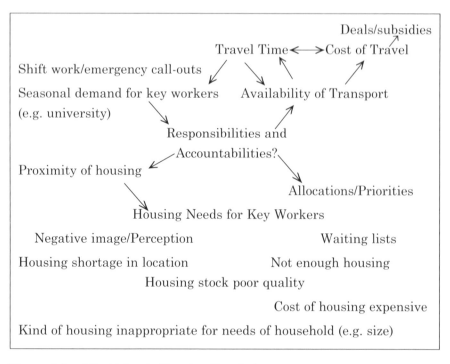

Figure 3.1   **Mind Map 1: Housing Needs for Key Workers**

In order to refine your mind map, you can group different areas of the map, for example, by using different colour pens and colour coding the themes. You might also want to use images, and other kinds of words, for example, a few headline statistics which seem to you to be especially noteworthy. You will probably fruitfully make a few attempts at creating a mind map, so don't rest on just the first one which you come up with.

   In these topics, we can see a number of possible question areas brewing:

- How is housing allocated to key workers, if at all?

- How important is the co-operation of public transport providers and what mechanisms are in place/could be developed?

- How do you persuade key workers to take temporary jobs and temporary accommodation? How does the provision of short-term accommodation affect social cohesion in the neighbourhood?

- Should key workers get the right kind of housing when other citizens do not?

- Who or what is responsible for addressing the problems of housing and key workers?

- How should housing be allocated?

However, while these begin to look like promising question *areas*, none of these are really research *questions*. Some lend themselves to a close description of process or procedures – but they lack critical engagement and are rather large and unwieldy. Others lend themselves to value judgements with no evidential base. Some initial questions might be relatively easy to answer by simply looking up the right source; for example, in this case, looking at statutory duties, policy documentation and undertakings made by organisations as employers, seeking to recruit staff, all gives valuable information as to the prevailing attitudes, norms, and obligations taken up by organisations. A dissertation question needs to explore a specific question which cannot be readily addressed by reference to material which is already in the public domain and which can simply be represented. You may also find that you are exploring an area which has already been researched, possibly recently and in depth. In order to finally decide on a research question, some initial reading around and exploration of websites is essential.

In refining research questions think carefully about what it is about the theme and topic which really interests you. Is it an ethical issue about how values are defined and enshrined in allocation mechanisms in the context of scarce resources? Or is it about really making a difference at the level of policy in practice, for example, how partnerships between local housing suppliers and employers can be negotiated to provide subsidies to the end user?

In any event, further steps are needed to refine the theme into a topic, and from the topic into a question. In order to do this, a second set of maps could be produced. The one in Figure 3.2 shows some of the main decision points which arise in narrowing down the topic into a question. Scoping the sample population is not only a methodological issue, in terms of helping you to work out how you will go about the empirical study, it can be helpful to think about this early on, since it helps to narrow down the area further. In this example of the key workers, rather than attempting to research all key workers everywhere, some selections can be made.

The Great Transformation: Turning Topics into Research Questions

From this, you can begin to refine the question area further. In this example, exploring the housing problems of key workers could be tackled in different ways, for example by demand or supply:

- I am going to explore the needs of junior house doctors who move to Kensington and Chelsea to take up their job and find that they need affordable housing within ten minutes' walk of the main building in which they work, but who cannot access it at this stage in their career, since they are based in one of the most expensive housing areas in the UK

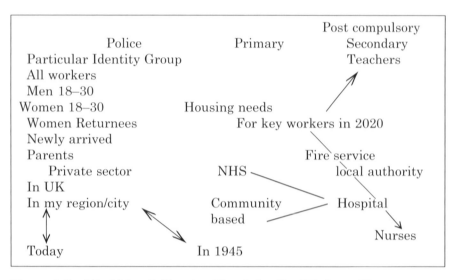

Figure 3.2   **Mind Map 2: Housing Needs for Key Workers (2)**

- I am going to establish the allocation mechanism for hospital flats, looking for issues connected to processes. For example, positive bias (towards the newly appointed member of staff with relocation needs) and negative bias (such as, race bias in the allocation procedure), and make recommendations for its improvement

By thinking ahead a little to how you might tackle the area, you might be able to further tighten up your research question.

Some Common Pitfalls

1) Too big!

One of the most common pitfalls, with the biggest negative consequences, is to define the research question in ways that are too big.

'Too big' means:

- Too broad – the scope of the project is so wide that in fact there is more than one project here. Limit your research question to one main concept or a couple of key variables. Don't set out to find out everything there is to know
- Too ambitious – while this can be linked to its breadth, too ambitious can also arise given the contexts of the research. This book is for students taking undergraduate degrees, who now need to do their dissertation. Students doing undergraduate degrees face a number of constraints, not least the amount of time they have available; the quality of time available; the money available to pay for any expenses; competing

---

Good questions are:

- Clear
- Specific
- Answerable
- Interconnected
- Substantially relevant

Figure 3.3   **What Makes Good Research Questions?**

Source: Punch (2005: 46)

demands on their time and capacity, including their energy, focus, interest, determination; the level and quality of skills and experience gained so far. This rules out some studies, such as longitudinal ones, or which require a large sample and a research team. However, don't avoid being 'ambitious', do talk your ideas over with your class and your supervisor, since there may be a way of dealing with the line of inquiry which makes the project more manageable

Remember: *It is important to recognise the distinctions between the requirements and expectations at different levels of study. Undergraduates are doing undergraduate research, not postgraduate. You are not expected to produce an original contribution to knowledge, nor are you expected to put together and run a research project which spans six countries and requires a team of researchers.*

2) Too vague!

'Too vague' means:

- The research proposed is presented as a topic or theme. Perhaps some work has been done in order to move it towards a research *problem*. But the next vital step is to shape a research *question*: this is a focused, researchable version of the research problem formulation

Ways of dealing with vagueness lie in getting more focused by formulating the problem as a line of inquiry. Tell-tale signs of research questions and titles which are insufficiently focused include the lack of specification of any particular setting, population, area, time frame, body of theory, concepts, variables, phenomena, or in summary, it is hard to tell what the research will actually look at from the phrasing of the question or title. Such vagueness will cloud your judgement when making critical decisions such as those about methodology, and conducting a literature search.

Remember: *Original research and fresh thinking can come from apparently 'small' questions.*

3) The proposed research project will tell us nothing new and is overly descriptive

- This pitfall arises where the student limits themselves to *describing* previous research which has already been done by others

Bringing together research carried out by others is an essential step in your production process, but the dissertation needs to go beyond this. A common but avoidable error is to produce a description of previous work, rather than a critical discussion which goes beyond the work of others. Thus there is the lack of any original element. Under these circumstances, the final dissertation handed in does not meet the mark. Rather, the student has produced an extended essay, albeit in much greater depth and with greater understanding than other coursework which they have previously done.

Remember: *The dissertation must contain an original element. While this can take many forms, including theoretical explorations involving library work, it is not an extended essay or a piece of coursework with extra reading.*

In summary, do not be discouraged from reaching for the stars: just make sure you have enough rocket fuel to get you there – and that you have done the necessary reading and learning, are being realistic about the time and energy you have to bring to the project, and are prepared to take the advice of the supervisor back at base.

Task 3.2

Draft Research Questions: Discussion Points

Working in small groups, consider each student's draft research question in turn.

What suggestions can the group make for:

(a) Tightening up – making the question more focused

(b) Adjusting it to better reflect what the student says they want to do

(c) Next steps – ideas for resources for the student to look at, places to visit, people to talk to?

Summary

- There are a number of ways in which you might identify your research topic:

- o   A course or academic area

- o   Drawing on life experience

- o   In the news

- o   Historical importance

- o   Eye-witness

- o   Local issues

- o   Country or region specific

- o   Tutor's inspiration

- o   Cyber inspiration

- The key challenge is to turn your general research topic into a research question

- What makes a good research question? It is:

  - o   Clear

  - o   Specific

  - o   Answerable

  - o   Interconnected

  - o   Substantially relevant

- Some common pitfalls are:

  - o   It is too big

  - o   It is too vague

  - o   It tells us nothing new and is overly descriptive

- Be adventurous – but listen to advice and take time to shape the question

Further Reading

Clegg, B. and Birch, P. (2007) *Instant Creativity: Simple Techniques to Ignite Innovation and Problem Solving*. London: Kogan Page.

Rudestam, K.E. and Newton, R.R. (2001) (2nd edn.) Chapter 2, 'Selecting a Suitable Topic', in *Surviving Your Dissertation: A Comprehensive Guide to Content and Process*. London: Sage.

Punch, K.F. (2005) Chapter 3, 'Research Questions' (and possibly Chapter 2, 'Some Central Issues'), in *Introduction to Social Research: Quantitative and Qualitative Approaches*. London: Sage.

Walliman, N. (2004) Chapter 3, 'What Will It Be About?' in *Your Undergraduate Dissertation: The Essential Guide for Success*. London: Sage.

Chapter 4

What Kind of Researcher Are You?

"Now, what I want is, Facts. Teach these boys and girls nothing but Facts. Facts alone are wanted in life. Plant nothing else, and root out everything else. You can only form the minds of reasoning animals upon Facts: nothing else will ever be of any service to them. This is the principle on which I bring up my own children, and this is the principle on which I bring up these children. Stick to Facts, sir!' Charles Dickens [1868] (2007)

If I can't dance, I don't want to be in your revolution.'

Emma Goldman[1]

This chapter considers the possible answers which you could give to the question: what kind of researcher are you? The question relates to your view of truth and knowledge; what they are and how they are established. The chapter considers the place of empirical research and positivism, and inductive and deductive approaches, alongside various perspectives on the scientific method. The chapter next moves on to consider how this translates to the personal stances of researchers, giving a few examples of how academics have thought about their role, and what thinking and writing means to them. This chapter isn't a comprehensive guide to this complex philosophical area. Rather, the aim is to provide some signposts which you can pursue independently. There is a more extensive reading list under Further Reading at the end of the chapter which you can explore at your leisure.

The Truth Is Out There: Empiricism and Theories

Empirical data on its own is not enough. We can collect data of every kind, but in the end we are left with numbers and words which carry little meaning in themselves. We need to do something with data in order to make it mean something. Empirical data can be conceptualised as a series of objects which potentially tell us truths of some kind, to a greater or lesser extent, about aspects of the world. They both represent, and are part of, the world. In their raw state, unjoined-up and untheorised, they tell us very little about the whole or any of its constituent elements. Such objects on their own are of somewhat limited use without bringing them together with theories. This can only happen if researchers make it happen. Researchers make decisions about collecting data, and then shape and interpret it using concepts and theories, their own and others.

On the other hand, theory with no evidential base is equally hopeless. Theories are not free-floating ideas with no connection to the world. They may talk with other theories more than with any empirical data collected by the theorist themselves, but they attempt to talk about and to the world in its real and constructed state. In disconnected 'theory' we find instead a series of ideas which, however interesting, provocative, and nice to look at, leave us none the wiser as to their usefulness, veracity or accuracy, representative truth, interpretative meaning, factual quality, or poetry.

Therefore, a central task of research is to find connections between the empirical world and theoretical frameworks. This should not be confused with the methodology adopted. There are all kinds of ways in which this might be done. After all, philosophers are just as interested as social policy analysts in making sense of the world: but they might do it differently.

How it is done can be broadly seen as a choice on several different axes defined by the starting point of the researcher and the kind of project with which they are engaged.

- Do we start with theories, and see how useful they are in making sense of what we might call 'real life'? Or should we start with 'real life', and see what frameworks we can generate out of it which will bring meaning and order to the mess?

- Is our aim to seek higher truths about humanity or to intervene in a local child care scheme?

- Should we collect the numbers of the newly divorced or ask the newly divorced how they feel about it? Each method will tell us something which the other one does not; yet neither method will tell us everything.

Questions of objectivity, scale and purpose are rife in doing research. In doing your dissertation, you will need to grasp some sense of the central debates and arrive at a view about where you stand in them. You will probably have already started to do this earlier in your studies. But in doing your dissertation, you will now need to link what might seem like quite abstract and philosophical principles to the decisions which you make about the kinds of research question you pose, and how you go about executing your study.

The Truth Is Out There – Or Is It In Here?

Positivist approaches start from the assumption that it is possible to step aside from the everyday social mêlée and observe, measure, record, and ultimately, theorise it. The world is assumed to be observable and is external to us. The assumption made is that the world is structured in ways which allow us to make observations, for example, it will have patterns, which will mean that making predictions and forecasts is possible. There is a philosophical assumption that it is ultimately one world with a physical reality which we all share.

In this approach, the social mêlée can be separated from the observer. For example, the social flow continues irrespective of whether the observer is present, or what they think of it. It is assumed that observers are capable of developing competencies as researchers. In the role of researcher, they become capable of developing a particular kind of competency, that of viewing reality in a relatively detached and unpartisan way. The circumstances of their making those observations and their personal situation, feelings, senses and attitudes will have no bearing upon the data recorded. This can be organised and ensured by learning and following particular techniques and methods. In that sense it doesn't really matter who has made the observation, provided that they are competent and follow the rules of making such observations in the same way as everyone else.

Positivist approaches generally assume that findings should be generalisable, i.e. research should be repeatable, and therefore theories which arise will hold true at least for some time. The kind of knowledge which can be generated should be specific and tightly defined, the simplest method and the simplest expressions of conclusions are preferred. Knowledge should be distilled and robust enough to withstand close examination and attempts of refutation. In the early days of positivism, the social universe was assumed to operate according to laws, and ideas were expressed in those terms, much as natural scientists assume and express the physical universe. This is no longer a key characteristic of positivist approaches.

However, highly positivistic approaches may aim to develop overarching theories which integrate systems and might ultimately see these kinds of theories as the most valid form of social knowledge.

Relativist approaches operate from a different set of assumptions. The key lies in whether or not researchers can separate themselves from reality. In fact, relativist approaches theorise our reality as in part a figment of our imagination, or at least, in more sociological terms, part of our social imagination and experience. The assumption made is that we encounter, observe and record reality in partisan ways. We interpret what we see in the light of our own assumptions and world views, experiences, social location, and expectations. Researchers here must also become competent in their ability to do this, developing higher order skills of collecting data which relate to meanings, and finding ways to interpret and shape meaning. Researchers in these traditions tend to assume that social knowledge is contingent and prone to change. Researchers can arrive at social understandings of the world which seem to hold true for some time and across many different kinds of social spaces, but time and society will move on, rendering these 'facts' out of date.

Relativist approaches assume that meanings of observations will change, melt, become hybrid, re-separate. Events, situations, processes and structures are available for review and revision in the meanings which we find in them. This also suggests that reality is more fragmented than it may first seem. It is less the case that there is one reality, rather there is our reality. Highly relativistic stances may assume that individual world views are so individualistic that it is virtually impossible to generalise, or to arrive at a coherent view of reality *per se*. This view has implications for how to approach research, since we can maximise our benefit by concentrating on micro levels of analysis, seeking out instances, cases, and settings each of which is beautiful and unique in its own right.

Task 4.1

Define and List Five Features: Positivism and Relativism

- Define positivism
- List five features of positivism
- Define relativism
- List five features of relativism

Deductive Versus Inductive Approaches

Deductive approaches start from the world as it is represented in theories and discourses. Beginning from the abstract and general level, researchers will test out data form the empirical world against their theoretical frameworks. They will look for where data strongly supports theory, as well as for gaps and problems, for example, where a theory doesn't quite or entirely work when applied to the real world. This is a positive thing, since it allows research to push forwards, refining, shaping, adding, removing theories, gradually building up a body of knowledge which is tried and tested. Where researchers find that the theory doesn't hold, then empirical data might be viewed as evidence which ultimately challenges and refutes the theory. Again this isn't necessarily a bad thing, since it ensures a robust and reliable body of knowledge is left standing. Positivist researchers gain insight from attempting to apply grand theoretical abstractions to the everyday empirical world; some of their insight is into that empirical world, and some into the theory itself.

Both inductive and deductive approaches are developed from a range of methodological approaches, each of which has its own strengths and weaknesses in terms of effectiveness Qualitative approaches tend to work at the level of meaning with the aim of developing understandings and work up theoretical explanations from there, while quantitative researchers will attempt to establish What? Who? How many? Thus, qualitative researchers will be better able to explain 'Why' than 'How' while quantitative researchers will be stronger working the other way around.

In practice, many researchers and writers of both grand theory and local understandings argue that doing research and developing frameworks is a process conducted as a loop. Researchers might go around the loop a few times in the course of doing a project, making use of the opportunity to refine and sharpen data and insights, learning something new in each time.

Task 4.2

Compare and Contrast an Inductive Approach with a Deductive Approach

Draw a diagram to express the differences between the two approaches. Aim to keep it simple: for example, show one process working from the top down, and the other from the ground up, or think about the steps researchers go through around a project process shaped like a loop. Consider whether there are any elements which both approaches share.

Two Researchers in the Playground

The stances you take in these kinds of debates will affect the kind of dissertation that you do and how you think you should go about it. You may be much more interested in making close observations of events over time to establish patterns than conducting an in-depth interview to piece together the meaning of the act to the individuals making those patterns. You may also prefer to test a theory in the real world or to construct a hypothesis, i.e. a theory of your own, than to start by entering the situation and trying to work out what is going on. However, there is a tension between this and the needs of the actual line of inquiry. There is a tension between formulating a good research problem, developing a line of inquiry which flows from it, and taking a stance and developing a methodology irrespective of your own personal stance as a researcher, and vice versa.

Neither deductive or inductive stances are right or wrong, both stances can lead to strong research projects which produce perfectly good findings. You are in good company whichever road you take: you can look up Aristotle, Plato, Galileo, and Bacon to see where they stood on these matters. There are some suggestions under Further Reading at the end of this chapter where you can explore this further.

Scientific Knowledge: Scientific Method?

Researchers do research for many different reasons and will have contrasting views of knowledge, of where it comes from and how it develops. There are several aspects to this debate which have a bearing on the decisions which researchers make.

The debate ask us to consider these kinds of issues:

- Whether or not the methods which researchers in the social sciences use are really *scientific*

- Whether this really matters – *should* research in the social sciences be carried out scientifically? Is it not more of an art than a science?

- What do we mean by *'scientific'*? How do we know if we are behaving 'scientifically'?

This debate stems dates back to the origins of the scientific method, and in part lies with the ways in which theory or knowledge (depending on your view) developed, splitting between increasingly sophisticated disciplines with specialised knowledge on the one hand, and a series of apparently fixed and 'known for sure' things on the other.

This will affect us in so far as researchers implicitly or explicitly believe that their research produces valid truth claims of some kind (bearing in mind the diversity of kinds which this might take). For some, the ultimate evidence for proving that research has been carried out with scientific objectivity is the use of proven, repeatable, scientific methods. For others, the question is defined in different terms; they may be equally exercised by the status of the knowledge, theory or understandings which are generated by research, their contingency, and porous, fluid nature.

In the footsteps of the pantheon of greats such as Locke, Hume and Kant, and the footsoldiers, who developed philosophical critiques of knowledge, researchers have to ask themselves if their research findings can be said to be permanently true; or in any sense true; if true, in what sense exactly? Furthermore, how can we understand the process by which knowledge develops into a body of knowledge? Do research findings accumulate brick by brick until we see the shape of the building? Even if we can arrive at a satisfactory answer to the process by which knowledge appears, it still leaves the problem of how we more precisely conceptualise the body of knowledge. The image of 'a body of knowledge' is itself an interesting one, with certain kinds of imagery and suggestions about connections and solidity. But other images might offer alternative ways of seeing which are equally interesting and exciting.

The Character of Social Research

Ways of thinking about knowledge and its connections to research (what is research? how and why do we do it?) are therefore diverse, with a long and complex history. Moving away from formal theoretical accounts, we can also inquire of those engaged in thinking and research for their answers. Here we will look at just a few, seeing through the eyes of the researchers themselves.

Discovery, Progress and Specialisation

The discovery model frames research as scientific endeavour based on a journey of enlightenment, which proves to be a force for good in society. It is an enlightenment theme which has survived, although it would be fair to say that it waxes and wanes in terms of fashion.

The following extract comes from an article published in 1947 which considers the place of scientific research in the development of religion. The extract is interesting, since the author is both excited by ideas and the abundance of knowledge with which he finds himself surrounded, while observant of the fragmentation of knowledge into specialised disciplines and areas. He also notes the professionalisation of philosophers, who by 1947 are no longer to be found drifting about the coffee houses of Europe waving pomade in the direction of the masses, but had begun to enter the labour market where they would do administration in universities as well as teach. He is therefore thinking about several different aspects of the production of knowledge. Nonetheless, he is implicitly working within a framework of discovery:

> When Wilhelm Wundt died, in 1920, it was said that the last of the scholars who 'knew everything' was gone. In former centuries massive minds could encompass most of human knowledge. Herbert Spencer, for example, was recognized as an authority in philosophy, psychology, sociology, anthropology, political science, education, biology, and geology; he wrote in

There is a tradition of thought which aims to develop a theory of knowledge, or if you like, a theory of theories. Here are four examples. These are the tip of the iceberg, and we cannot possibly do justice to them here. However, each of them had something interesting to say. Some further lines of investigation can be found in the books suggested under Further Reading at the end of the chapter.

1) Karl Popper

Popper considered that most theories can be corroborated by at least some empirical evidence which stands in their favour. However, he noted that some theories undoubtedly accumulate more evidence in their favour, and thus gradually become stronger and more believable over time. In parallel, weaker theories fade and shrink away. As the evidence base for those theories wanes, so those theories become what Popper called falsified, literally meaning, shown to be false. Popper's logical conclusion is that we should recognise the theories which stand the test of time. Therefore, empirical study is very important since we use this to generate evidence bases and find out which theories or bits of theories can be falsified. It also means that tracts of our knowledge base are somewhat temporary, since some theories of the day are liable to be falsified in the future. However, a core body of long-standing, robust knowledge develops over time.

See: Popper (2002) *The Open Society and Its Enemies.*

2) Thomas Kuhn

Kuhn conceptualised the development of scientific knowledge as 'a series of peaceful interludes punctuated by intellectually violent revolutions' in which from time to time 'one conceptual world-view [or paradigm] was replaced by another.'

Not for Kuhn the careful accumulation of theory and knowledge. But instead first the accumulation of theory and knowledge (which stands the test of time) within established paradigms of thought. During this phase scientific endeavours flesh out the paradigms, they don't challenge them. But such paradigms are ultimately vulnerable to challenge and are prone to being overturned. Kuhn argued that scientists might go off in all directions, but only some of them will discover anything interesting and unique. Most of them will keep plugging away within the existing paradigms. Occasionally, one or other of them, or perhaps a little knot or circle, will discover or conceive of something which is entirely new, which runs against the contemporary beliefs and knowledge of the day. In effect, this is the discovery of an outside which lies beyond the paradigm. The paradigm can't explain or accommodate it. The 'revolution' in thought to which Kuhn refers is not necessarily won by persuasion or violence: it is rather more to do with power struggles about the validity of paradigms amongst the thinkers of the day.

See: Kuhn (1996) *The Structure of Scientific Revolutions.*

3) Foucault
Foucault deconstructed knowledge by seeing it as part of the social and institutional setting in which, and through which, it became expressed. He argued that knowledge and theories weren't really 'the truth' as such but can be understood as systems of thought represented as discourses which frame reality, and to all intents and purposes, become it.

Foucault developed his ideas about knowledge through doing empirical studies (for example, famously of clinics), exploring the extent to which discourses themselves ultimately provide and become certain kinds of structure. Discourses become operationalised in and through institutions and everyday life, in powerful, controlling forms. The discourse is the institution which becomes the reality to its inmates and staff. This led him to distrust and disown scientists, doctors and so on, and led him to attack what he saw as the hypocrisy of those who claimed truth in the name of scientific progress.

See: Foucault (2001) *Madness and Civilization.*

4) Patricia Hill Collins
Patricia Hill Collins developed a highly innovative and radical view of knowledge as conceived from the standpoint of the speaker, framed by power relations. She argued that the historical location of black women was found in largely subaltern relationships in particular to white men. These subaltern relationships render them invisible in knowledge systems, including those claimed to be scientific, and their views, understandings and social knowledge are silenced and hidden. Therefore, far from being a 'progressive' force for liberation, knowledge systems and the kinds of truths which are generated by them in fact are oppressive structures which reproduce all of the relations of domination found in society. These include the relations of power found between black women and white men.

The strategy should then be, argues Collins, to relocate black women at the centre of knowledge. This would allow for the emergence of new kinds of social knowledge, including specially black epistemologies. This throws up new kinds of truths while also exposing existing knowledge as white, male, and Eurocentric. The theoretical consequences entail the development of knowledge informed by the intersection of race, class, and gender. The methods

(Continued)

(Continued)

> used by which we come to know what we know are transformed, moving away from a colonial model of researcher and the researched, to an inclusive, partnership model which includes the researched who become active in the research process.
>
> See: Collins (1990) *Black Feminist Thought: Knowledge, Consciousness, and the Politics of Empowerment.*

Figure 4.1   **Science, Truth and Knowledge: Four Perspectives**

all of these fields. But today few men are expert in more than one field of knowledge. Knowledge is increasing at so fast a rate that most scholars find it difficult to keep abreast of the developments in even one department of learning and at the same time do a fair share of the world's work as teacher, physician, administrator. This amazing increase in knowledge is the result of the present emphasis on research. The greatest discovery ever made by man was the discovery of how to discover. The scientific method in its various phases is responsible not only for our growing knowledge of the world but also for the increase in the world's population, for the lengthening of human life, for the comforts which surround us, for the speed of our travel, for the promptness of our news, and for the destructiveness of our wars. Research is the symbol which the historian of the future will use to explain the explosive energy of the last hundred years.

Source: Williams (1947: 3)

My Research: Connecting Social Selves to Social Research

As C. Wright Mills rather famously suggested in 1970:

> The sociological imagination enables us to grasp history and biography and the relations between them within society. That is its task and its promise. (1970: 12).

While this comment relates to sociology, it is nonetheless interesting, and important to recognise the connections between the personal and the research project on the one hand, and the social and political character of the inquiry on the other.

Motivation to, and rationalisations about, research, writing, debating, and arriving at understandings are operationalised by individuals who often explain the meanings of their activities in terms of their contexts.

The so-called 'cultural turn' which swept across the social sciences and humanities from the sixties onwards presented a major challenge to scientific concepts of neutral stance and the assumed invisibility of the person. The concept of the personal (and political) moved centre stage and the range of social locations from which researchers write, and the impact of that on research became more evident. Many researchers write from particular standpoints rooted in their biographies and identities which inform their wish to bring about social understanding, insight and change. This is reflected in the kinds of research questions that are asked, how research is done, and has consequences for the kinds of knowledge, theory, or understandings which are produced.

Researchers often give clues as to their stance and motivations for research. In this first example, Beverley Skeggs discusses her reasons for making her well-known exploration of class and gender:

> The motivation is also partly autobiographical and produced from my experiences of marginalization:

> I read a woman's book, meet such a woman at a party (a woman now, like me) and think quite deliberately as we talk: we are divided: a hundred years ago I'd have been cleaning your shoes I know this and you don't. (Steedman, 1986: 2)

> My mother's sister was a domestic servant when she was young, it was just over sixty years ago. My mother avoided the same fate because she was younger. ... The writing of this book was fuelled by passion and anger. I watched 'class' analysis disappear from feminism and cultural studies as it became increasingly more of an issue for the friends I had grown up with, the people I live(d) with and the women of this research. (Skeggs, 1997: 14–15)

Karen Brodkin in her study of *How Jews Became White Folks and What That Says About Race in America* also connects her line of inquiry to her own and others' experience, this time showing us how inquiry emerges and crystallizes over a period of time:

> Writing about Jewishness was the last thing I expected to do when I started this project. What began as a rather distant study of the ways that race, ethnicity, class and gender combine to construct Americans (what we used to call a unified theory of race, class and gender) turned into an exploration of what the changing places and meanings of Jewishness tell us about Americanness ... readers should know that my qualification as a Jew – growing up in a secular Jewish family and spending much of my life in leftist academic and political circles – are a mix best described as Jewish lite, Jewish late, or nouveau Jew. I have spent the better part of my last decade fumbling around in libraries, at conferences, and in conversations, trying to make my own Jewishness visible and understandable. (2004: ix)

However there are other views: in contrast here is an anti-personal and anti-genealogical comment from Andrew Sayer:

...Insofar as this is a book of critiques, I should perhaps point out that I am more interested in ideas than who might have authored them and more interested in their evaluation than in their history. By and large I therefore avoid questions of how particular authors are to be interpreted. (2000: 3)

Researchers' Obligations

Marx argued that it is the task of the philosopher to not only describe the world but to change it, an idea which has survived. Such connections between politics and social research and social theory are expressed in a diversity of ways, as we began to see in the previous section. This raises issues about the extent to which researchers and thinkers are bystanders or are people who could, and indeed should, get involved.

Here is Alex Callinicos reflecting upon social theory with an interesting comment on theory and its place in the world:

> One virtue of widening the intellectual horizons within which social theory is considered is that it may make it more difficult to sustain certain prejudices. Thus three intellectual historians seeking to draw attention to some neglected nineteenth-century British political thinkers echo the Thatcher government's disdain for the social sciences, which they associate with 'such sociological nabobs as Comte, Durkheim, and Weber'. ...It should be clear enough by now that social theory is an irredeemably political form of thought. As a revolutionary socialist, Marx sought to realize in his own life the unity of theory and practice which he defended philosophically. Tocqueville was an ambitious but frustrated participant in French parliamentary politics during the 1840s ... fundamentally, however much Weber may have sought to resist this conclusion, social theories at least implicitly evaluate as well as analyse, and offer political solutions to what they describe. (2005: 4–5)

Political and ethical dilemmas often present responsibilities to the educated classes (who at times have been targeted on account of their education) more generally, who then arrive at a point where they feel that they should 'take sides'.

In this abridged extract, the Korean sociologist Hyun-Chin Lim discusses some of the dilemmas which he encountered in his lifetime of study in different national contexts, and how he addressed them at different points:

> When I was discharged from the military in 1976, I was trying to figure out what I would do, and studying abroad was one of my options... However, I felt a sense of hypocrisy ... since I had always been talking about Korean independence and autonomy. In particular, there was no way to explain it to my friends who had endured so many hardships as activists in the student movements ... [Afterwards] I was not comfortable when I completed my studies in the United States and stood in front of a classroom in Korea ... The sacrifices of the students who resisted the

new military government under Chon Tu-hwan were great, but they were not satisfied with their studies. I felt that we were committing another historical crime as we sat by and watched them. Eventually, this caused intellectuals to stand up and fight for social reform. I realised how difficult it is to bring about social reform when I was a founding member of civil society groups such as the Nara Association for National Policy, the Citizens' Coalition for Economic Justice, and the Citizens' Coalition for Political Reform. (2007: 51–152)

Feminist Challenges: The Personal As a Political Project

Feminist approaches to epistemology and methodology are alive and kicking, with their own genealogies. See for example:

* Roberts [1971] (1997) *Doing Feminist Research*
  This is a classic collection of papers which explores feminist research

* Ramazanoglu and Holland (2002) *Feminist Methodology: Challenges and Choices*
  An exciting and challenging book that explores scientific method and enlightenment legacy alongside postmodern arguments and feminist epistemology; a second, smaller section looks at doing feminist research

* Harding (2003) *The Feminist Standpoint Theory Reader*
  A collection of papers exploring feminist standpoint theory from the seventies and eighties and where we are today

* Letherby (2003) *Feminist Research in Theory and Practice*
  For an up-to-date survey and critical discussion

The Politics of Research Projects in Politics

Doing research for a research project in the discipline of politics presents its own difficulties when it comes to a consideration of whether or not doing political research is, as it were, actually political. It raises issues about how we might view politics as a discipline, and how we might go about viewing the truth claims of researchers and thinkers about politics. Most students of politics will find classic texts with a more philosophical bent helpful, but two useful books for more general readers, perhaps from other disciplines, are:

* Marsh and Stoker (2002) *Theories and Methods in Political Science*
  This is a useful book giving an overview to the connections between methodological approaches and frameworks such as behaviouralism and institutionalism which are in turn connected to the epistemological issues arising

- Leftwich (2004) *What is Politics? The Activity and Its Study*
  This book is probably too basic for third year students of politics, but is
  a useful introduction for students from other areas approaching social
  and political issues without a background in political theory or political
  science, or wanting to do a research dissertation from a political standpoint

Research and Real Life: Occupation and Applications to Problems in Policy

The relationship between research and policy is a sometimes vexed one,
since it can be difficult to close the gap. However, doing research which
can be used by others is one of the drivers of research, and dissemination
and influence are viewed as among its most important aspects. Here is a
description of an attempt to close the gap between research and policy by
founding a journal to provide an avenue for dissemination:

> *Criminology & Public Policy* was born when Jeremy Travis, then
> Director of the National Institute of Justice (NIJ), recognizing the
> need for a vehicle for the user-friendly dissemination of policy-
> relevant research, put out a request for proposals (RFP) for the
> development of a new journal that would have increased the rele-
> vance of criminological research at the heart of its mission. Travis
> was frustrated that so little of the policy-relevant research, much of
> which NIJ had funded, translated into meaningful policy change. In
> his original proposal submitted in response to the RFP, Todd Clear
> envisioned a journal that would operate differently than the tradi-
> tional peer-review journal while still maintaining the credibility and
> integrity that comes with the double-blind peer-review process. The
> proposed journal would have as its mission bridging the gap between
> policy-relevant research findings and criminal justice policy. (Clear
> and Frost, 2007: 633)

Richard Titmuss is often credited with playing a major role in establishing post-war social policy research in the UK, prompting the emergence
of departments of social administration and subsequently social policy
alongside the transformation of the thinking about the training and
development of those working in the public sector. His particular view
was that while he was not against the pursuit of ideas as such, disciplines such as sociology's main purpose was ultimately to provide fodder
which could inform real interventions in society to mitigate inequalities
and poverty. (See Titmuss, 1950, *Problems of Social Policy*.)
   The world of informing, intervening in, and influencing policy and government research has its own standpoints and matters of debate. In the UK, the
advent of the New Labour government's modernisation project has
raised new issues about the complex relationship between users, citizens,

consumers, institutions, academic research, the knowledge of service users, and policies. This has been one of the drivers in pushing effective research and community engagement centre stage. A discussion of the impact community engagement of the New Labour modernisation project on government social research and policy communities can be found in Bochel and Duncan (2007).

User involvement in services and care, both as direct users and in terms of their participation in, and even control of, policy formation and governance has moved centre stage in increased recognition of the particular kinds of knowledge which users develop and their potential contribution.

The issues of engaging users with policy and practice include:

• The kind and amount of service provided and the extent of user input into its construction and provision, and feedback and review subsequently

• User participation in the formation of policy instruments

• User participation in, and control of, settings, institutions and systems which deliver services

• Ethical issues of informed consent

• Ethical and quality assurance issues of governance and accountability

Specialisms in community engagement and service user involvement have developed. See for example:

• Brafield and Eckersly (2008)

  A discussion of, with practical suggestions for, conducting, an ethical and effective consultation exercise with a vulnerable group

• Consumers in NHS Research Support Unit (2000)

  A report which aims to brief and update researchers on the co-production of knowledge and understanding and a role of service users

• Clark et al. (eds) (2005)

  A discussion about involving children in services aimed at them, the title of which, 'Beyond Listening', indicates the stance taken

Relating your interest in social analysis and critique to your occupation is also a factor in choices about research. Many occupations are defined in terms of their aim to achieve and manage social change and social justice. Many occupational groups are users of research and understandings generated by social scientists of all kinds and many organisations use, produce or commission research themselves. Health and social care as well as education, local authorities and statutory bodies are good examples.

In the following example, the field of social work is discussed by the International Association of Schools of Social Work and International Federation of Social Workers in these terms:

The social work profession promotes social change, problem solving in human relationships and the empowerment and liberation of people to enhance well-being. Utilising theories of human behaviour and social systems, social work intervenes at the points where people interact with their environments. Principles of human rights and social justice are fundamental to social work. (Crawford and Walker, 2004: viii)

From this flows a commitment in the social work profession to developing highly skilled professionals who can 'develop a rigorous grounding in and understanding of theories and models' (ibid.) in order to navigate social work as a 'complex activity with no absolute "rights" and "wrongs" of practice for each situation' (ibid.).

See under Further Reading at the end of this chapter for some more suggested readings.

Task 4.3

What Kind of Researcher Are You? Discussion Points

1) That which we might broadly define as 'the social sciences' typically generates particular kinds of understandings and knowledge. On balance, how would you answer the question 'What are the social sciences good for?'
2) What kind of researcher are you?

Summary

- Connecting empiricism with theories is essential for undergraduates doing a dissertation. You might not make a fully empirical study (i.e. you might do a theoretical dissertation), but in all dissertations you should develop some sense of the reasons for your choice and how you relate to the philosophical issues raised

- Positivism: the truth is out there and you can discover it by following scientific methods

- Relativism: the truth is in here as well as out there, we make sense of reality in specific and partisan ways

- Deductive versus inductive approaches: in the first, start at the top with the theory and test it out by a case on the ground; and in the second, start at the ground with the case or instance and work back up to theory

- Do the social sciences practise scientific methods? Should this be the norm?

- What is social scientific knowledge, and how does it develop?

- Four examples (from a potentially large list) were taken: Popper; Kuhn; Foucault; Hill Collins

- There are a range of reasons and motivations for doing research: discovery; autobiographical; the anti-personal; the political; the developmental including in professional terms; to make an intervention in policy

- Why do research? What does research and theory mean to me?

Further Reading

Becker, S. and Bryman, A. (2004) *Understanding Research for Social Policy and Practice: Themes, Methods and Approaches.* Bristol: Policy Press.

Beresford, P. and Croft, S. (2001) 'Service Users' Knowledges and the Social Construction of Social Work', *Journal of Social Work*, (1) 3: 295–316.

Blackburn, S. (2001) *Think! A Compelling Introduction to Philosophy.* Oxford: Oxford Paperbacks.

Bochel, H. M. and Duncan, S. (2007) *Making Policy in Theory and Practice.* Cambridge: Policy Press.

Burke, A. (2000) *A Social History of Knowledge: From Gutenberg to Diderot.* Cambridge: Polity Press.

Cudd, A. and Andreasen, R. (2004) *Feminist Theory: A Philosophical Anthology.* Oxford: Wiley-Blackwell.

Descartes, R. (2007) *Discourse on Method and the Meditations.* London: Penguin.

Goldblatt, D. (2004) *Knowledge and the Social Sciences: Theory, Method and Practice.* London: Routledge.

Gomm, R. and Davies, C. (eds) (2000) *Using Evidence in Health and Social Care.* London: Sage.

Okasha, S. (2002) *Philosophy of Science: A Very Short Introduction.* Oxford: Oxford University Press.

Pampel, F.C. (2000) *Sociological Lives and Ideas: An Introduction to the Classical Theorists.* London: Palgrave Macmillan.

Pirsig, R.M. (1999) *Zen and the Art of Motorcycle Maintenance* (25th anniversary edn). London: Vintage.

Sayer, A. (1999) *Realism and the Social Sciences.* London: Sage.

Sedgwick, E.K. (2007) *The Epistemology of the Closet.* University of California Press.

Williams, M. (2000) *Science and Social Science: An Introduction.* London: Routledge.

Note

1   Emma Goldman was a famous female Russian anarchist in the twentieth century.

Chapter 5

Writing the Research Proposal

Overview

What is a research proposal?

The components of the research proposal

Research Proposal Checklist: WHITTLE

- What
- How
- Importance
- Timely
- Title
- Literature
- End result

Giving and receiving feedback about your own and others' research

Ethical considerations in close-up

Risks to the researcher

The researched at risk

Guidelines from professional associations

Equalities for all

This chapter is all about writing the research proposal. You should draft a proposal, however roughly, as part of reading this chapter. It is suggested that designing, proposing and writing the research project is a process of whittling away at the design, approach and concepts, returning to each part of the proposal a few times in order to get it right. Time must be spent on developing the proposal.

Each section of the proposal is discussed. Firstly, you are asked to work at your research question a little more; then to look at aims and objectives.

You need to identify the major concepts and theoretical frameworks with which you will work, and design a methodological approach as well as conduct an initial literature search and reflect on ethical issues. One of the suggested Tasks is to discuss the proposed project with your colleagues. This is partly to learn about giving and receiving constructive feedback as well as seeing your work through the eyes of your colleagues, who might have useful suggestions to make.

What Is a Research Proposal?

Good research proposals both give an overview of the project and a well-informed discussion of the nuts and bolts of the proposed research. There is a persuasive element to research proposals. In part, although you are only proposing a project, you need to show that you have thought it through and can do it. Research proposals should demonstrate to the reader that:

- You can see how your proposed project connects with the literature and is informed by, and builds on, the current state of research in specific and constructive ways

- You are proposing a properly worked out, thought-through, viable and timely piece of research

- You are aware of the strengths of your proposed approach and possible limitations

- You have weighed up the ethical issues involved

- Your research will lead to original findings

  The research proposal is extremely important. A good proposal lays the foundations of good research and it is worth investing time and effort into getting it right. Skimping on details may well mean that you end up covering core tasks downstream when you would rather be collecting data or developing your arguments. Proposals which are still too broad at the stage of their submission tend to lead to issues around trying to conduct research effectively within the timescales allowed.

  Developing your research proposal is a good opportunity really to get engaged with your chosen area. Be inspired! Get interested and begin to carve out your own interests. It is also an opportunity to work differently with your academic tutors, perhaps deepening and broadening your understanding of their specific research interests as well as research more generally. In many universities you will find that working up your proposal allows you the space to develop your research relationship with your supervisor(s) and dissertation module leaders.

Components of the Research Proposal

Research proposals cover key areas in common; however, you may find that your department, school or university sets out particular requirements,

- A clearly defined research question
- A persuasive argument that the research is important and worthwhile
- The researcher has identified their philosophical stance, possibly standpoint and style of research, for example positivist, feminist etc.
- The researcher can link their proposed project to a wider field of study and show how their work adds to it
- The researcher has designed a methodological approach which is viable, reliable and valid
- The researcher gives reasons for their choice of specific methods, discussing strengths and limitations of the approach
- How the research plan is to be executed has been well worked out: the nuts and bolts of doing the research, including a project plan, has been provided
- There should be some consideration given to whether or not ethical issues arise, and how they will be addressed
- There is a strong bibliography containing:

    o Recent research reports including journal publications
    o Works by the leading researchers in the field
    o References to the methods literature and debates
    o Works relating to ethics

Figure 5.1   **What Makes a Good Research Proposal?**

including a format or style, as well as indicating the relative importance attached to each section or component (often reflected in the marking scheme). You should check the requirements of the research proposal, and make sure that you seek an academic tutor's advice or feedback before submitting it.

The key areas which are generic to most research proposals are:

1) *Title*

The title of the dissertation should reflect the well-defined aims of the research.

You might find that acceptable titles of research seem long and convoluted to you. Your instinct might be to try to make a title attractive as though it is the title of a book or website. But research write-ups are in a different category of media. It is perfectly acceptable and even necessary to use long and perhaps 'tedious' titles. The title needs to tell a researcher enough to decide whether to pull up the abstract. The abstract needs to tell the researcher enough to decide whether to read the whole research write-up. Because of this, titles are often rather long and specific.

You can make your title more focused by several means:

- By identifying the setting; for example, the organisation under investigation; the neighbourhood or country; the time in which it is set if historical etc.

- The actual research question, if pithy, often makes a good title; a subheading can also be used with it

- By being concrete about what it is that you are researching; for example, a study of white girl gangs aged 14–15 years old in Swansea

Further Focusing the Title

Example 1: Why are all the managers white at Moon Bank Inc.?

This looks like an initial question which has prompted the research. It is rather too broad and is really a research topic rather than a closely defined question which can be answered. It is true that the researcher has observed and problematised a facet of an organisational structure. However:

- The title is vague and rather general. It invites a big, sweeping analysis which could include all sorts of things, for example, a section which tries to express the history of the slave trade and colonialism could appear in the project. On the other hand, an evaluation of the current systems of stratification could also appear. Yet to include both is a massive project

- The research to be carried out is not particularly clear, The research could be a philosophical or polemical piece, or it could be an evaluation of staff recruitment, selection, and promotion policy and procedures at the bank. These are quite different kinds of projects which different readerships would enjoy

- It is also rather broad in scope – *all* of the managers might refer to managers of every grade, and if the bank is a large organisation, then perhaps the proposal is of a global analysis

- Finally, it may be based on a faulty premise which undermines the research as a whole. It might be found in empirical data that not *all* of the managers are white – although there may be a significant white majority. On the other hand, if it is true that there is a 99–100% white management then this could be a highly interesting dissertation, as it still would be if it were 75%. In this case, it might be wise, and indeed a powerful statement, to find out the correct statistic and include it in the title

Example 2: All change: the need for radical intervention at Moon Bank Inc. to enable BME managers to take their place in the boardroom

This is a potentially stronger title because it tells the reader:

- Who or what the research is about (BME presence in the boardroom of Moon Bank Inc.)

- More clearly what the research will investigate (strategies and interventions to enable BME achievement)

- That the scope of the research is clearer than in the first example (it is about managers crossing the white ceiling into the boardroom)

- That the research is located at Moon Bank Inc., although this might still be a large global organisation so it is still rather large

- Something of the flavour of the project: the first phrase 'All change' suggests a policy change or intervention of some kind.

However, the title is still not quite right. For example, to what extent has the researcher assumed that a course of action is required before they have done the research?

Example 3: All change: an evaluation of the frameworks in operation at Moon Bank Inc. which aim to facilitate BME managers to take their place in the boardroom: a case study of two branches in Liverpool and Cardiff

Task 5.1

Titles

Firstly, what comments might you make about Example 3? How else might you reword it?

Secondly, using artistic licence, construct a title for a piece of research which explores recycling practices in your supermarket.

2) *Aims and Objectives*

    a) Typical aims include making a contribution to:

- A debate and academic thinking on a subject

- A body of research on a topic

- Policy or other kinds of interventions, so that the research is action-orientated

An example starting point for working out one of the aims might be:

- To evaluate the formal and informal processes of promotion within Moon Bank

This is a better aim than:

- To work out why white people get promoted so often at Moon Bank

b) Objectives are more specific to your study and include the key research questions. Research objectives must be clearly articulated; should be specific; narrow; there shouldn't be too many of them; should all relate to each other.

Examples could include something like this:

- How much is the degree of support given to possible candidates influenced by informal networks?

- Do all candidates have an equal chance of finding out about forthcoming promotion opportunities?

3) *Introduction to the Research Topic*

This section should explain what the research topic is and why you have chosen it. It should include the reasons why the research is being conducted, i.e. why it is important and why it is timely to conduct this research now. Try to find some evidence of recent interest in the topic (e.g. in the news, or in the organisation's documentation, as well as any debates in academic journals and the public media) which will help you to show that your chosen topic is important. This section should give the background to the proposal.

4) *Literature Review*

This section should locate the proposed research in the wider field of literature. The aim is to allow the reader to understand the contexts of your research, and what contribution your research will make to it. At this stage, the review will necessarily consist of a survey or overview of the field. Doing this initial literature review will help you to refine the research further and will enable you to see how others have approached the task of empirical investigation in terms of methods used. Even though this is the initial stages of doing a literature review and the final version in the dissertation will be much longer and more thorough, it is important to clearly connect the literature to your own substantive inquiry.

Figure 5.2 shows both unsuccessful and successful literature reviews for a research proposal from Brimingham University.

5) *Research Design*

This section should include the following:

- The research methods to be used: how will data be collected and analysed? Explain why you have selected your particular method(s), whether it/they have been used before in existing studies on the topic, and what the advantages and limitations were when used before, and what they might be in your proposed research

Unsuccessful Literature Review

Foucault's works looked at mental illness, asylums, and the archaeology of knowledge. Roy Porter's and Edward Shorter's histories of psychiatry and psychology show that definitions of mental illness have differed across time and place. Ernst and Swartz record that under colonialism, science and medicine contributed to racial, class, and sexual discrimination. Feminist writers Chesler and Showalter who have written on psychiatry will be important for this study. Post-structuralist and post-modernist approaches to the construction and representation of identities will be used. Post-colonialism's concern with the 'subaltern' and the suppression of 'subaltern voices' will be significant.

Successful Literature Review

This study will draw on diverse approaches to the history of psychiatry, and to the origins of segregation in southern Africa. Histories of psychiatry and psychology have shown that, although having a probable partial biochemical basis, the criteria for the definition of mental illness have differed across time and place. The history of science and medicine in both Europe and in the colonial order provide a means for exploring the role of biomedicine (including psychiatry) in contributing to racial, class, and sexual discrimination. Feminist analyses of the centrality of gender, and critiques of psychiatry and psychology, will be a key axis around which this study is formed. For example, while men of all races formed the majority of inmates at the Natal Government Asylum in nineteenth-century Natal, women were deemed to be particularly prone to particular forms of mental illness.

Post-structuralist and post-modernist approaches to the construction and representation of identities, and to the articulation of power, will provide a means of deconstructing the 'texts' and discourses which are an important part of this study. In particular, the works of Michel Foucault on mental illness, asylums, and the archaeology of knowledge will be considered. I recognise, however, that the application of Foucault's ideas in the African context is problematic. Post-colonialism's concern with the 'subaltern' and the suppression of 'subaltern voices' will be reflected in attempts to 'hear the voices' of the institutionalised.

Figure 5.2 **Sample Literature Reviews for a Research Proposal from Birmingham University: The Research Topic is 'The History of Mental Illness in Natal in the Period up to 1945'**

Source: www.ssdd.bcu.ac.uk/learner/writingguides/1.07.htm

- Research methods not being used – explain the reasons for your rejection of other methods, and what, if you have chosen them, you might have gained/lost

- Explain how you are positioned in the research as the researcher. For example, your stance as a researcher, and how this has affected the kinds of questions posed and the methods which you have selected

6) *Ethical Considerations*

All research involving human and animal participants must be considered in the light of the ethical issues which are raised. You will probably find that your university has particular regulations which govern how ethics should be handled. You must ensure that you find out what they are, and work within them. A more detailed consideration of ethics is found towards the end of this chapter.

For now be sure that your proposal addresses the following issues:

- How will you go about gaining your participants' consent?

- How will you be able to demonstrate that your participants have given informed consent, i.e. know fully the implications of what they are consenting to, as opposed to simply agreeing to be researched?

- How will participants' confidentiality and anonymity be maintained?

- Specifically, what will you do with the data you collect, including personal details?

- How will your participants have access to the results of your research?

For a further discussion of consent, please see Chapter 9, under the heading 'Consent'.

7) *Conclusions and Recommendations*

It is vital to aim to draw a conclusion. All project proposals must show that this is in the intention, and show how the conclusions will relate the proposed aims and objectives. A way of approaching this at proposal stage is to identify some of the potential including theoretical, methodological, policy or other issues. You might also indicate that you would expect to make recommendations, especially if this is a policy-orientated project.

8) *Time Scales/Project Plan*

Research proposals usually contain a project plan of some kind. You should check the assessment requirements to see how much depth is needed at this stage. Break down the research process into stages and allocate a fixed time period for each stage, indicating the time budget (how many days, weeks or number of hours) you intend to spend on each activity. You should also aim to include the main landmarks of the various stages which you will go through in the project.

Providing a project plan demonstrates that you have scoped the project and have enough resources to ensure that you will bring the project to a successful conclusion.

9) *Pilot or Feasibility Study*

Most undergraduate dissertations do not require a pilot or feasibility study, although you may find it helpful to do one, if you can do it in time. If you do, then do include information about this in the research proposal, and don't be afraid to indicate where you learned about mistakes as well as what worked well.

10) *Bibliography*

This should be set out in the usual way and should include the most important and relevant publications for your research. It should include references to:

- Context and background reading

- Literature and previous studies undertaken including bang up-to-date journal articles

- Literature on the research methods you intend to use

- All online sources used including dates of search

- Ethical issues

As you can see, having even two or three references relating to each bullet point would already produce a bibiliography of 12–15 sources, and the scope is much wider than for ordinary coursework assignments.

Refining and Shaping the Proposal: Whittle Away

In order to get your proposal right, be prepared to spend some time on it, shaping and paring it down, revisiting its component parts to get them right. See Figure 5.3.

Giving and Receiving Feedback about Research

A good way to whittle your research proposal is to share it with others and get feedback. Learning to give and receive feedback about research is a valuable lesson, and well worth pursuing.

1) **What**: What is the research question – are you sure that you are proposing a refined and shaped question rather than a topic area or even broader theme?
2) **How**: What methodologies have you selected and why have you rejected others? What is your philosophical stance as a researcher?
3) **Importance**: Why is the proposed research important? What are the target audiences who are most likely to find this research important?
4) **Timely**: Why do you think that this research should be carried out now?
5) **Title**: Does the reader know what the project is about from the proposed title?
6) **Literature**: Have you identified the key *academic* research which has been carried out in this field so far? Do you clearly show how your proposed research relates to existing literature and builds upon it?
7) **End result**: When you have completed this piece of research, what will the end result be? Are the aims of the research clearly defined?

Figure 5.3   **Research Proposal Checklist: WHITTLE**

Task 5.2

Giving and Receiving Feedback about Research

Working in small groups, share draft research proposals.

The author of the proposal should remain silent and listen to the rest of the group as they:

- Identify two strengths of their proposal
- Identify two weakness of the proposal
- Discuss which sections need further work
- Consider the ethical issues which arise, choosing one proposal which raises complicated and/or interesting ethical issues

At the end, the author should get the right to reply.

Move on to the next person.

Task 5.3

Learning to Talk About Your Research: Personal Reflection

Learning to talk about your own and others' research can be regarded as a particular skill. It requires a mode of self which needs to be listening, constructive, undefensive, open and honest, reflexive, sensitive and engaged.

Ask yourself, what did you learn from giving and receiving feedback about your own and others' research? What did you learn from the interaction of the rest of the group about your own and other's projects?

Ethical Considerations in Close-up

As more research has been carried out with real people, so there has been growing concern over the ensuring protection against harm on the one hand, while recognising the need to allow research to occur on the other. Post-war concerns were sparked by Nazi experimentation on prisoners, but in fact were compounded by subsequent research practices, for example those shown by the Milgram experiments (see Milgram and Bruner, 2005), which demonstrated the extent to which deference to authority figures led educated, responsible, and modern members of the public, when placed in social roles in the research project, to carry out (as far as they knew) acts of violence. Concerns have become crystallised into debates concerning, and more work focusing on, the question of ethics in research. There are two aspects to this: safeguarding the rights and safety of both the researcher and the researched.

Risks to the Researcher

The problem of risk to the researcher is a tricky area. On the one hand, live research introduces an element of uncertainty and opportunity. In order to make the most of the research, researchers will often need to go 'off piste', which may involve getting into situations which they did not anticipate and for which they may be ill prepared. Secondly, the nature of the research project may itself necessarily involve risk. Arguably, many a research project would never have happened if the risk had been duly weighed up and presented to risk-aversive departmental supervisors and university committees. Finally, risk is a socially constructed concept regulated by institutions. What might be perceived as high risk today may not have been viewed as such yesterday, and vice versa tomorrow. Thus the process by which risk becomes recognised and the social and institutional relations through which it arises and is evaluated also means that different kinds of risks are subject to greater regulation and scrutiny at different historical moments.

On the other hand, risk is with us and as a new researcher setting off into the unknown you do need to take heed of it. It is suggested that a pragmatic approach is taken: wherever possible you should seek to minimise your risks and maximise your opportunities, and be clear about the level and kind of risk which is within your threshold. This means thinking things through carefully beforehand. See 'Hazards' in Chapter 9 for more about this.

The Researched at Risk

Equally, it is difficult to always be able to accurately assess the risk of a research participant, since the reaction of participants to research when all goes well or badly is unknowable. Furthermore, while it is possible to guard against accidents, many events are not within the gift of the researcher. In other words, accidents will happen. As a rule of thumb, the guide is to seek to safeguard the rights and dignity of the researched. Carefully consider how you would ensure ethical participation in your research project, as detailed in Figure 5.4.

Ethical participation is:

- Voluntary

This includes the right to withdraw from the research process or any part of it, at any point, without giving a reason. Participants need to sign a consent form (see Chapter 9 for 'Consent' and Appendix 3 for an example of a consent form). Please note that special arrangements need to be put in place where research participants are unable to sign a consent form, or their consent is uncertain, or they are deemed particular vulnerable.

- Informed

The participant should know what the research is about, its aims and purposes, and how their contribution will be used. Please note that you need to give consideration to what you will do if you wish to carry out unobtrusive research, for example, by participant observation, where the participants do not know that they are being researched until after the fact (if ever).

- Safe

The participant should not be put at risk by your actions, this being defined as both physical and psychological.

- Confidential

Participants should be able to leave the research process confident in procedures which will keep their identity and contact details confidential if they are expecting this, for example, that their contributions will be anonymised in write-ups. You need to think about what you will do with personal details, for example, how long to keep them and their disposal.

Figure 5.4   **Ethical Participation by Humans**

Box 5.1 contains sources of further assistance on ethics from professional associations. Please note that ethical procedures need to be followed in working with animals – albeit not the signing of consent forms.

Box 5.1   Ethics: Guidelines from Professional Associations

Social Research Association	www.the-sra.org.uk/
– look for: Ethical Guidelines	ethical.htm
British Sociological Association	www.britsoc.co.uk/equality
– look for: Statement of Ethical Practice, in the 'Equality' section	
The British Psychological Society	www.bps.org.uk/the-
– look for: Code of Conduct and Ethical Guidelines	society/the- society_home.cfm
Economic and Social Research Council (ESRC)– look for: Research Ethics Framework	www.esrc.ac.uk
National Health Service: National Patient Safety Agency – look for: National Research Ethics Service	www.nres.npsa.nhs.uk

---

Box 5.2   Specific Help Re: Research Involving Animals

American Psychological Association, Committee on Animal Ethics and Ethics – look for: Guidelines for Ethical Conduct in the Care and Use of Animals	www.apa.org/science/anguide.html
Nuffield Council on Bioethics – look for: Our Work, – and then: The ethics of research involving animals	www.nuffieldbioethics.org
Medical Research Council – Look for: The use of animals in research	www.mrc.ac. uk/index.htm
Animal Procedures Committee	www.apc.gov.uk

Equality and Difference

Finally, the broader area of equality and difference is one in which you should reflect in designing your research. In turn, as a researcher, you too have rights. You may feel that your equal rights have been or could be breached. There are a number of sources of help in addition to the above, including guidelines found at:

- The Equality and Human Rights Commission (www.equalityhuman rights.com)

Summary

- What makes a good research proposal?

  o A clearly defined research question

  o A persuasive argument that the research is important and worthwhile

  o The researcher can link their proposed project to a wider field of study

  o The researcher has designed a methodological approach which is viable, reliable and valid; and can give reasons for their choice of methods

  o How the research plan is to be executed has been well worked out: the nuts and bolts of doing the research, including a project plan, have been provided

  o There is a strong bibliography containing: recent research reports including journal publications; works by the leading researchers in the field; references to the methods literature and debates

- What does a research proposal contain?

- A research proposal contains a research question, reports on initial work, and a developed plan for carrying out the research. It includes:

  o A title
  o Aims and objectives
  o An introduction to the research question
  o The literature review
  o A research design
  o Selection

- o Nuts and bolts: how, where, what, why, when
- o Ethical considerations
- o Conclusions and recommendations
- o Time scales/project plans
- o Details of a pilot or feasibility study
- o A bibliography

WHITTLE down your research proposal:

- o What
- o How
- o Importance
- o Timely
- o Title
- o Literature
- o End result

- Giving and receiving feedback about research:

  - o What did you learn from giving and receiving feedback?

- Don't forget ethical considerations:
  - o Risks to the researcher
  - o The researched at risk
  - o Guidelines from professional associations

- Equalities for all

Further Reading

Bell, J. (2005) Chapter 2, 'Planning the Project' and Chapter 3, 'Ethics and Integrity in Research', in *Doing your Research Project: A Guide for First-time Researchers in Education, Health and Social Science.* Maidenhead: Open University Press.

Berg, B.L. (2007) *Qualitative Research Methods for the Social Sciences.* New York: Pearson International.

Hakim, C. (2008) (2nd edn.), *Research Design: Successful Designs for Social Economic Research.* London: Routledge.

Kenyon, E. and Hawker, S. (2000) '"Once Would be Enough": Some Reflections on the Issue of Safety for Lone Researchers', *International Journal of Social Research Methodology*, 4 (2): 313–27.

Welland, T. and Pugsley, L. (2002) *Ethical Dilemmas in Qualitative Research.* Aldershot: Ashgate.

Chapter 6

Finding Resources and Doing the Literature Review

Overview

What is a literature review?

Effective searching

What makes a good source?

Types of sources and their relative strengths and weaknesses

- Online sources
- Internet sources: health warnings

Building the literature review

- Hooks
- Anecdotes
- Main concepts
- Use the original texts

Reviewing texts from a different moment in time

Help with academic writing style

- Example: how to introduce and link texts

The literature review is a key building block in the academic challenge which you mount in the whole of your dissertation

This chapter turns to researching and preparing the literature review. It explores the purpose of the literature review and gives some tips on producing a good one. This includes working with a range of sources and different ways of finding and accessing them, such as via online gateways and sources.

The chapter encourages you to critically evaluate the usefulness and reliability of sources. Next, the chapter turns to consider how to build up the literature review, providing some tips on linkages, giving the review some
pace, and referring you to Chapter 12, Drawing Conclusions and Writing Up,
for further thoughts about grammar and English for academic purposes.

What Is a Literature Review?

The literature review in undergraduate dissertations, like postgraduate
ones, will deserve its own dedicated chapter. A second kind of literature
review will also be done for the methods section of the dissertation, which
again will also have its own dedicated chapter. In order to complete your
dissertation you may feel as though in effect, you have to do two literature
reviews: one for the substantive area of inquiry, and a second one, albeit
shorter, for methods! This chapter considers the main literature review.
    A literature review:

- Aims to critically evaluate the literature and bulid on what has gone before

- Brings together the landmark studies with recent research

- Connects the state of the literature to your inquiry, providing an
  understanding of, and a basis for, your own study

Importantly, the review is not an extended discussion, in the manner of
an exceptionally long essay. It is a critically engaged discussion which
brings together literature including previous empirical research from different sources and times, with different approaches and findings, into an
engaged whole. One key thing is to ensure that what you select for inclusion takes forwards your own line of inquiry, and that you seek to add to
understanding through your critical engagement – not merely reproduce
the critical understanding of others.
    By the end of the literature review the reader should be able to see:

- What work other researchers have carried out and the major issues or
  questions which are debated within the field. You should aim to group
  together works which share a similar inquiry or reach similar conclusions
  and point up where the substantive points of disagreement and debate lie.
  Avoid describing each earlier work in a long list

- The 'gap' in knowledge and understanding which you say exists in the
  field and which you claim your project begins to address. This might well
  include something relating to methods as well – you can return to pick this
  up later in more depth in the methods chapter itself

- How your research question will work within that gap

- That you have a sound understanding of the area of work, and are critically engaged with its debates. That you have reasons for the selections

which you have made, and the review as a whole is a convincing part of the argument of your dissertation as a whole

By the time you have completed the literature review, you should be able to:

- Say which journals are key to your inquiry

- Be able to name at least some of the leading researchers in the area

- Pass comment on the most recent studies

- Have grasped the main ways in which people have gone about doing research in your field, for example, which qualitative and quantitative methods have been used

Holding these aims in your head is vital to the success of the review. You should try to avoid a long description of the work in the field. You will see when this is happening, since you will produce a list-like chapter, rather like an annotated bibliography. Bringing texts together and analysing them in the light of your own inquiry is the second key component. This requires you to synthesise work, thus avoiding the silo approach to academic discussions, where literature is arranged in small sub-groups, each splendid and interesting, but with no overall connection.

Literature reviews are in the end individualised assemblages, unique to the question that you have posed. Once you have assembled the few key texts, you may be surprised by the range of other work which you can fruitfully bring in. But bear in mind that this is true for all of the other researchers before you. The key to your selection of their work is the relevance to *your* inquiry rather than the relevance to *their* inquiry. This can be hard to separate out at the beginning of things. Something to avoid is a critically engaged and lively review of the literature which works through the ongoing debate – yet never connects to your own. A central task is to work through the possible linkages. At the drafting stage keep a weather eye for strong links which you can return to later in the dissertation while noting weaker ones which once briefly included, can be left at the roadside.

Remember: You must show how your own question links into the wider literature; the literature is interesting in so far as the light it can throw upon aspects of your research problem. Not making the connections between them and your own work will lead to an extended essay. However well executed, and however much you personally learn from doing an extended essay, you will end up with a debate that you have staged from the vantage point of a watching audience. A good literature review is one in which you enter the fray, even if you do subsequently find yourself exiting ungracefully pursued by a bear.

Hide and Seek: Effective Searching

Not uncommon outcomes of first searches are:

1) Thinking, I can't find anything much: it seems as though not that many people have researched this.

   It is unlikely that there really isn't anything much at all that you can use. The common solution here is to work on the technique that you are using to make searches, to avoid for example:

   o An ineffective choice of key words e.g. using layperson's language rather than concepts

   o Ineffective searching technique, e.g. using 'and' or 'if'

   o Not searching in the right places, for example, relying on Google rather than using databases of learned journals

   o Finally, electronic searches are not the only way to search. Specialist archives in small, local museums and libraries for example may not be wholly online, while others may not be available to the general public and will require that you gain formal access before use

2) Thinking, there are far too many references: how can I possibly choose between them?

   This is more likely, although less likely than you may imagine. The starting point is to consider how the different works relate to your research question and their relevance in terms of approaches and findings. This involves reading purposively and sifting through a certain amount of not particularly useful stuff. Make good use of abstracts, and do be prepared to scan a lot of material.

   In terms of actually cutting down the sheer volume of digital resources which might spring up in responces to an enquiry, the common solution is to work with more advanced search features in order to search for linked words.

   Secondly, you could choose to concentrate on the classics, in the first instance, some of which will be founding works plus the key interventions, which can be added to the most recent work (including the most recent reviews of the field). Finally, you need to reconsider your research question with a view to checking that you haven't designed a project the scope of which is still far too large.

Remember: Make sure that you have included recent research papers. These are usually found in peer-reviewed academic journals. You will need to search the most recent editions of key journals in order to achieve this. In some cases you might also be able to reference conference papers, and it is worth browsing the internet to see what the latest conferences have been. It might be worth contacting conference presenters directly to request a copy of their paper if it hasn't yet come out in

> - Authoritative sources
>   Identify the most frequently referenced and highly esteemed
> - Up-to-date sources
>   Be sure to find the most recent publications of research
>   findings in academic journals
> - Accurate sources
>   Make sure you that you correctly record the reference: correct
>   volume, issue, page numbers, and year of publication
> - Confidence in your sources
>   You and others should have confidence in the selection and
>   coverage of sources

Figure 6.1   **What Makes a Good Source?**
Source: based on Race (2003: 120)

conference proceedings. Most researchers will be more than happy to provide this – as long as you reference their work.

Types of Sources: Different Texts Do Different Things

There are several different kinds of texts which you will find useful in preparing your literature review. It is important to recognise their relative strengths and weaknesses; almost all of them are useful, but different kinds of texts can be used for different purposes ranging from their critical and academic contribution to being sources of data in their own right.

Task 6.1 sets out some of the different types of text which you are likely to encounter. Complete the table, identifying the main strengths and weaknesses of the different texts, and consider whether or not you might be able to use them and how, for example, as an authoritative source versus an interesting set of raw data.

OnLine Sources for Rich Literature Reviews

The advent of the internet and digitalisation has brought the possibilities of online materials, available 24/7 and often free or at economic prices. Today, a series of databases have been established which provide gateways to online resources of books and journals as well as providing bibliographic information and the location of texts which can then be ordered. Figure 6.2 shows just a selection of them.

Task 6.1

Types of Text: Strengths, Weaknesses and Their Possible Uses

Type	Access	Strengths	Weaknesses	Possible Uses
Academic books and journals	Libraries; internet databases; specialist collections			
Reports; informed discussion documents	Libraries; internet databases; specialist collections; think-tanks; charities; consultancies; third sector and public sector bodies; independent research organisations; private corporations; foundations and trusts			
Major government departments and agencies; public records offices; some public services; private corporations	Some have limited access, through government archives; full public or subscription access to digitalised online collections is now possible; the land registry (for a fee); Companies House (for a fee)			

Task 6.1

(Continued)

Type	Access	Strengths	Weaknesses	Possible Uses
Restricted access public and private services	Health, education, criminal, vehicle and traffic data, credit and expenditure data			
Parliament and other bodies of governance	Ranges from records such as Hansard (UK government) through to regulatory bodies, quango			
Photographs; diaries; paintings and sketches; shopping lists and bills; letters; calendars; travel accounts	Personal collections are sometimes available to the public; sometimes there is agreed access to the researcher			

ASSIA	Applied Social Sciences Index and Abstracts
BEI	British Education Index
CINAHL	Cumulative Index to Nursing and Allied Health Literature
COPAC	Consortium of University Research Libraries Online Public Access Catalogue gives access to catalogues of large academic libraries
ERIC	Department of Education, USA, searchable database
H-Net	H-Net Humanities and Social Sciences provides database on reviews of academic books
INTUTE	Intute: Social Sciences provides a gateway to a vast range of high quality web resources by links as well as its own publications (previously called the Social Sciences Information Gateway, SOSIG)
SciELO	Scientific Electronic Library Online: Social Sciences edition; literature from developing nations with a focus on Latin America and the Caribbean
Sociofile	Sociology, Anthropology, Social Work, Education, Health and Psychology journals
SSCI	Social Sciences Citation Index, lists works which cite a particular other work
Theses.com	Index to Theses with Abstracts Accepted for Higher Degrees by the universities of Great Britain and Ireland
UNESCO	Offers a database for education
WorldCat	The bibliographical records of 50,000 libraries

Figure 6.2   **Online Academic Sources for Literature Reviews**

Box 6.1   Online Sources: Secondary Survey Data

Your university library will allow you to access a series of academic databases including some of those shown in Figure 6.2 plus many others. You will need a password in order to access them – but once arranged, the databases will be free of charge to you, and you will be able to access and download materials.

In preparing your literature review it is very important that you ensure that you do find out what sources you can access locally, including specialist digitalised archives and galleries that your university may look after or have connections to.

In addition, you should be aware of the range of survey data which you will be able to access on-line. This is the case for both

> qualitative and quantitative methodologies, and will be useful in many literature reviews.
>
> Chapter 7 looks in more detail at surveys online; see under 'Secondary Sources: Surveys' in the first section, 'Quantitative Techniques'.

As well as searching journals and books, you will also want to include up-to-date research reports, and some basic data if available, for example, statistics. There are some useful sources in Appendix 1 which go beyond the usual academic sources.

Box 6.2 Internet Sources: Health Warnings?

The databases and portals shown in Figure 6.2 are of peer-reviewed publications appropriate for use in academic work. Unless the material has been through a peer-review process, there is no guarantee of its quality. However this does not mean that it is necessarily of poor quality. Task 6.1, Types of Texts: Their Strengths and Weaknesses, has allowed some discussion of the reliability of texts. Today, there are a multitude of websites which make truth claims in different ways: however, their status is contested. A good example are Wikis.

For a sceptical stance on the digital revolution, see: Keen, A. (2007), *The Cult of the Amateur: How Today's Internet is Killing Our Culture and Assaulting our Economy* (London & Boston: Nicholas Brealey Publishing). The BBC Newsnight discussion about this can be accessed at:

www.bbc.co.uk/blogs/newsnight/2007/06/the_cult_of_the_amateur_by_andrew_keen_1.html. For alternative perspectives there are a host of websites and discussion groups, as well as blogs which take up Keen's arguments. Google: 'Keen'.

Putting the Literature Review Together

The literature review needs to engage the reader from the outset. While it necessarily uses academic language and conventions, you need to ensure that a non-specialist (although trained in academic language and conventions) can follow it. It may be tempting to write ten words where one will do, but using plain English, paying attention to grammar and the structure of your work, and thinking about how best to convey the importance and urgency of your area are all welcome to readers of literature reviews.

Using Hooks

Strong hooks are attention-seeking headlines which frame the review or any particular section within it. These should not be newspaper-style sensationalism, but grounded in the research area.

- The use of statistics is often very effective:

   Over 40% of young Bangladeshi men are unemployed. The comparable unemployment rate for young White men was 12%.

   Source: Muslim Council of Britain (MCB) from White (2002) from ONS (www.statistics.gov.uk, www.mcb.org.uk/library/statistics. php#4 10/03/08)

- Timeliness

It is important to remind the reader why the research should be done now, and why they should therefore keep reading the review.

A spur for research into climate change, for example, was the launch of the UK's £1bn research funds for the *Living With Environmental Change* programme in London (on 18 June 2008), the aim of which is to generate the evidence base needed to press for increased environmental controls. The evidence base needs to be generated in a 'timely' manner – since there is not much time left to persuade the world of the case, it is argued.

- Relevance

Is the research important? Does it have consequences? Consider the case of: Campbell (2003), *Iraq's Weapons of Mass Destruction: The Assessment of the British Government* (www.number10.gov.uk/output/Page271.asp)

Help with Drafting the Literature Review

We return to writing-up later in Chapter 12, but pause here to suggest that in order to get the literature review right, you will need to be prepared to go through it several times. Unlike an essay which you will work on and then submit within a short time frame, and thus be unable to amend subsequently, you will probably find that the literature review which you initially draft will need to be amended in the light of the outcomes of the research that you subsequently conduct. While it is desirable to try to pin down as much of the review as you can early on, it is important to remain flexible, and be prepared to revisit it later. This can feel onerous, especially if you are busy with other tasks involved in doing a dissertation, so you may instinctively be reluctant to revisit the literature review. However, you will be able to make it more stronger and persuasive after doing your empirical research.

Remember: An effective approach is to produce a draft literature review early on, and to aim to return to it subsequently downstream.

Using Anecdotes

Anecdotal accounts can bring the text to life but can become wearisome if overused. Here, Steven Kern has successfully used an anecdote to introduce and communicate the bare bones of one of the world's most complex debates:

> In an autobiographical sketch Einstein recalled two incidents from his childhood that filled him with wonder about the physical world. When he was five years old his father showed him a compass. The way the needle always pointed in one direction suggested that there was 'something deeply hidden' in nature. Then at twelve he discovered a book on Euclidean geometry with propositions which seemed to be about a universal and homogeneous space ... These early memories embodied two opposing views about the nature of space. The traditional view was that there was one and only one space that was continuous and uniform with properties described by Euclid's axioms and postulates. ... New ideas about the nature of space in this period challenged the popular notion that it was homogeneous and argued for its heterogeneity. (1983: 131–132)

Building the Review: Start a Section with the Main Concepts

A core characteristic of good literature reviews is the solidity of the critically engaged discussion. The review should aim to be robust enough to withstand at least some adversarial challenges, even though it may not, at the first few attempts, be the world's most beautiful artefact. Taking time to set up the section, beginning with the age-old task of defining the key terms, has much merit as an approach.

Take for example the extract which follows in which Margaret Ledwith starts by defining the concept of hegemony and how this can be interpreted and thus staged for her purposes, as setting up the problem of consent:

> Gramsci's analysis of the concept of hegemony is profound. Hegemony is the means by which one class assumes dominance over the masses in society. Traditional Marxism emphasised that this was achieved through coercion, the way in which the state

exercised control through the law, the police and the armed forces. Gramsci extended this understanding by identifying the way in which dominant ideology, as a form of ideological persuasion, permeates our lives through the institutions of civil society. By these means, dominant attitudes are internalised and accepted as common sense, and thereby legitimised in the minds of the people. Not only did he develop the notion of consent within a Marxist framework, but he analysed hegemony as 'the entire complex of practical and theoretical activities with which the ruling class not only justifies and maintains its dominance, but manages to win the active consent of those over whom it rules' (Gramsci, 1988: 244). Cited by (Ledwith, 2007: 121)

Find and Use the Source Texts

Do not merely accept the received view of an author's work. Always locate and carefully read the key works yourself, and find good reviews of those texts which tease out the variety of interpretations and uses made of them over the years. Remember that uses are made of texts not of the author's own choosing. The use of ideas is not under the control of their originator, not least, long after they are dead. Take for example certain ideas of Charles Darwin, discussed here by Derek Heater:

> Indeed, insofar as the nineteenth century can be said to have transmitted any legacy regarding world citizenship it is a collection of confused ambiguities. Darwinian biology was vulgarised into the doctrine of 'the survival of the fittest' and so helped to propagate the concept of mankind [sic] not as potentially unified but as violently racially divided. That such an interpretation was the very reverse of Darwin's own beliefs did not prevent the widespread acceptance of this parody. For, in his *The Descent of Man*, he had in fact written:
>
>> As man advances in civilisation ... the simplest reason would tell each individual that he ought to extend his social instincts ... to all the members of the same nation, though personally unknown to him. This point being once reached, there is only an artificial barrier to prevent his sympathies extending to the men of all nations and races.
>
> (Darwin, in Laurent, 1987, cited by Heater, 2006)
>
> The unabridged version of the extract set in the context of the passage can be found in *The Descent of Man,* one of Project Gutenberg's free ebooks available online at www.gutenberg.org/dirs/etext00/dscmn10.txt.

Reviewing Texts from a Different Moment in Time

A further set of issues arises with the unfolding of events including political and theoretical interventions over time, which renders texts historical artefacts embedded in their historical conjuncture. Viewing texts through the lens of history allows the benefit of hindsight to later generations but can lead reviewers to adopt something of the higher moral ground, sometimes quite rightly although equally, sometimes perhaps in a rather uncritical and unreflexive manner given the almost inevitable demise of their own thinking in due course.

The approach offered here by Eriksen in his discussion of the impact of feminism on anthropology, treads a middle, but critical, ground. He both adopts a critical stance towards the invisibility of gender issues in Malinowski's work on the one hand, while reminding us of his contribution on the other:

> Gender was for a long time relatively neglected in anthropological research, which is perhaps surprising, since gender identity may well be the most fundamental basis for personal identity. Malinowski, who has often been praised for his ethnographic detail, is now said to have neglected important women's institutions completely and exaggerated the contribution of men to the reproduction of Trobriand society (Weiner, 1988). In many other classic studies too, social actors are more or less seen as equivalent to social men. (Eriksen, 2001: 125)

Situating Key Texts and Characters in Their Intellectual Moment

Making connections between genealogies of thought, art and cultural currents is another challenge. Here is a good example by Merlin Coverley. Coverley discusses the post-war period showing the hiatus between the end of one phase of surrealism, closed as he argues by Nadeau's book, and the emergence of the *Situationist International* with the colourful character of Guy Debord, which he argues followed:

> By the end of the Second World War the surrealist movement was effectively over and the publication of Maurice Nadeau's *History of Surrealism* in 1944 provided its epitaph. Surrealism had failed to deliver on its ambitious promises to reform society and allow all to share in the apprehension of the marvellous that

it had revealed....Movements as diverse and ephemeral as Cobra, the Lettrist International and the Imaginist Bauhaus formed a new avant-garde fuelled by new revolutionary sentiments but they were hampered both by a lack of direction and, indeed, members... it was only with the emergence of the *Situationist International* in 1957 that a momentum for change began to appear. From 1957 until the riots of Paris in 1968, the situationist movement, under the firm, if not tyrannical, grip of Guy Debord, produced a series of statements that defined terms such as psychogeography, the derive and detournement for the first time... (Coverley, 2006: 81–2)

There are a number of texts which can assist you with situating books and their writers in their moment (with interpretations); here are a few suggestions:

- Pampel (2000) for Marx, Durkheim, Weber, Simmel and George Herbert Mead

- Sedgwick (2007) for Melville, James, Nietzsche, Proust, and Wilde

- The 'For Beginners' series by Pantheon books. Includes Marx, Freud, Einstein, Darwin

Remember: If you are specifically working on an intellectual history, do ask your tutors for suggestions.

Contextualisation: Setting the (Significant) Scene

A common challenge is how to effectively introduce the main elements of the historical contexts which will frame the discussion, without devoting a lot of time to it. Large-scale, complex scenarios and situations need to be set out in order to convey their importance but usually only briefly, so that the main business can commence. The rub lies in the need to keep it brief, while demonstrating the significance of the contexts.

In the following extract, the writing style is characterised by a spare text and carefully chosen words which convey the issues with clarity. There is a judicious use of headline statistics; and the author Peter Calvocoressi sticks to a simple chronological order which allows him to set the scene of the fall of France in World War II in just one paragraph:

The French capitulation in June 1940 was psychologically, although not logistically, inescapable. The French government and some of its forces, particularly naval and air forces could have been removed to North Africa and did start to do so. But logistics are not enough. France did not wish to fight on. It was stunned by the scale and shame of its defeat and it feared anarchy. A quarter of the entire population were refugees; close on 2 million were prisoners or missing; 300,000 had been killed or badly wounded ... The government was in disarray and there were rumours of a communist seizure of power in Paris, frightful visions of a Second Commune and a repetition of the lacerations which had followed that other defeat at German hands seventy years earlier: *La Debacle*. (Calvocoressi, 1997: 95–6)

Writing Style and the Academic Challenge: How to Introduce and Link Texts

Firstly, there are technical issues with writing styles. For example, it can be challenging to write without undue repetition of the few key phrases with which you have become most familiar. Figure 6.3 contains some suggestions for phrasing styles from the excellent website at Manchester University, the *Academic Phrasebank*, which sets out many relevant and useful examples of how to discuss literature. The website is well worth a visit before you hand in your draft literature review.

Secondly, there is an academic challenge in the literature review. Assembling a review is in effect assembling an academic argument, at the heart of which lies a challenge. In making a literature review, you are critically engaging with what has gone before, synthesising areas, challenging existing orthodoxy, seeking to extend debate, and identifying issues which you wish to pursue further. The component parts of the review must then hang together in a sustained, academically rigorous manner with a logical flow.

The dissertation as a whole is a persuasive, argumentative, exploratory narrative, and your literature review needs to pick up and connect your research question with the area of work in which it fits, while exposing the gap you seek to fill or the problem which you wish to raise. Looking forwards, your methods chapter needs to logically flow out of them both: the methods chapter takes forward the project as further defined and elucidated in the literature review. In building up your literature review, you are building up your argument for doing the dissertation in the first place, and are showing why you are doing it in the way in which you have chosen to. When working on the draft, remember this. Be clear about your reasons for selecting works, and how the critical points you make about them support your dissertation as a whole.

General descriptions of the relevant literature

A considerable amount of literature has been published on X. These studies ...
The first serious discussions and analyses of X emerged during the 1970s with ...
The generalisability of much published research on this issue is problematic.
What we know about X is largely based upon empirical studies that investigate how ...
During the past 30 years much more information has become available on ...
In recent years, there has been an increasing amount of literature on ...
A large and growing body of literature has investigated ...

Reference to what other writers do in their text (author as subject)

Smith (2003) *identifies* poor food, bad housing, inadequate hygiene and large families as the major causes of ...
Rao (2003) *lists* three reasons why the English language has become so dominant. These are: ...
Smith (2003) *traces* the development of Japanese history and philosophy during the 19th century.
Jones (2003) *provides* in-depth analysis of the work of Aristotle showing its relevance to contemporary times ...
Smith (2003) *draws our attention* to distinctive categories of motivational beliefs often observed in ...
Smith (2003) *defines* evidence based medicine as the conscious, explicit and judicious use of ...
Rao (2003) *highlights* the need to break the link between economic growth and transport growth ...
Smith (2003) *discusses* the challenges and strategies for facilitating and promoting ...
Toh (2003) *mentions* the special situation of Singapore as an example of ...
Smith (2003) *questions* whether mainstream schools are the best environment for ...
Smith (2003) *considers* whether countries work well on cross-border issues such as ...
Smith (2003) *uses* examples of these various techniques as evidence that ...

Figure 6.3   **Introducing and Linking Techniques: Examples from the**
Academic Phrasebank

Source: www.phrasebank.manchester.ac.uk/sources.htm

Summary

- A literature review:

  - Identifies the state of research in the field
  - Provides a critical evaluation of the literature:

    - It situates the literature in its contemporary moment and shows how this affects both its production then and reading now
    - It shows how the work links to the intellectual contexts of its day and of nowadays

  - Links the literature to your research project, showing its place and potential contribution

- Searching:

  Searching is an essential task to produce a good, rich literature review. The keys to effective searching are:

  - Know where to find the sources which are best for your project
  - Understand the relative strengths and weaknesses of your sources

- Online sources:

  There is an enormous range of sources, some of which carry health warnings. Learn to use academic databases well and save yourself many hours of work.

- Build up the literature review by using:

  - Hooks
  - Anecdotes
  - Main concepts
  - The original texts

- Be critically engaged with your literature review. Remember:

  - Review texts in their historical moment
  - Situate texts in their intellectual moment
  - Contextualisation: setting the scene

- Help with academic writing style:

  There are a number of sources of help, including Chapter 12 of this book.

- The literature review is a key building block in the academic challenge which you mount in the whole of your dissertation.

Further Reading

Aveyard, H. (2007) *Doing a Literature Review in Health and Social Care*. Maidenhead: Open University Press.

Becker, H.S. (1998) *Tricks of the Trade: How To Think About Your Research While You Are Doing It*. Chicago: Chicago University Press.

Fink, A. (2005) *Conducting Research Literature Reviews: From the Internet to Paper*. London: Sage.

Hart, C. (1998) *Doing a Literature Review: Releasing the Social Science Imagination*. London: Sage.

Chapter 7

Research Design: Projects and Their Needs

Overview

Research design: approach with confidence!

The litmus test: will the reader be persuaded?

Validity; reliability; representativeness and generalisability

Research design: common pitfalls

Time is a major problem

Triangulation: what it is and why it is a good idea to do it

Design research as a working whole

Approaches to research: different kinds of projects

Refreshing qualitative and quantitative methods

Snapshot of their strengths and weaknesses

Qualitative and quantitative: combination or separation?

Approaches to mixing methods

In this chapter, we consider research design and how this can help you to achieve your project. Beginning with the litmus test of a research design (will your reader be persuaded?), the chapter moves through the key concepts such as validity, reliability, generalisation and triangulation which you need to grasp in order to successfully demonstrate that the research which you propose will be robust. The chapter identifies the characteristics of a good research design before examining the diversity of possible approaches to doing a research project. These are: Case Studies; Surveys; Grounded Theory; Narrative Research; Ethnographies; Action Research; Theoretical Explorations; and Comparative Approaches. Following this, we refresh our memories about qualitative and quantitative methods and explore the possibility of using a mixed design with both.

Research Design: Approach with Confidence!

Students are often a little daunted by approaching their first significant independent research project. However, independent research can be rewarding and you should feel encouraged that learning how to design and execute research, like most things in life, is a matter of practice. Far from being new to this, in almost all degree programmes you will have already encountered research methods and will have already been carrying out research and writing it up. You will have already produced coursework with mini literature reviews; carried out independent research in exercises and case studies; completed small pieces of research, and will have practised writing up and presenting work, including its constituent elements such as a bibliography. However, research design may feel like something new in the sense of bringing together all of these elements.

The research design is a vital step which links the steps taken so far (the formulation of the research problem and the development of a question, working up the aims and the objectives; doing the initial literature review) to the next stage, which is actually doing this research. As such it is an important bridge which can substantially support your dissertation project. The research design will set out the research methods which will be pursued to execute the research. It should show how the constituent parts of the research process (the pieces of the jigsaw), fit together, what each piece contributes to the whole, and the choices which have made selecting the pieces and asembling them into the whole.

Research design should show the type of design which has been created; the researcher's role in the research and their underlying assumptions; the actual methods which are going to be used including sampling and data analysis techniques; reasons for the selections made and the limitations of the research which will result.

It is important that the research design is detailed and specific. It is at this stage that the nuts and bolts of doing the research are thought through as well as the larger question of overall approach.

The 'Litmus' Test of the Research: Will the Reader Be Persuaded?

When people read a research design, they have certain issues in their minds:

1) Will the proposed methods produce the kind of data needed in order for the researcher to address the research question including the aims and objectives?

2) Will the specific methods produce the kind of data which the researcher claims they will?

3) Can this research be conducted in both an ethical and timely manner?

4) Is the researcher aware of the imperfections and problems in the research – and have they taken them into account?

5) Will this research tell us something which we didn't know before?

6) Will the research pass the test of validity – will it be reliable, robust, representative?

7) Does the researcher know where they are located in the research, and how they will address the issues arising?

In order to get this right, you must be prepared to read widely and deeply. For an undergraduate dissertation, it is reasonable to expect to look at:

- Research methods textbooks which give overviews of research methodology
- Specialist methods texts which discuss the chosen method, e.g. surveys
- Examples of methods which have been used in previous studies (which you can do as you are preparing your literature review)
- Look carefully at what the researcher did; the reasons for their choices, what the outcomes were, including limitations

Remember: *you must research the method – as well as using the method to do the research!*

Time Challenge: Design the Research

A common issue encountered by students undertaking their first independent research project in the contexts of doing a dissertation, is time. Time is probably the biggest obstacle for students to navigate. This is because of:

- The realisation that research is interesting: once started, you would like to do more of it!
- Growing confidence: you can do this – it isn't rocket science
- Developing a better sense of the potential of the project, once the project is under way, and realising what you could do
- Overestimating what is required and failing to stop in time
- Underestimating how long everything will take until you get underway
- Conflicting demands which fall in the moment of greatest demand of the degree programme as a whole, i.e. the final year

A good research design can significantly offset many of these issues while allowing space to get the most out of doing a dissertation. Above all, however, do remember that you are doing the dissertation in the context of a wider programme of study. On the one hand, there should be the expectation that extra work will be required to get it done, but on the other, it is vital to recognise when enough is enough, and come to a halt.

Here are some wise words from experienced researcher Catherine Hakim:

The short timescales imposed on a dissertation or thesis mean that costs, time and feasibility are the overriding factors in the choice of design and subject. The requirement to complete the project successfully within the permitted time means that practical considerations always take precedence over theoretical issues or the search for innovation. (2008: 149)

Remember: *Take time to design your research – and build in a good allowance of time at every stage.*

Validity; Reliability

The design will ensure that the research project is:

- *Reliable*: If this method were used again to research this sample, it would produce the same or similar enough results
- *Valid*: This choice of method was the right one for the task: it is fit for purpose. This will be demonstrated by your data set – you need to end up with the right kind of data and the right amount of data

These two concepts deal with different things and yet are interlinked. The overall research design must deliver data and it is upon that data that conclusions, ultimately, rest. A weak design produces weak data and limited conclusions, with question marks raised about validity and reliability. Researchers may choose traditional or innovative methods, but if either are poorly realised they can't get the results that they need.

Representatitiveness and Generalisability

The concept of representative refers to the extent to which the project's findings can be generalised to other similar case. Some researchers would argue that all research ought to be representative, but others may suggest that representativeness sits upon a continuum – at one end lies what is (relatively) securely representative, while at the other lies specifics to the unique case which give an insight into the case, but are not generalisable.

It is suggested that students concentrate on working through the issues of reliability, validity, and representativeness as far as they can to the best of their own and the project's limits.

> The most common pitfalls are:
> - Methods-led work: students work back to front choosing the methods first and research question second. The method should always follow the research question
> - The pool of methods is too limited, for example, to what the student has already experienced and feels most confident to use

- Grabbing a possible topic area and making a cursory research design, to subsequently find that it is altogether too boring, complex or simply unmanageable!

- Choosing a method which is appropriate to the research question, for example, deciding to make a survey of local users to ascertain car parking needs at a local school, but marred by poor execution (the researcher waits at the school gates out of hours and therefore doesn't meet any users) or which can't be executed (empirical research has to be carried out in a particular time which coincides with the school holiday period). It is at the research design stage that these sorts of nuts and bolts issues need to be thought through and anticipated. You might need to reject what in its own terms is a perfectly good method, if you can't actually carry it out, for example, you choose interviews but can't access any research subjects from your target group

- Choosing a method of poor fit, (deciding to use a questionnaire with closed qustions and tick boxes to ascertain how local residents *feel* about the impact on their child of a death through bullying at the local school) but which can be well executed (the questionnaire is prepared in time, the researcher well prepared, sensitive to the local situation). This will produce a well executed survey with lots of the wrong kind or quantity of data

- Starting to research without thinking through each of the steps (for example, the researcher conducts an interview but has underestimated the time needed for transcription) and needing more resources or missing out steps altogether; 'the Who, What, Where, Why and How?' questions have not been addressed

Figure 7.1   **Research Design: Common Pitfalls**

Box 7.1   Triangulation

Triangulation is a technique where the researcher uses more than one method, object or subject in order to check the robustness of the original data sets. Therefore, triangulation is a tactic whereby the researcher generates a few different data sets in different ways, and compares them. The researcher will work out a position broadly lying in the middle of the various data directions, i.e. will take a fix. This prevents the researcher from being (mis)led by outliers or unique cases which would otherwise skew the data. Triangulation can sometimes be done as a check on the effectiveness of the sample frame selected, and can also check how effectively data has been collected.

Designing Research Projects: The Importance of the Whole

In thinking through your dissertation, it is important to conceive of it as a working whole. Working through the stages of turning a potentially interesting topic into a rich research question, and then thinking through which methods would best produce the data set which you need in order to address the research question will all help you to get a good result. Writing up your findings is the final leg of the project, and this should be understood as part of the whole.

Remember: Design the research methods you will use as a working package – the package needs to deliver the best data set that you can obtain both in terms of its richness and its best fit to the research question. Do not be methods led! Be inquiry led. Also, do be open to trying out methods, you might be pleasantly surprised by their diversity and what you learn from each.

Approaches to Research: Different Kinds of Projects

There are various ways to approach your project design. The choice of approach will depend upon balancing:

- Methods which best fit your specific research question

- Your stance in research, in epistemological and personal terms: what kind of researcher are you?

- The aims of the research: for example, in-depth understanding or action-based interventions

- The time and other resources which you have available

In this section, we consider some of the main approaches which you might take:

- Case studies

- Surveys

- Grounded theory

- Narrative research

- Ethnographies

- Action research

- Theoretical explorations

- Comparative studies

1) Case studies

Case studies seek to uncover the unique elements of their case and to gain an in-depth insight into how something works; why something is how it came to be; specific features of a character or situation and so on. Case studies are often favoured by undergraduates doing their dissertation. The advantages are that case studies:

- Allow the exploration of one case in some depth which is rewarding (although relatively narrowly focused)

- The case can be designed so that it is eminently manageable given other constraints such as time

- Can be used with other methods

- Can be compared with case studies conducted by other researchers

However, it is not all plain sailing with case studies. While they are relatively narrowly defined, it can be difficult to establish their start and end point (Bell, 2007), and to know what to exclude becomes a major research problem. Secondly, it can be difficult to make generalisations from case studies. While this is not always the aim, nonetheless, it can mean that case studies are limited in their usefulness.

2) Surveys

Surveys are a common approach to quantitative research. Surveys ask the same questions of a selected population, and their answers are compared. The data generated in this way will reveal social patterns, and will carry some explanatory power of particular kinds.

Much social research is still conducted by surveys, and their enduring popularity lies in their:

- Flexibility: for example, a range of sampling strategies means that the researcher may be able to specify their chosen population quite accurately and will be able to find and survey them

- Surveys can show which variables are at work in specific inter-relationships, for example, which variables are more or less important and with what consequences

- A lot of data can be relatively quickly gathered; delegation of collection can be made to relatively unskilled collectors; much of the data work can be handled by software, provided that the survey has been well designed (i.e. with this in mind) in the first place

There are some disadvantages to surveys, however. A key one is in fact their lack of explanatory power in the sense that surveys can be very poor at providing reasons, i.e. at answering the why question, rather than what, who, when or where questions.

3) Grounded theory

Grounded theory is famously associated with Glaser and Strauss (see Glaser and Strauss, 1967, and Glaser, 1992, for the first and last of many publications). It rests upon the principle of gathering qualitative data from which theory is generated.

Typically, the researcher will begin collecting data: analyse it, looking for any emergent categories; collect some more data and see how this fits with the their idea of possible categories so far and work out whether any new ones or amendments to existing ones are required. The researcher will then carry on collecting the data until the categories are 'filled', i.e. where no new significant ones are emerging and we are no longer learning much from continuing to fill existing categories.

However, generating and working with data over a period of time is a challenging task which takes time and thinking through to arrive at plausible interpretations. For committed and enthusiastic student researchers, this is a good choice of strategy which can yield excellent results. However, for those with a more instrumental view or perhaps with much less time, this might not be such a good choice for their dissertation.

4) Narrative research

Narrative research rests upon the concept that people structure their experiences in narratives, foregrounding their key issues and what they mean to them as they do. Narrative inquiry seeks to work out the dominant storylines and paradigms of meaning which are in operation, accessing the conceptual world of the research participant and gaining insight into the structures and processes which have shaped it over time.

A typical inquiry takes the form of interviews, often open-ended. Life history interviews are a kind of biographical inquiry which rest on facilitating participants to, literally, tell their story. Other varieties include group interviewing, oral histories, working with personal documents and so on.

This kind of inquiry has been used variously in the social sciences, including in anthropology, sociology, and political sociology and represents a potentially perfectly manageable and attractive project for you to attempt. However, life histories in particular come with a health warning: gathering someone else's story generates a great deal of data! Willing research participants with great stories to tell make great research participants but there is a labour involved in the careful transcription and analysis of data which follows.

5) Ethnographies

Ethnographics can provide the richest data of complex density, more so than perhaps any other qualitative method. Much of the original ethnographic work in anthropology and other approaches to understanding human life was conducted and published as closely detailed studies of specific communities and tribes. The principle was to grasp the structure of social life including its symbolic and organisational systems, such as rituals and economic exchange. Through the twentieth century ethnography left the shelter of anthropology and today is used to explore all manner of social associations including gangs, families, youth cultures, and communities in a vast array of social settings from hospitals and offices to neighbourhoods, marketplaces, and football grounds.

Typically, a researcher will identify a good community or site or field, in which a social system of some kind is in operation. In order to work out the subtleties of the organisational system they might observe unobstrusively from the sidelines, but are more likely to seek to participate in the goings-on. A key task is to make sense of the governing and organising systems by accessing the structure of meanings from the actors' perspective, for example, by the analysis of discourses and rituals and the basis and operation of systems of stratification and rule, etc., such as exchange and significant beliefs.

Ethnographies can be enormous fun since it provides an opportunity to poke your nose into somewhere that you wouldn't otherwise be able to go. Such encounters with worlds other than your own are intellectually challenging and inevitably broaden your horizons. However, again, you need to reflect upon the time required to really get to grips with a social setting. Be prepared for a lot of hanging about in the first instance and quite intensive writing up, reflection and analysis later.

6) Action research

Action research projects aim to take social action as part of the project. You might develop a line of inquiry; make investigations; arrive at recommendations for action; and then seek to facilitate those actions, or you may take actions as you go along. Action research projects then, as their name suggests, focus on making interventions which are informed by research, and which in turn inform the research findings. The key difference between action research projects and those projects which generate data, analysis, and understandings is the point at which the research is used. In action research projects, the data is used as part of the project with the research typically playing a leading or facilitative role. This aim contrasts with a process of dissemination which leads to action downstream.

Students often report that they find action research invigorating; identifying the project and taking action for change is an intrinsically empowering and rewarding experience. Provided, again, that the project is manageable, this could be a good avenue to pursue. Action research will bring new experience and give an opportunity to learn about some of the practical and theoretical problems which arise when setting out to make a difference.

7) Theoretical explorations

Theoretical dissertations can be attractive for those who enjoy grappling with social theory and philosophical problems. However, a true theoretical dissertation is not a literature review with an extended discussion of the main points raised. Theoretical dissertations might sound attractive, typically removing the need to collect empirical data with all that that involves, but they are stretching in their own right, and will take just as long. The explanation lies in the kinds of reasons for not doing empirical study, and the kinds of opportunity offered by doing a purely theoritical one:

> ... although political theories are more or less always culturally and temporally bound to an extent, they are far less so than political issues which arise out of the empirical world. Consequently it is possible for instance to compare and contrast the Platonic view of human nature with the Marxist one. There would, of course, be far less point in comparing and contrasting the contemporary political issues of Plato's empirical world with those of Marx's empirical world. (Silbergh, 2001: 153–4)

8) Comparative studies

Comparative approaches are common in some fields, for example, comparative politics in political science and political sociology, and comparative social policy and welfare states. Longitudinal studies (i.e. studies conducted over years) also have an intrinsically comparative element. Given the constraints under which undergraduates are working on dissertations, comparative studies generally work well where there is a good literature to use, useful secondary sources possibly including a good (large-scale; well funded; developed over time; led by reputable agency) data set which can be readily drawn upon.

It is relatively difficult for students to make a full comparative study of situations or systems, for example, in two states, during the time allowed for dissertation work if empirical work is undertaken. If you aspire to that, you might be better off considering a comparative literature review which frames an empirical case study made in one state, rather than attempting a large cross-national comparative study.

Refreshing Understandings of Qualitative and Quantitative Methods

Social research is conducted by gathering and analysing empirical data systematically. A range of methods are used to do this:

1) Qualitative methods
   Qualitative methods aim to develop understandings of meanings. They often rely on interpretation, a methodological act which in turn

requires theorisation, and which can be conducted in different ways with different outcomes. Qualitative methods generate so-called 'soft' data: words, images, sounds, feelings and so on. There are particular methodological approaches to gathering and working with these, for example, the techniques of visual sociology as set out by Prosser (2006) are particularly effective for gathering data from printed images as well as settings such as the organisation of a room. Qualitative researchers may tend towards taking an interpretivist stance in the research process.

2) Quantitative methods

Quantitative methods aim to identify and make sense of patterns in data, using measurement and exploring connections, for example, by attempting to establish cause and effect between different variables. Quantitative researchers will typically adopt scientific methods, testing models and hypotheses in the real world with empirical data.

Quantitative researchers link variables and assess the relative importance of each one to the others, crudely, to establish what effect one has on another. So, identifying variables and measuring their relative importance is the key to much quantitative research, and data collection techniques are largely designed to capture the data needed in order to arrive at relative measurements. Quantitative methods generate so-called 'hard' data such as numbers, and their variations, and connections are mapped using statistical analyses. Data is collected in numerical form, although it can be expressed using all manner of diagrams, charts and mathematical models. Researchers may tend towards taking a more positivist stances in the research process.

Huberman and Miles characterise the two approaches as orientated around variables (quantitative methods) which attempt to establish the most likely relationships between them, and cases (qualitative methods) which attempt to establish '...specific, concrete, historically grounded patterns common to a small set of cases' (1994: 436). Therefore, quantitative methods can also generate large data sets with many variables, requiring a multivariate analysis, which literally means an analysis of many variables. However, this does not mean that qualitative researchers work with small datasets, (even though they do work with small numbers of cases). In fact qualitative methods typically generate large data sets, bringing their own challenges of sorting, cross-referencing and categorising.

In both quantitative and qualitative research, there is a considerable diversity of methods or techniques which can be used. These range from tried and tested methods which form the bedrock of many research projects, alongside novel and innovative approaches. Table 7.1 provides a snapshot of tried and tested methods.

Method and whether quantitative or qualitative?	How will the method be used in this instance?	Benefits and drawbacks of applying method in this instance	Suggestions for alternative or complementary strategies

Table 7.1   Snapshot of Common Methods

Method	Qualitative or Quantitative?	Characteristics, Benefits and Drawbacks
Postal survey	Quantitative	• Low cost • Response rate can be poor • Answers may be incomplete • Responses are pre-coded and must be simple so people can understand them – sometimes this means the quality of information gained is lower than from other methods
Telephone survey	Quantitative	• A cost-effective method of achieving a robust sample allowing generalisations to be made • Responses are pre-coded. Certain groups do not have access to the telephone, so may be excluded from the sample • It is difficult to ask sensitive questions over the telephone • Works well with employers
Face-to-face survey	Quantitative	• Can include open questions as pre-coded • Can achieve a robust sample allowing generalisations if sufficient numbers are surveyed

Table 7.1

Method	Qualitative or Quantitative?	Characteristics, Benefits and Drawbacks
In-depth interview	Qualitative	• Expensive and time-consuming to administrate • Ideal for gathering sensitive information or exploring complicated issues • Rich and detailed information can be gathered • Interviewers are allowed more flexibility • Answers to open questions can be difficult and time-consuming to analyse
Focus group	Qualitative	• Expensive and time-consuming to administrate • A group discussion with around 8–12 people • Usually lasts between 1 and 3 hours • Capitalises on interaction between participants • Participants are not representative of the wider population, which does not allow for generalisation • Useful for gathering sensitive data • Requires careful and unbiased analysis
Case study	Qualitative	• The researcher gains understanding of a specific person's experience through an in-depth interview • Provides good quotations and rich data • Can bring alive other research, such as survey data • Findings cannot be generalised to a wider population

Task 7.1

Methods of Choice: Relative Benefits

Now construct your own table using methods which you or your classmates have been considering, identifying their strengths and weaknesses in the contexts of the specific research projects which you are currently considering:

Qualitative and Quantitative: Combination or Separation?

Historically, and to some extent it is still the case today, you will find that many researchers specialise in one approach rather than another. The explanations are partly found in the kinds of research that they like to do, and thus the method(s) of best fit which will produce the best data for their projects. Another, associated, aspect of this lies with an epistemological choice, i.e. their approach will reflect their preferred stance as researchers in the research process. However, yet another aspect lies in the researchers' expertise which builds up over time.

The level of specialisation in the different methods needed to carry out good research asks a lot of individual researchers, who need to be able to develop their expertise across several different approaches and methods, especially as the projects which they take on become larger and more complex. It takes time and a determined, focused effort to become competent in all forms of research methods. The reality is that most researchers will develop strengths and weaknesses in different approaches and will have different degrees of experience and familiarity with them.

In summary, you may find that there are clear divisions between researchers who think of themselves as being in the various camps of qualitative and quantitative research. However, you will also find many researchers either aspire to, or in practice work with, both kinds of approaches. In planning your research design, you should bear in mind that a combination of methods is required for many projects in order to achieve the aims of the research investigation.

Remember: The choice of methods and their combination i.e. the research design, essentially relies upon matching the method to the research problem. As Punch points out:

1) Triangulation.
   Triangulation can be used by conducting studies using both methods, and cross-checking the results.
2) Qualitative research improves insight into quantitative research.
   For example, by providing meanings and understandings which contextualise the data.
3) Quantitative research improves the quality of qualitative research.
   For example, by using a survey to identify members of a sample who are subsequently interviewed with more accuracy than other methods such as the snowball method, allows.
4) Both methods are used to provide certain kinds of data which only each is capable of providing.
   For example, one part of the study may collect data about car park usage while another part of the study may collect drivers' perceptions of car park accessibility.
5) Different methods can provide insight into the two dynamics of structure (quantitative data) and process (qualitative data).

For example, one may reveal the housing class of a sample while the second may reveal how members of the sample came to live in that accommodation.

6) Agenda setting.

Quantitative research is more closely defined by the researcher, while qualitative research allows greater leeway to the researched. A mixed methods approach allows for the researcher to set the agenda on some issues, and in addition to pick up issues as presented by the researched.

7) Generalising from findings.

Generalising from findings can be problematic in the case study approach of qualitative research; this might be partly addressed by a quantitative component. *Vice versa*, using a qualitative component may allow a more in-depth analysis of a few cases to enrich the data set and thus understanding.

8) Qualitative research answers the question 'Why?'

Quantitative data sets show causal relationships between variables and their relative importance, but do not provide explanations as to why that should be. Qualitative components to a research design can begin to colour this in.

9) Spanning the macro-micro divide.

A mixed methods approach might allow the researcher to use both large scale data sets which provide insight into major social trends and structures, while a local case study using qualitative methods allows the researcher to access social dynamics at micro level. Integrating these can allow researchers to develop rich insights into, and further developments of, theories and concepts.

10) Phases of the research project.

Different methods might be the best fit at different phases of the research project, especially in projects which are conducted over a long period of time. Long-term longitudinal studies benefit from running the loop which draws out connections between macro and micro levels of investigation.

11) Hybrids.

A quantitative research design staged as an experimental study contains some elements of qualitative research.

Figure 7.2   Approaches to Combining Quantitative and Qualitative Methods

Source: Punch (2005: 241), based on Bryman (1992: 59–61)

...it is useful to focus on the main direction of influence as being from question to method. Otherwise we run the risk of starting with methods, and adapting research questions to them. (2005: 238)

In terms of approaches to developing mixed methods, see Figure 7.2, which presents Bryman's well-known views.

This summary of combined methods allows for hybridity. This is exemplified in some of the points which Bryman makes, for example, that in working with qualitative research, quantitative measures (such as often, many, frequent, few) are often brought in, while quantitative researchers, in order to make sense of their data, in practice work through a level of meaning. A key rationale however, is the possibility of triangulating your results; using a different method and/or data set allows you to look for evidence which affirms and undermines your original findings.

Summary

- Research design should be led by the needs of the project, not by what you are familiar with or most prefer

- It is important to conceive of the research design as a whole package, using more than one method if needs be. Look for positive opportunities strengthen your data set in any ways you can

- The most common pitfalls include:

  o Methods-led problems: being unresponsive to the needs of the project; not being adventurous and lacking confidence
  o Not thinking things through: having good ideas which are not worked out – not considering which methods will produce which data sets and to what use that will data be put. Logistical problems can also arise – where the design presents too many hurdles to be carried off well

- Time can be an issue – for example overestimating what is required and not knowing when to stop – or underestimating how long everything will take and running out of time

- Validity – right method, right place, right kind of data, right quantity

- Reliability – the project is repeatable. If it were repeated, it would produce broadly the same or close enough results

- Representative – not all studies set out to be representative: decide beforehand whether or not this is an aim. If it is, then ensure that you have got the right sample and have collected the right kind of data

- Triangulation: check your reading or interpretation of the data against readings of alternative data. The truth should lie somewhere in between, not list to one side

- The litmus test: is the reader persuaded? Does the reader accept the research or are there substantial questions hanging over it?

- You can choose between several different kinds of projects. Some of the more common ones for undergraduate dissertations include:

- o Case studies
- o Surveys
- o Grounded theory
- o Narrative research
- o Ethnographies
- o Action research
- o Theoretical explorations
- o Comparative approaches

- Qualitative and quantitative methods:

  - o Qualitative – meanings; cases; explorations; from the ground up
  - o Quantitative – measurements; relationships; patterns; from the hypothesis down

- The big debate for years was between the value of qualitative versus quantitative methods. They are both useful – for doing different things. In any event, one possible way forwards is a combination, i.e. a mixed methods approach drawing on the excellent approaches to this problem by Bryman (1992). (See also Bryman, 2008.)

Further Reading

Bryman, A. (2008) (3rd edn.) *Social Research Methods*. Oxford: Oxford University Press.

Cresswell, J. W. (2002) (2nd edn). *Research Design: Qualitative, Quantitative, and Mixed Methods Approaches*. London: Sage.

Hakim, C. (2008) *Research Design: Successful Designs for Social and Economic Research*. London: Routledge.

Kennett, P. (2001) *Comparative Social Policy: Theory and Research*. Buckingham: Open University Press.

Robson, C. (2002) *Real World Research*. Oxford: Blackwell.

Tashakkori, A. and Teddlie, C. (1998) *Mixed Methodology: Combining Qualitative and Quantitative Approaches*. London: Sage.

Chapter 8

Collecting Data:
Quantitative Methods

Overview

Collecting data: the variety of methods of collection

Primary and secondary sources:

- Primary data – you collect yourself
- Secondary data – you use data collected by someone else

Surveys:

- Using secondary sources
- Doing your own surveys
- Sampling:

  - Random
  - Nth number
  - Stratified
  - Convenience

Administering surveys by post and phone: the effects on the sample

The general problem of bias

Research instruments: the questionnaire:

  - Setting questions
  - Re-using questions from other sources
  - Design: physical appearance

Tally sheets: unobtrusive data collection

This chapter focuses on quantitative methods. The larger part of the chapter deals with surveys, including using secondary sources as well as conducting your own surveys. There is a discussion about how different mechanisms for administering surveys such as by post or phone will affect the sample and findings. Following this, we move on to designing questionnaires, including a detailed section on setting questions and some tips on making your questionnaire attractive and easy to use. Finally other quantitative methods are considered, particularly tally or score sheets, which are a quick and easy way to collect data in an unobtrusive way.

Collecting Data: A Variety of Methods

How you will record data is a key issue: get it right and this will be enormously useful when it comes to making sense of your data when you bring all of your records together. Getting it wrong may lead to incomplete datasets and difficulties in reconciling their apparently discrete meanings.

There are two kinds of data which you will collect and use:

- Primary data – you collect this
- Secondary data – you use data collected by other people

Primary Data

You should discuss with your tutor and class the different ways in which you can collect your data; however, some common appraches to primary data collection are:

- Field notes which include your own observations, thoughts, feelings, interaction including dialogue, what you sense etc.
- Maps and diagrams: drawn on site, these could include the placement of furniture, office layouts, streets and public spaces, the journeys of people, animals, vehicles, objects
- Tally or scoring sheets, a means of recording observed behaviour from which it is possible to work out patterns
- Surveys: typically using questionnaires with a prescribed set of questions, which can take different forms and will elicit different responses
- Interviews: recorded (for example by digital recorder), photograph, film etc., and with materials generated in the interview process by the research participants
- Time logs, diaries, budgets etc.: the research participant collects their own data which reveals a high level of detail, micro decision-making, and allocations of time to different kind of tasks
- Documents: letters, diaries, photographs, postcards, newspapers, 'official' documents such as annual reports and policy statements

Secondary Data

Secondary data refers to your use (or re-use) of data collected by other people.

The common source of secondary data are:

- Government sources of published statistics
- Associations, for example, trade unions, professional associations and membership groups, political parties, interest groups and agencies
- Statutory and charitable bodies
- Large, reputable, well-established global organisations such as the EU or UNESCO
- Archive organisations and documents

As you can see, the diversity of data collection which you might obtain lends itself to a range of quantitative and qualitative techniques. This chapter will concentrate on quantitative techniques, and Chapter 9 will concentrate on qualitative techniques.

Quantitative Techniques

Secondary Sources: Online Surveys and Compendiums of Data

In practice, much of the data that you can access nowadays will meet the needs of at least part of your research project. You might well find that it will suffice for all of it. There is a wealth of data sets available, and many useful compendiums such as bulletins, fact sheets, and yearbooks, news updates and so on. Data is easier to access than ever before, with more sophisticated searches and ready-made inquiries and reporting available which you might well be able to use quite successfully.

The advantages of using secondary sources include:

- Learning from others about good question formats, sampling strategies which have worked, possible response rates
- You can frame and complement your research with data which has already been collected
- Being able to use them as your main method: this might be the only alternative in some cases, especially for practical reasons of time and cost as well as methodological reasons, for example, historical timeframes

Some of the disadvantages of using secondary sources include:

- The social construction of reality by the choices of categories, measurement teachniques, and the write-up is out of your hands
- The data was collected to meet the aims of research projects which do not share the aim of yours
- Changing definitions over time and between places might present issues of comparability
- The margin of error and quality of errors might be unknown or misjudged

Even so, before setting off to do your own project, do take time to familiarise yourself with the range and quality of the surveys and datasets readily on offer. Table 8.1 shows some examples of the range of accessible surveys and compendiums of data which are generally regarded as robust and dependable.

Remember: It is always worth checking for secondary sources first, not only to frame and contextualise your research but also with a weather eye to the potential usefulness of the datasets in fulfilling much of the needs of your research project. Both undergraduate and postgraduate students may find that there is plenty of good data around that is fit for purpose – and most websites today have improved with user-friendly, online search and reporting facilities.

Task 8.1

Using NOMIS

NOMIS provides data about labour markets in Britain since 1971, and can be found via the Office for National Statistics website. The NOMIS site will collate and present data in a range of ways, including maps, graphs and diagrams, and spreadsheets. You can select sets of summary statistics which package data by geographical area, presenting labour market profiles either by ward, local authority, or parliamentary constituency. These are a good, quick, easy starting point. Alternatively you can go freelance using the Wizard enquiries to obtain more detailed data defined by your specific choices. Using Wizard allows you to make comparisons between different areas of the dataset and so on. There is an Advanced Query option. Once you have become familiar with NOMIS and what it can do, this is quite useful.

The first task:

- Find NOMIS
- Choose the Summary Statistics tab
- Find Local Authority
- Enter your postcode

  a) What percentage of people are economically inactive?
  b) What percentage of the population have no qualifications?
  c) What is the hourly pay of full-time workers? How does it compare with the GB average?

The second task:

- Find NOMIS
- Choose the Detailed Statistics tab
- Find Wizard Query
- Find Jobs Density
- Make choices of selection, clicking on the Next tab when a selection has been made, until a table appears. You can also request a map, which is interesting

Table 8.1   **Secondary Sources: Examples of Where to Find Good Online Data**

The National Centre for Social Research	Various surveys including British Social Attitudes (see Box 8.1) and the Health Survey for England. Look under topic areas, e.g. ageing, disability etc. Also look for the Survey Methods Unit which deals with methodological issues.	www.natcen.ac.uk
The Office for National Statistics (now governed by the UK Statistics Authority)	General Household Survey; Labour Force Survey; Social Trends; Regional Trends.	www.statistics. gov.uk
The Centre for Longitudinal Studies	National Childhood Development Study, 1958 cohort; British Cohort Study 1970; Millennium Cohort Study.	www.cls.ioe.ac.uk
Scottish Government	Scottish Health Survey; Scottish Household Survey; Scottish Crime and Victimisation Survey; Scottish House Condition Survey; Public Attitudes to House Condition Survey. Also look for the link to Scottish Executive Research which has its own pages, and the Index of Multiple Deprivation reports.	www.scotland. gov.uk
Northern Ireland Statistics Agency	Central Survey Unit; Census; wide range of topics is considered here etc. Look for the Northern Ireland Longitudinal Study (NILS) and the Northern Ireland Neighbourhood Information Service (NINIS).	www.nisra.gov.uk
Welsh Assembly Government	A wide range of topics are covered including demography, health, housing, education, training, agriculture, industry, the economy, local government, transport, the environment and the Welsh language. Look for: 'statistics' under Topics. Also look for useful compendiums and bulletins e.g. StatsWales.	www.wales.gov.uk
World Health Organization	A wealth of data on matters including mortality; health.	www.who.int

Table 8.1

	systems; lifestyle-related diseases; also look for Health Atlas, and useful Fact Sheets.	
The Social Sciences Data Collection based at the University of California at San Diego (SSDC)	Portal collating many rich sources of data on the USA and the world. Includes the US Census; election and polling studies. Some sources are unavailable to non-SSDC subscribers.	www.ssdc.ucsd.edu
General Social Survey	American attitude data. The main areas covered in the GSS include socioeconomic status, social mobility, social control, the family, race relations, sex relations, civil liberties, and morality. Also look for the Roper Centre.	www.gss.norc.org
Inter-University Consortium for Political and Social Research (ICPSR) at Michigan	The world's largest archive of social sciences data.	www.icpsr.umich. edu/ICPSR
Council of European Social Science Data Archives (CESSDA)	Portal to research in Europe including links to many key databases; data surveys, election studies, longitudinal studies, opinion polls, and census data. Look for the European Social Survey; Eurobarometers; and the International Social Survey Programme.	www.nsd.uib. no/cessda
European Union website	A dense website with data on Euro themes: general and regional stats; the economy and finance; population and social conditions; industry; agriculture and fisheries; external trade; transport, environment and energy; science and technology.	www.epp. europa.ec.eur

(Continued)

Table 8.1   (Continued)

Look also for key indicators;
also useful annual publication,
search under Eurostat Year
Book – this provides access
to very useful smaller
compendiums of data including
The Pocketbook which contains
the Key Figures on Europe.

Box 8.1   Spotlight on the British *Social Attitudes Survey*

The *British Social Attitudes Survey* is an example of a large-scale, long-term, regularly conducted government survey.

Since 1983, the National Centre for Social Research has conducted annual surveys into changing attitudes in Britain. The results are published annually in the report *British Social Attitudes*, which is also available online.

The *British Social Attitudes Survey* collects data on a very wide range of areas, from gender issues, healthy diets, and civil liberties, through to marriage, family and friends, local government, the countryside, education, transport etc.

Over time, topics change and are redefined, new ones are added and older lines of inquiry fall away. The shifts in definition, tone, discourses and so on makes the *Survey* itself an interesting source of data. However, an undoubted richness lies in the content of the responses as well, i.e. the data on offer. The website provides access to many of the lines of inquiry and can generate comparative data, which saves time when working with the reports in hard copy.

Below is an example of the kind of data which can be obtained, comparing responses to a line of inquiry pursued twice in the *British Social Attitudes Survey*, in 1995 and 2003.

Example

How much do you agree or disagree with each of the following statements?

'Immigrants take jobs away from people who live in Britain.'

	BSA 1995	BSA 2003
Strongly agree	13.69%	11.81%
Agree	33.37%	31.25%
Neither agree/disagree	25.43%	24.5 %
Disagree	19.26%	24.08%
Strongly disagree	4.91%	4.50%

Source: British Attitudes Survey Information System
www.britisocat.com/BodySecure.aspx?control=BritisocatMargin
als&addsupermap=LBIMMIGRT3&varnocache=0.76327672530
61394

Website

www.britisocat.com

Challenging Numbers: Things to Know about Data Sets

While useful, data generated in these datasets cannot be taken at face value. There are questions to be asked by researchers when working with data. These include:

- Who has produced it?
  This raises issues about who paid for it; vested interests; credibility

- Do the numbers stack up?
  This raises issues about what is claimed and whether the evidence supports such claims. Avoid fallacies – either those of others, or making your own through an incorrect reading or application of data

- How was the data collected and what are its limits?
  It is good research practice to always discuss data collection procedures, problems encountered, and the limits of the study set in train by the research design. Know what the data is and where it comes from, before attempting to use it in your study. Consider what bias from the perspective of your study might be built in, and consider how categories are socially constructed

- They can be structured in different ways in order to allow relatively spontaneous, open responses (semi-structured) or more directed, closed responses (structured). You can also use scales to gain views or perceptions of the action. See examples of the kinds of questions which can be asked in Figure 8.1.

Disadvantages of surveys include:

- Once you've started you must finish. Unless you treat your first set as a pilot study you are on a course of action which is inflexible; changing direction means that you risk making your study invalid
- They are not good at uncovering meanings, feelings, awareness, motives etc.
- Generating a lot of data: this can often be coded (see next chapter) and managed using software

---

Box 8.2   Spotlight on Social Trends

Social Trends is a useful compendium of data with pithy and useful commentaries. Various areas are examined including demography; households and families; education; the labour market; distribution of income; expenditure patterns; health; welfare; crime; housing; the environment; transport; changing lifestyles; inclusion.

Compilation Sources

Note that a list of all of the major government surveys, data sources, archives etc., used is contained at the back.

   Table 8.2 shows examples of a few entries in the compilation sources, which demonstrates the richness of their range, as well as providing useful information about their sampling frame, frequency of data collection, response rates and so on.

Source: Social Trends 38 (2008: 16)

Website

www.statistics.gov – look for the product *Social Trends*

Doing Surveys: Practicalities

Often, the data available is not the right kind, amount, or accessible. This means that you need to collect your own. For many people, surveys are synonymous with using quantitative methods, although as we will see later, observation techniques can also yield quantitative data.

Table 8.2   Examples of Government Sources Used in *Social Trends*

Source	Frequency	Sampling Frame	Type of respondent	Coverage	Effective sample size (most recently used in *Social Trends*)	Response rate (percentage)
Annual Survey of Hours and Earnings	Annual	HM Revenue and Customs PAYE	Employee	UK	142,000 employees	82
Census of Population	Decennial	Detailed local	Adult in household	England and Wales	Full count	98
Families and Children Study	Annual	Child Benefit Records	Recipients of child benefits (usually mothers)	GB	6,367 families	84
National Passenger Survey	Twice yearly	Passengers at 650 stations	Railway passengers	GB	50,000 individuals	37

Source: Social Trends (2008)

The advantages of surveys are:

- They can be used to collect data from a large number of people
- They are good for asking questions requiring factual answers

Designing Questionnaires: Setting Questions

Ensure that all of the research instruments which you use are clear to readers, easy to use and can be used in the same way over and over again. Group questions together into themes (for example, have one section on car parking availability; a different section on charges) and put the most important questions first (in case the respondent doesn't complete the whole questionnaire). Include a section for the respondent's details, such as demographic information (for example, whether they are male or female) and their relationship to the survey (for example, in the case of a survey concerning car parks, is the respondent a driver or a passenger).

- *Example: structured question*

  >Did you find a car parking space within ten minutes?

  Yes / No / Don't Know

- *Example: semi-structured question*

  >How did you go about trying to find a car parking space?

  'I drove up Porter Street but there wasn't anything there, then I went around the back of Carport and there was a space but I was too late. In the end I went to the meters by the library.'

- *Example: scaled questions*
  Your questions will allow you to collect different kinds of quantitative data:

  o In categories
  For example, patient, doctor, visitor, receptionist, cleaner. These are nominal categories which don't have a mathematical relationship unless you assign one.
  o Ordered values
  This is where people can select from categories such as 'strongly agree' or 'disagree'; 'tallest' as opposed to 'shortest' etc. These are categories which do have a mathematical relationship, indicating for example whether people or things are heavier or lighter; taller or shorter; bigger or smaller; stronger or weaker.
  o Scale values
  A few examples of scale value categories are between 16–21 years old, 22–27 years old, 5–10 kg or 11–16 kg. These are categories which can be accurately put into an order.

An Example of Using a Scale – the Likert Scale

The Likert scale is a common device used to prompt responses, where the respondent selects a point on a continuum. Likert scales generally use five measurement points or choices, although some applications also use an additional category or two, for example 'Don't know'. The key quality is that they avoid the trap of using too few categories, such as three. When faced with three possible choices, there is a tendency for respondents to plump for the middle one. Using an uneven number and aiming for around five choices, i.e. providing a sufficient range, pushes respondents to make a choice while not overwhelming them with options. A Likert scale can be arranged in a list, such as the one below, or sometimes the selection points might be arranged as a horizontal bar with numbering attached to each choice, so that 'Not at all successful' might equal 1 and 'Very successful' would equal 5. The bar approach can speed up the data collation stage.

How successful were you at finding a car parking space in town today? Please tick one of the following:

Not at all successful	☐
Not particularly successful /	☐
Fairly successful	☐
Quite successful	☐
Very successful	☐

Figure 8.1   **Kinds of Questions: Structured; Semi-structured; Scaled**

You will be able to do different things with the data achieved, either manually or by using a software package such as SPSS – it is well worth you building your coding design into your questionnaire design. You will need to work out what you will do with the data as part of designing the instrument to collect it.

It is important to spend time on devising the questions: see Table 8.3 on setting questions.

Online Resources for Accessing Surveys and Designing Excellent Questionnaires

In order to assist you to design excellent questionnaires, see the sources available online in Figure 8.2, Useful Sources for Working with Surveys.

1)   The STILE questionnaire database and useful links available from the Higher Institute for Labour Studies

The STILE questionnaire database provides access to an international selection of organisational surveys and the questions that are currently in use. You can run queries to find the ones best suited to your purposes. For instance, surveys can be selected by use in particular countries and by their design criteria such as questions suited to longitudinal studies. In 'advanced research' you can specify additional criteria such as languages or type of scale. There is a link from each question to the survey where it comes from. You can also print your selection for your ease. (See: www.stile.be/HomeAndNews.htm)

2)   Question Bank: University of Surrey

The Question Bank is an information resource in the field of social research, with a particular emphasis on quantitative survey methods.

The website has been designed to help users locate examples of specific research questions, and to see them in the context within which they have been used for data collection. It is intended to assist with the design of new survey questionnaires, the search for data for secondary analysis, and the teaching of survey research methods. It is funded by the Economic and Social Research Council in the UK. (See http://qb.soc.surrey.ac.uk)

Figure 8.2   **Useful Sources for Working with Surveys and Designing Excellent Questionnaires**

Table 8.3   **Setting Questions: Pitfalls and Fixes**

Example Question	Problem	Fix
Did you not go to the match with James who didn't want to go?	Too difficult to understand without further explanation	Avoid using negatives, and simplify and divide questions if you need that information: Did you go to the match? Was that with James? Did James want to go to the match?
Do you come here often?	Open to misinterpretation: invites a range of responses (comical; offence and so on) none of which are the kind of response that you are looking for	Clarify the question, use neutral language and be specific about what you want to find out, for example: How often do you visit this shopping centre? i) Every day ii) Twice a week iii) Once a week iv) Once a fortnight v) Monthly vi) Annually vii) Never been before viii) Other
What would it take to persuade you to re-use your plastic bags?	Makes assumption: that the respondent is not re-using bags	Be specific about what it is that you want to find out: i) Are these new bags or did you already have them? ii) Explore reasons
Are you flying to France and then changing for Vietnam when you get there?	Asks at least two questions in one; invites an answer to only one part or a confused response, possibly with accompanying explanations which may/not be clear	Again, simplify the questions, splitting them up into easy to understand and answer queries: i) Are you flying to France? ii) Will you be flying on to Vietnam? iii) When will you be flying on/how long will you stay in France?

Table 8.3

Example Question	Problem	Fix
So, you were 49 years old or was it 50?	A potentially sensitive question asked boldly; might also be too specific for respondent to answer easily or smoothly since if respondent does not view this as a sensitive question, they might be hard pressed to quickly work out the correct answer. In either case, the question invites some inaccuracy in the response	Allow greater vagueness on the part of respondents; ask permission for information by showing how this would help you. For instance, phrase it: May I check my understanding so that I am clear: about how old were you would you say at that point?
When you found the £10 note on the floor, did you do the right thing and hand it in to the shop assistant?	A leading question loaded with value judgements: invites inaccurate or confused reply unless affirmative	Decide what the true line of inquiry is about. There are two options here: (1) Rephrase the question to focus on the behaviour not the attitude in the first instance; and then use prompts. For example: What did you do when you saw the £10 note? Do you recall what went through your mind? (2) Pose the question as a vignette: People sometimes come across money lying on the ground. What do you think they should do when they find: i) £10 lying in the street ii) £10 lying on a shop floor

(Continued)

Table 8.3   (Continued)

Example Question	Problem	Fix
		iii) £10 on the stairs at a birthday party in a friend's house
Did you enjoy the film? Yes quite a lot Mainly Not really	An incorrect use of scales. Firstly use five rather than three choices, since there is a tendency for respondents to drift towards the centre or middle choice. Secondly use language which is less ambiguous – 'Mainly' is too vague and open to too many interpretations	I really enjoyed the film. Do you: Strongly agree Agree Neither agree nor disagree Disagree Strongly disagree
How much do you earn in salary a year? (excluding bonuses, savings interest or dividends, benefits and pensions): £10–15k £15–25k £26–40k £41–70k £71–180k	This attempt at using scale values to generate factual data needs to be staged with intervals which are: • Consistent • Meaningful In this instance, at the lower end a few thousand pounds carries a relatively greater social significance than at the upper end	Less than £5k £6–10k £11–15k £16–20k £21–25k £26–30k £30–35k £36–45k £46–55k £56–65k £66–75k £76–90k £91–105k £106–120k £120–150k £150+

Task 8.2

Devising Questions

Imagine that you are conducting an opinion poll investigating political beliefs. Devise five questions which would allow you to investigate public opinion relating to foreign policy.

Share them with your colleagues.

What different questions formats were used, and in what combinations (for example, what proportion of closed to open questions)?

What sources of inspiration were used?

What different scales were used?

How persuasive were the rationales for their choices presented by your colleagues?

Designing the Questionnaire: Appearance

When designing your questionnaires make sure that you have got your audience in mind. You need to make everything very straightforward for them. This isn't patronising, but recognises that:

- You are very close to your research, and what seems like common sense to you might well be rather mysterious to others
- People aren't always very good at following instructions!

Tips on Physical Design

- Write for your audience. The audience are the research respondents – not your university tutors, friends or family
- Avoid jargon, sophisticated phrasing, and overly complicated questions; this will just bamboozle your respondents, especially if they are trying to complete the questionnaire quickly
- Don't give your respondents 'difficult' tasks to do, for example, questions requiring mental arithmetic or exercises requiring spontaneous drawing, unless you have been able to pilot the study and know that this is presented in a way which definitely works
- Make sure that your questionnaire is quick to complete, to ensure that respondents do make it to the end
- Avoid 'over-designed' questionnaires with fancy fonts; lots of colour; a high level of decoration; borders; patterned paper etc., this will confuse your respondents
- Use plain white paper and a simple to read font size of at least 12 and perhaps 14 points
- Use as few sheets as possible, the less the better
- Test your questionnaire out on a few people from different social groups including acquaintances: a hall porter; a friend; someone at work. Take heed of their queries and hesitations – these are signs that they didn't immediately understand the instructions or questions, and take on board any

other data or feedback on offer, for example, the length of time it took for them to do it etc.

Remember: Beauty is in the eye of the beholder – and words are in the eye of the reader.

Look at Appendix 2 to remind yourself of the 'readability' issue which you will need to address in the design of your research instruments and any covering documentation, such as information sheets.

Task 8.3

Evaluating a Survey

- Find a survey: this might be a customer satisfaction survey; a public information survey; an online media inquiry; a local survey relating to services
- Complete it
- Reflect upon its design from all points of view: the kinds of questions, layout, readability, how long it took you to do, etc.
- Identify two improvements which you would make. Give reasons for your choices

Administering the Survey: Finding a Sample

In theory, perhaps the best approach is to attempt to access the whole population. In practice, this is extremely difficult, for issues of time and cost, as well as generating huge and unmanageable data sets. Thus, the need to draw a sample arises. The sample needs to be large enough so that there is some security in terms of the breadth of the sample which is likely to gain coverage and which allows generalisations to be made. However, samples are by nature sub-groups, so thought has to be given to working out where and how to find a sample.

The first step is in deciding which segment(s) of the whole population you will seek to access, i.e. your sampling frame, a methodological decision determined by the needs of your research project. But the second task is to actually track people down, persuade them to participate, and maximise the chances of them doing so. See Table 8.4, Methods for Finding a Sample, as the first step.

Administering the Questionnaire: Maximising the Sample's Response

Surveys can produce a significant non-response. This is so even for surveys with government or corporate backing, substantial resources, a well-organised system to carry them out, and with incentives and penalties for respondents. Without resources and publicity it is impossible to achieve a whole population response, but even mobilising a sample to reply can be difficult.

Surveys can be conducted in different ways such as by post, email, in person or by telephone. These methods can be quick to carry out and relatively cheap in terms of the costs per unit of data. However, different methods used for different kinds of audiences will increase or decrease the chances of a good response rate. You need to match the approach with the likely behaviour of the group in which you are interested. For example, the received view is that conducting questionnaires by telephone can increase the response rate over alternatives such as the postal questionnaire, although neither produces such a high response rate as face-to-face interviews. Response rates to questionnaires carried out for the purposes of social research may be as low as 10–15% (Denscombe, 2003) while in market research this may be even lower, at less than 5%. Mobile phones might be better suited to some audiences than others, while ringing home phone numbers of established, mature households means that your call will be abruptly ended. In person research conducted on a railway station concourse full of hurrying passengers produces a worse response than in the station waiting room.

Conducting Surveys by Post

Postal surveys can produce good quality responses, since those that commit to completing and returning the questionnaire may well spend time actually filling it out. However, notoriously, postal questionnaires are generally returned by relatively small percentages of the population, as low as five per cent is not uncommon especially if the questionnaire is complicated. Thus, to gain an adequate number of responses, the researcher generally has to build large samples into the design, increasing the cost and complexity of carrying out the exercise, and might have to send out the questionnaire more than once, or send a

Table 8.4   Methods for Finding a Sample

Sampling Method	Description	Best Uses	Potential Drawbacks
Snowball sampling	Each new subject refers the researcher on to further subjects	To access hard to reach	Relies on the judgements of various participants which may not be consistent and thus present groups which are unsystematically defined or consistently biased in a particular direction
Random sampling	All subjects have an equal chance of being selected	Increases representativeness of the sample	Difficult to define the parameters of the whole population and difficult to definitely include all possible candidates in the whole population from which to select, therefore may produce bias
Nth number sampling	Every nth name is selected for inclusion in the sample	Can be a quick and easy selection method to use when handling large amounts of data, for example, when using a database	Need to be sure that the way that the data is sorted and presented contains no particular order, i.e. that its order is truly random
Stratified sampling	Sub-groups are defined in the data, and the number of subjects selected from each group is weighted according to the overall importance of the sub-group to the population as a whole	A good way of checking the power of sub-groups which otherwise distort readings due to their increased probability, for example, of being selected, or their propensity to be selected	Need to be sure that the definition of each sub-group does not lead to bias in terms of creating or overstating significance; also need to ensure the allocation to each sub-group is accurate

Table 8.4

Sampling Method	Description	Best Uses	Potential Drawbacks
Convenience sampling	Sample is selected because they are available, easy to find, co-operative etc.	Good for rough and ready sampling and quick checks; can produce results which resemble the outcomes which would have resulted from a more rigorous sampling more closely than it may be supposed	Introduces bias due to social characteristics of the readily available as compared to the hard to reach: the researcher cannot know whether the outcomes from a more rigorous approach would have been very different or not

reminder for completion. This is also the case when using email. A quick and easy-to-complete online questionnaire (to the right audience) can achieve a higher response than traditional snail mail. However, a long questionnaire which crashes halfway through does not produce any favours.

Conducting Surveys by Telephone

Telephone surveys tend to produce a better response rate, especially if the researcher has been able to use a gatekeeper to obtain lists of potentially interested respondents. For example, a researcher working through a list of members of a club or association which has given consent to the research and has forewarned its members may get a much better response than when cold calling names from a telephone book. In both cases, it would be possible to attend to the socio-geographical dispersal of the sample, this being much more difficult with face-to-face interviewing which may be affected by the constraints of the interviewer's capacity for travel and availability. Yet Figure 8.3 demonstrates some of the issues around sampling which arise for both telephone and postal questionnaires.

Telephone interviewing:

Some groups are automatically excluded:

1) Those without a phone (social exclusion bias)
2) Those who are ex-directory (creating gender and middle class bias)

Some groups are less likely to respond at certain times, days, dates, seasons, for example:

1) Faith communities
2) Shift workers
3) Carers (gender bias)
4) During major holiday periods

Postal Questionnaires:

Groups are more likely to respond:

1) Where respondents feel strongly about the topic, for example, when there is a local opinion survey of proposed planning permission in the high street
2) If they are well-organised; with time to complete the questionnaire
3) When they have a good level of literacy; they can cope with the questionnaire without further explanation

Some groups are less likely to respond:

1) The busy and generally stressed may not see questionnaires as a priority
2) If the questionnaire touches on subjects which are considered sensitive for the population on the basis of, for example, invasion of privacy; embarrassment or shame; sex, religion, politics; financial matters, especially income, debt or tax related

Further decisions by the researcher can affect the sample and outcomes: what kind of telephone to use – mobile or land line? Should we use snail mail or email? But note that while these choices will influence the social characteristics of the sample selected and thus the kinds of data obtained, decision-making such as this can be used to specifically target populations.

Figure 8.3   **Social Factors Which Affect Sampling**

Box 8.3   Spotlight on the Census

The Census dates from 1801, and has occurred every ten years apart from 1941 when it was disrupted by war. The Census Act of 1800 was passed amidst fears that the growing population would outlive the food supply, prompted by the debate following the publication of Thomas Malthus' essay on the 'Principle of Population' in the late eighteenth century. The original data collection was carried out by the Overseers of the Poor in England and Wales, and schoolmasters in Scotland. In 1841 the Registrar General's post took control of the Census.

The collection aims to collect data from 100% of the population, with penalties for non-completion. In order to achieve maximum returns and to avoid imposing penalties, a system of door-to-door visits and postal returns has been devised and perfected using Area Monitors and other workers.

The questions posed, their shifting definitions and the sometimes controversial public debate surrounding them are themselves interesting data. Take for example the question in 1871 which asked respondents to declare if they were 'lunatics, imbeciles or idiots' (this was abandoned in 1881). Today, current debates surround how best to define and count various categories, what ethical issues are raised in doing so, and whether doing the Census is even necessary or within the principles of human rights. Controversies take place around specific lines of inquiry including religious belief and practice, and ethnicity and nationality. Censuses are found not just in the UK and USA but all over the world. Google, for example, the Census in Nigeria 2006.

Samples of Anonymised Records (SARs)

The SARs are a recent innovation. They allow researchers to access samples of survey data (between 1% and 5% of the population) without needing to access or deal with the whole of the census. Drawn from the 1991 and 2001 Census, the SARs allow multivariate analysis of the full range of categories found in the Census.

Further information relating to SARs in particular can be found at the Cathie Marsh Centre for Census and Survey Research (CCSR)

Websites

www.ccsr.ac.uk
www.census.ac.uk

Bias in the Response

Bias in the response is generally caused by:

- Decision making over administering the questionnaire which causes a concentration of responses to come from some groups rather than others
- Non-responses as a result of refusal: this is itself an important source of data, indicating taboo subjects, obstruction, and political resistance
- Miscommunication of the research question: this can be systematic, indicated by significant numbers of respondents apparently misunderstanding the question
- Demographic bias which is built into the questionnaire or the process by which it is administered

Uncovering Demographic Bias

When designing your questionnaire, decide what demographic factors it is useful to know: age, gender, race, religious identity, gender, postcode and so on. When looking at datasets, do checks on these demographic groupings. Look for:

- Over representation, or heavy clustering: a large percentage of respondents were from a particular group
- Under representation – the absence of groups including hard to reach groups
- Selective responses – a particular group 'refused' a particular question or set of questions

Dealing with Bias

In order to deal with bias, a few steps can be taken:

- Identify possibilities of bias and either take steps to mitigate it, or take steps to use it as a vehicle to obtain certain data from certain respondents. For example, keep a rough tally sheet of respondents so that you can seek out those who are at risk of becoming under represented
- Reflect upon whether using a split method for conducting surveys would be useful, for example, using mobile phones for 14–19 year olds, and postal surveys for 40–55 year olds. If a split method is used, then the consequences of this for the integrity of the data and bias which might arise need to be evaluated in the data analysis and the findings reached:

  o Ensure that all research instruments used are geared to levels of reading and speech which are lower than university undergraduates might assume. This increases accessibility. See Appendix 2 for some information about 'readability' including a couple of examples of measurements of reading ages. The likelihood that more respondents will interpret the question in the same way.

- Weight the data during data analysis. This is to compensate for the influence of under- or over-represented groups

Data Collection by Observation: Record Cards and Tally Sheets

There are alternatives to collecting data by questionnaires. Alternative techniques do different things, for example, tally sheets allow researchers to collect data relating to behaviour by observation, with limited or no interaction with the (unwitting) research participant. This allows a system

Table 8.5   Tally Sheet: The Dental Surgery Waiting Room

Location: Wood Cross, Hartford Road
Date: 11 Nov 2006
Time of Arrival: 3 p.m. Departure: 5.30 p.m.

Behaviour	Incidents
Read a newspaper or magazines	1111
	1111
	111
Used mobile phone	1111
	1111
	1111
	1111
	11
Browsed at surgery leaflets, treatments, costs etc.	1111
	11
Made further enquiry of receptionist after initial wait	1111
	1
Returned to car park	111
	1111
Ate and drank	1111
	1
Went outside for a cigarette	1111
	111

of scoring which has been used in various ways, for example, recording children's play behaviour; hospital visits; traffic flow; use of shopping centres; animal–human interaction.

Tally sheets typically contain a system of categories and tick boxes, which can be speedily completed in a systematic way. An example can be seen in Table 8.5, Tally Sheet: The Dental Surgery Waiting Room.

The advantages of tally sheets are that they:

- Allow the researcher to capture events while in mid-flow
- Allow the researcher to allow speedy data capture
- Are non-invasive: don't interrupt the flow of events
- Are not influenced by interaction with the research participants
- Can be used unobtrusively

The main disadvantages with tally sheets are that they:

- Don't access meanings and can't explain 'Why?'
- Are carried out without the research participants' knowledge or consent
- Allow certain events and objects to be captured but not others: are somewhat inflexible

Nonetheless, tally sheets can be a useful technique to use in a dissertation, even if they are not the only method used. They are quick and easy to use and produce a solid data set which can be pondered over later.

Summary

- There is a wide and critically engaged literature about quantitative and qualitative research techniques with which you should be familiar

- The most common quantitative technique for data collection used by students is surveys although sometimes it is possible and preferable to use survey data from secondary sources (provided that they are reliable), for example, national surveys. There are a number of good secondary sources of survey data, and nowadays these are more easily accessible online

- There are alternative strategies for recording data including the use of tally sheets or logs. These allow the researcher to record observed behaviour in an unobtrusive way. They are quick and easy to use, although they do not provide meanings or allow research participants to contribute, making them research subjects rather than participants

- A key challenge in doing successful surveys is linking your questionnaire to your sample. Sampling techniques vary; each has its own strengths and weaknesses in terms of bias and effectiveness. Ensure that you choose the sample that best fits your research question:

  o Random: all subjects have an equal chance of selection
  o Nth number: every nth number (e.g. every 25th name) is selected
  o Stratified: samples are divided between sub-groups and a proportion selected from each sub-group depending on their importance in the sample as a whole
  o Convenience: respondents are easy to locate and access; they are 'to hand'

- Having selected your sample, you then need to work out the best way of reaching them. Different approaches might mobilise some social groups more effectively than others. How you administer the survey (by post, in person, by phone, by email and so on) will affect the data which you collect. For example, doing so in person at the school gates will allow you access to waiting parents but not to parents at work

- The general problem of bias can be created by a number of factors, including where:

  o The sampling technique itself is wrong
  o The method of administering the questionnaire affects the sample
  o Non-responses are too numerous and invalidate the study
  o The questions are ambiguous or the 'wrong' kind (for example, closed instead of open) and produce poor quality responses

- You need to design your own research instruments: The most frequently used one is the questionnaire. Be careful how you set questions, and consider re-using and adapting questions from other sources such as Question Bank

Further Reading

Bryman, A. (2008) (3rd edn) *Social Research Methods.* Oxford: Oxford University Press.

Creswell, J.W. (2002) (2nd edn) *Research Design: Qualitative, Quantitative, and Mixed Methods Approaches.* London: Sage.

Czaja, R. and Blair, J. (2005) (2nd edn) *Designing Surveys: A Guide to Decisions and Procedures.* Thousand Oaks. California: Pine Forge Press.

Fowler, F.J. (1995) *Improving Survey Questions: Design and Evaluation.* London: Sage.

Hakim, C. (2008) *Research Design: Successful Designs for Social and Economic Research.* London: Routledge.

Robson, C. (2002) *Real World Research.* Oxford: Blackwell.

Chapter 9

Collecting Data: Qualitative Methods

Overview

The variety of qualitative techniques:

- Interviews of various kinds
- Observational inquiries, for example, of interaction and problem solving
- Case studies, which explored a particular setting, situation, organisation, institution, unit, arena, network, system in-depth
- Visual methods including the analysis of images, and tracking the production, consumption, and journey of objects through material culture
- Ethnographies

The biographical turn

Using documents

Oral history; life history

Doing interviews

Time logs and diaries

Visual methods

This chapter focuses on mainstream qualitative techniques that are located in a framework of biographical inquiry and lived experience. Examples of good practice are suggested in each section which explore, using documents: life histories; oral history; and data collection for these by interviews. Guidance on doing both one-to-one and group interviews is provided alongside discussions about structured, semi-structured and focused techniques. Another form of data collection is considered, that of time budgets, logs, and diaries which allow for detailed record keeping, often by the research participants themselves. Finally, the chapter considers visual methods.

This chapter, like chapter 8, explores a rich area, and does not seek to be comprehensive. There are suggestions throughout of possible avenues for further exploration as well as more detailed texts and additional suggestions under Further Reading at the end of the chapter.

The Growth of Qualitative Methods

Qualitative methods are well established in the social sciences and cognate disciplines. Qualitative techniques are good for working out meanings, feelings, attitudes, perceptions, and understandings. They are becoming increasingly diverse and are used in a much wider range of inquiries as methods become popular. Conventionally, techniques of qualitative data collection include:

- Interviews of various kinds

- Observational inquiry, for example, of interaction and problem solving

- Case studies, which explore in-depth a particular setting, situation, organisation, institution, unit, arena, network, system

- Visual methods including the analysis of images and settings

- Ethnographies have become more widely used in a range of fields

- Approaches which cut across these categories, such as working with material cultures (objects, their meanings and their journeys)

- Social networking and other kinds of novel community and identity interaction also present fresh opportunities for developing new approaches

The Biographical Turn

Qualitative methodologies have a long history. The use of biographical materials, in the case we are about to examine of letters between migrating family and community members, is largely associated with the Chicago School. Its pantheon of classics includes Thomas and Znaniecki's [1918–21] (1958) *The Polish Peasant in Europe and America* (Angell, 1945).

Box 9.1 Thomas and Znaniecki's [1918–21] (1958) *The Polish Peasant in Europe and America*

Thomas and Znaniecki were part of the Chicago School famous for the urban sociology of the 1920s and 1930s, a form of symbolic

(Continued)

(Continued)

interactionism grounded in the significant social change which Chicago underwent as it changed from a small town to a major urban conurbation with a large migrant population.

Thomas and Znaniecki's particular study was of the immigrant Polish population who arrived in the USA and Chicago in significant numbers from the late 1880s onwards, the world that they had left behind and their adjustment and settlement in Chicago. The newly arrived communities recorded their experience in diaries, stayed in touch with the folks back home by letter, were reported upon in local newspapers, and talked to the curious sociologists who found in the docksides of Chicago a rich social life, perfect for their investigations into how the community worked as a community: its rules, norms, decision making, roles taken, and so on.

Please note: the original research was published in five volumes, but a condensed version is available in one slim volume (see above).

Approaches since have made use of many different kinds of biographical objects and texts neatly conceptualised as the 'documents of life' (Plummer, 2001).

The life history approach, broadly defined, was boosted by the social changes of the sixties and seventies, and this has subsequently been conceptualised as a 'biographical turn in the social sciences' (Chamberlayne et al., 2000). However, not all qualitative approaches are connected to biographies as such.

The use of personal documents is argued by Plummer (2001) to represent a means of developing a critical humanism which places human subjects at the centre of the social sciences. As he correctly observes in the second edition, humanism critiqued by poststructuralists, postmodernists, multiculturalists and so on. However, qualitative methods are good for retrieving the otherwise silenced or invisible accounts of social life. This is positioned by Plummer as way into the 'underground' history of life subjects although others see such silence as a function of the subordinate social locations in systems of stratification.

Using Documents in Your Research

Documents which can be used in research are practically of any kind, including:

- Diaries, including internet versions such as blogs

- Letters, emails, exchanges

- Personal belongings (possessions)

- Archives, photo albums, pictures and portraits

Documents can be:

- Found, exchanged, lost, purchased objects

- Made by the researched

- Made by the researcher

Documents can literally mean paper documentation, or any assembled materials which can be 'read' for their inner meanings. As with quantitative methods, there are pre-existing data sets and good secondary sources which might be sufficient for your needs. An example is the Mass Observation Archives at Sussex University (see Box 9.2). It is worth you having a good look at possible sources before collecting your own (even though you might find that you do need to collect your own).

Box 9.2   Example Resource: The Mass Observation Archives

The Mass Observation Archives contain records from the Mass Observation Social Research Organisation which started in 1937. The three founding men, Madge, Harrisson and Jennings, aimed to produce 'an anthropology of ourselves'. The project recruited volunteer researchers who recorded in detail everyday life, including the various goings-on in their towns (for example, what happened at town meetings; events at the football ground; the social life of shops etc.). The archives stem from the first main period of collection (1937 to the 1950s); the second period since 1981, and funded via donations; and have links to other collections, and so on. The archives are in the library at Sussex University.

Website

www.massobs.org.uk

Life Histories

Life histories are a particular genre of biographical qualitative methodology. The tradition includes many well-regarded works such as:

- *Tuhami: Portrait of a Morrocan* (Crapanzo, 1985)
  Life history of a Morrocan tile maker giving insight into his symbolic and material world

- *The Jack Roller: A Delinquent Boy's Own Story* (Shaw, 1966)
  Life history of a young man in the 1930s with an interesting first section by Shaw

- *The Children of Sanchez* (Lewis, 1961)
  The life of Jesus Sanchez and his four children, giving insight into the social context and everyday life in a poor area of Mexico City

Such narratives or stories (Miller, 2000) can be considered as a form of storying, a '...normal human activity, contributing to the maintenance of self and the passing on or transference of key cultural and personal elements' (Chamberlayne, 2000: 9).

The key methodological and epistemological issues which are raised include the part which the researcher plays in calling up and shaping the narrative data which is produced (Stanley, 1992) (Geertz, 1993). The narrative data is produced within specific social contexts, and as such has been 'assembled from the meaningful categories and vocabularies of settings' (Gubrium and Holstein, 1995: 47). In addition, there are considerable methodological difficulties for the researcher and their audience who grapple with the extent to which the tale presented is authentic, which generally means how closely it corresponds to reality. See Box 9.3. for a brief overview of the famous Lewis–Redfield debate.

Box 9.3   The Robert Redfield– Oscar Lewis Dispute

Robert Redfield and Oscar Lewis both made ethnographic studies of the Mexican village of Tepoztlan, but reached different conclusions.

Redfield graduated with a PhD from Chicago, married Robert Parks' daughter, and took up a post in anthropology when the department split into two (anthropology and sociology). Redfield produced studies of what he conceptualised as folk societies changing under the influence of modern times (for example, with the development of new technology, urbanisation processes and so on). His study of Tepoztlan found a closely-knit community with a high degree of shared culture, making gradual adjustments in response to modernising pressures.

In the 1950s, Oscar Lewis repeated the study. He found that the community was internally heterogeneous, with important internal differences of wealth, power struggles and so on, which conceptually suggests in general that communities are subject to variation. Until then, anthropology and other disciplines had worked within a framework of assumptions that communities are largely homogeneous in themselves, and heterogeneous from one another. Furthermore, he placed a much greater emphasis on the importance of the social structure.

Two studies of the same community which arrive at different conclusions are instantly of interest and so these studies became a source of controversy. They point up both the limitations of research and the extent to which individual researcher perspectives and culture will affect seeing. However, they also show the opportunities in doing research to develop original and competing conceptualisations of reality.

Key References

Lewis, O. (1951) *Life in a Mexican Village: Tepoztlan Restudied.* Illinois: University of Illinois Press.
Redfield, R. (1930) *Tepoztlan, a Mexican Village: A Study in Folk Life.* Chicago: Chicago University Press.

Life histories are often taken of individuals, but studies such as *The Children of Sanchez* show the inter-connectedness of life courses, and ultimately show us something of a collective and social reality. Miller for example sees this as a virtue, arguing that 'the maintenance of the fiction of the atomized individual becomes untenable with the adoption of a biographical perspective' (2000: 2). Bertaux and Delcroix eloquently articulate the need to work out the social networks within, and through which, lives are lived and which show us part of the whole, or an aspect of the whole which we did not know before. Methodological implications include that life histories must be collected from different parts of the network, so that '...they illuminate and reflect upon each other like the gems of a necklace' (quoted in Chamberlayne et al., 2000: 74).

Working with Oral History

Oral history performs many social and individual tasks including:

- Giving a voice to the otherwise silent, or 'hidden from history'

- Presenting alternative views of history from the otherwise established and well-known

- Preserving community and local histories

- Contributing to people's sense of personal and community identity

- Enriching the communication of the real-life stories behind exhibits, for example in museums and galleries

- Educational purposes more generally

As a methodological approach, oral histories also come wtih health warnings. For example, issues to consider typically include their general reliability, as well as specific issues around gathering accounts from subjects who might be suspected of being intrinsically unreliable witnesses (interviewing a con artist about their activities for example). There is then a question over motive and context which might substantially affect the accounts (interviewing a whistle-blower for example) for more worldly reasons than co-constructions of reality. However, these issues do not preclude doing oral history, and can largely be reconnected to the substantive debates of all qualitative methodologies which raises issues relating to the philosophical stances of the researcher (see Chapter 4, What Kind of Researcher Am I?).

Most countries have their own oral history society, as well as belonging to an international oral history society. The Oral History Society in the UK has an excellent website with links and further information, including practical advice. According to the Oral History Society:

- Oral history is the recording of people's memories. It is the living history of everyone's unique life experiences

- Oral history records people's experiences on sound and video tape. It is a vital tool for our understanding of the recent past. No longer are we dependent only on the written word

- Oral history enables people who have been hidden from history to be heard, and for those interested in their past to record personal experiences and those of their families and communities

- Oral history is new and exciting because it is interactive: it is shared history and a rare chance to actually talk to history face to face

- Oral history preserves everyone's past for the future

Source: www.ohs.org.uk/index.php

For an excellent introduction to oral history see Paul Thompson's (1978) *The Voice of the Past: Oral History*. You can find another rich source of data in the British Library's collection of oral history in the Sound Archives (see Box 9.4).

Oral histories have been used in all sorts of studies autobiographically and by researchers. Take for example Studs Terkel's many works, including his account of hard times (1970). Oral histories have been used in accounts of sexuality, see Friday (1976); in medicine and health studies, see Cornwell (1984); and local area histories, see for example the current and ongoing study of King's Cross Voices Oral History Project.

Box 9.4   Example Resource: British Library Sound Archives: Oral History

Including both audio and filmed histories, and an ongoing programme of collection and investigation, the British Library collection is rich in historical and contemporary materials from life histories; descriptions of everyday life; rituals; and examples of dialects and regional accents.

There are a number of potentially interesting links from the website which you might use for your project, including access to:

- Local and regional groups and their collections in the UK
  For example: the Ambleside Oral History Group; Bracknell Forest Heritage; the Exmoor Oral History Archive; the Refugee Communities History Project; the collection at the Ulster Folk and Transport Museum and so on

- Groups and collections in the USA
  For example: the Library of Congress American Memory; the Civil Rights Oral History Project; Voices of the Colorado Plateau; Rhode Islanders' Oral History of 1968; and The Vermont Folklife Center

- Groups and collections throughout the rest of the world
  For example: the Oral and Pictorial Records Programme in Trinidad; the Brazil Oral History Association; the Mexican Oral History Network; Oral History Association of Russia; and the Centre for Popular Memory at the University of Cape Town, South Africa

- Holocaust oral history
  For example: the British Library Voices of the Holocaust archive; and Vad Vashem Holocaust Martyrs' and Heroes' Remembrance Authority, Jerusalem, Israel

Online at:
www.bl.uk/nsa

Interviews: Life Histories, Oral Histories, Individual and Group Interviews

There are several different ways of going about collecting data for:

- Life histories
- Oral histories
- Individual interviews
- Group interviews

1) Structured interviews

Structured interviews are planned and organised interviews, where the interviewer will prepare a set of questions (an interview schedule), and will work through them in a systematic way:

- Posing the questions in the same running order in each interview

- Taking approximately the same length of time per interview

- Ensuring that they use the same language each time

- Conducting the interview under similar circumstances

The structured interview will be in the control of the interviewer to a greater extent than other forms of interview, and the interviewer will be seeking to find responses to specific, targeted questions.

2) Semi-structured interviews

Semi-structured interviews combine planned and tightly defined questions with more free flowing ones, allowing a greater degree of spontaneity and some flexibility for the interviewee to raise issues themselves. The answers sought will generally be more open-ended and broader in scope, and the interviewer's behaviour will involve more prompting, follow-ups and returning to issues raised earlier in the interview than perhaps is the case in more structured interviews.

3) Freeform interviews

Freeform interviews are unstructured, and issues raised are entirely those chosen by the interviewee, as is the length of time which it might take to fully expound them. Freeform interviews are usually used for life history collections, and can be conducted in a series over time. There are particular debates and techniques for life history collection, for example, see the Biographic Narrative Interpretative Method (BNIM) which features particular strategies such as the interviewer not seeking to interrupt the flow of the interviewer's speech, and will later look at two tracks of analysis: the actual lived life on the one hand, and the telling of the life, (its 'performance') on the other (Wengraf and Chamberlayne, 2006).

See Figure 9.1 for Do's and Dont's of conducting interviews.

Group Interviews

Most interviews are conducted one-to-one, but sometimes there are advantages to group interviews, which allow the researcher to access the interaction of the group and the group's views – as a group. This should not be confused with aiming to save time, where the interviewer seeks to 'kill lots of birds with one stone' by interviewing several individuals at once. Group interviews focus on interviewing the group, not the individuals who compose the group.

Focus Groups

Focus groups, usually accredited to Merton (see Box 9.5), are according to Templeton '...a small, temporary community, formed for the purpose of collaborative enterprise of discovery' (1985: 5). Bloor et al. suggest that a specific benefit is the group's ability to generate understandings since 'The group is a socially legitimated occasion for participants to engage in "retrospective introspection" to attempt collectively to tease out previously taken for granted assumptions' (2001: 5/6). Bloor (2001), Wilkinson (1998 and 1999), and Bryman (2001) all agree that focus groups enable participants to bring forward their own concerns and themes, since they may talk to each other rather than talking to the researcher. Their behaviour, for example, prompting, contradicting, clarifying and colluding, is itself a form of data which speaks of many things: impression management; power relations; the construction of identites and so on. Thus focus groups can provide you with unique insights into the social life of the group. But the power of the group to structure and organise its meanings can itself also be regarded as a weakness of focus groups. After all, this may well mean that the group process in fact shapes interaction and creates a particular kind of bias, a group effect, which distorts the nature of the raw data which it generates.

Focus groups typically bring together between 6–12 people and will provide a structured discussion which typically includes most if not all of the following:

- Welcome and introductions (consider using an ice-breaker)

- Explanation of the research and reassurances about what is involved

- A Q&A period of semi-structured interviewing by the interviewer

- A focused exercise, probably using stimuli such as pictures, text, a little task for the group to do; the whole group will do it

- The collection of contact details and basic demographic information such as gender, age etc. (if/as required)

- The signing of consent forms

- Remembering to record the conversation

Remember: Due to the number of people involved, you need to allow plenty of time for all to speak in the session. Make use of your facilitation skills for example, by providing break points so that quieter members of the group can participate, and allow longer than for a one-to-one interview: it is harder to organise larger groups.

Box 9.5 Merton, Fiske, and Kendall (1956/1990)
           The Focused Interview: A Manual of
           Problems and Procedures

Focused interviews in the form of focus groups, which allow researchers to record interaction, responses, and meanings in a

(Continued)

(Continued)

systematic way, came out of the Bureau of Applied Social Research (BASR) at Columbia University, founded by P.F. Lazarsfeld, Robert Merton and Patricia Kendall after the Second World War. The origins of the idea are found both in the growing market research needs of the burgeoning mass consumer society and the twentieth century interest in psyche and attitudes, as well as specifically the Office of Radio Research in which Paul Lazarsfeld asked groups of participants to respond to extracts of radio programmes. Such techniques were used during the war by the US Army Morale Division (in which Merton briefly worked), for example to ascertain responses from army personnel to training and propaganda films.

The book by Merton et al. contains detailed instructions about how to put on a focus group, and some of the methodological issues which arise. The *Manual* is still useful today and is worth reading if you are seriously thinking of running a focus group.

Time Logs and Diaries

In the UK, one of the earliest studies using logs was that by Pember-Reeves (1990). *Round About A Pound A Week* attempted to record the minutiae of everyday life of the working-class households in Hackney, London, at the turn of the twentieth century. All sorts of details were recorded, such as the items of food bought and consumed (including the menus on offer) and how or where; budgeting; the organisation of the household such as washing and sleeping arrangements, and so on. Collecting data at this level of detail revealed all manner of interesting insights and challenged prevalent myths, such as the assumed level of alcohol consumption by such households (high levels were disproved by the expenditure and consumption data). It was to inspire further investigations of poverty, fleshing out more abstract, polemical demands for change, and helped to raise awareness of the usefulness of close, detailed, empirical studies which provide evidence for claims and demand for change.

Perhaps the merits of the study include the general principle that we can still take from it today: it showed what could be achieved by a mixture of willing respondents; researchers working consistently and systematically as part of a team; and the commitment to return to the field to collect data at intervals over a period of months and years.

Although not as popular in the USA, there is a specific Russian genealogy of time use studies from which we can also learn. One of the earliest applications of note was that by Sorokin and Berger (1938). In

- You must record the interview; use a digital recorder and don't rely on your mobile phone!
- Ensure that you inform your participants of the research and have obtained their consent – also make sure that the participant knows that you are recording, how and why you are doing it, and what will happen to your recording
- Give thought to where you will do the interview; try to find somewhere quiet where you will be undisturbed; make sure that the layout of the room or seating is comfortable and appropriate
- Get to the venue early – never let your respondent wait for you (they might well be discouraged and leave if you are not there to meet them) and if needs be leave a message with receptionists or doormen, or notes on doors etc., if they need to find you within a building (it is better to meet them at the entrance however)
- Don't be surprised if your interviewee is late or doesn't turn up or isn't at home after all – don't tell them off, however tempting; you need to be patient, persistent and smiley to get interviews
- Be well organised: think through whether you will need to provide refreshments and pay for any petty expenses
- Make sure that you obtain/check the contact details, and if you need any demographic data (for example gender, race identity, housing tenure, age, educational level, religious belief, sexual orientation etc.) that you have a prepared sheet which can be quickly and easily filled out
- Allow time for transcription, i.e. typing up the data that you have collected – and more time for its analysis. Transcription can take time, especially if the interview was long or involved a lot of people
- Be quite clear about the kind of strategy which you are adopting: structured; semi-structured; one-to-one; group etc.; carefully prepare your interview schedule beforehand; and do explain to the group what sorts of things you are going to do and ask them about, so that they don't sit there worrying about it!

Figure 9.1   Interviews: Do's and Don'ts of Conducting Interviews

any event, since then, time budgets, diaries, logs and so on have become an established method for collecting data which provides close detail and is under the researcher's control. These means are used by establishment sources as diverse as the BBC and panel studies in the UK, as well as in smaller scale studies, notably by feminist researchers exploring the gendered division of labour. They are currently also popular in health, research, for example, in alcohol, and nutrition studies where they also help to raise the awareness of the log-keeper themselves. For examples see Gregory (1990), and Bianchi et al. (2000).

The basic technique is that the research participant makes their own data records, for example by keeping a log of the different activities over a day; who does what, when; journeys; a list of who they meet or kinds of interaction and exchanges (such as economic, for example expenditure). If health-related, then the log might record exercise or dietary events; issues of well-being, stress, state of mind, for example feelings throughout a day or over the course of events. The researcher collects the records (after some judicious monitoring during the collection to make sure that all is on track) and treats the record as raw data. See Table 9.1.

The advantages of logs include:

- Co-production of research: the research participants are active and engaged, responsible for a major part of the programme's success

- The researched learn about their own behaviour through keeping these kinds of records

- The level of close details which can be obtained, and their accuracy given that records are kept as the participants go about their business

- Recording valuable data is relatively quick and easy, without the transcription issues which arise with long, complex interviews

- Quite large samples can be taken simultaneously, more so than in other methods which require the presence of the researcher

Issues with time logs include:

- Decide who is doing the reporting: autobiographical approach versus other member of the household, class, or workplace etc.

- Detail can be difficult to obtain, for example, an entry might read 'work', or 'went to Glasgow'. Further, complementary, inquiry by interview may be needed

- False reporting, for example, not recording alcohol intake or consumption of chocolate cakes; the provision of alibis to explain time spent doing undercover activities; genuine over- or under-estimation, for example of miles walked or impact of exercise bike

- Some data might be lost, for example 'washing-up and listening to radio and feeding the dog' might only be recorded as 'washing up' or 'household chores'

- Memory – if the diarists simply forget what they were doing or forget to record it!

Visual Methods

Visual researchers will use all kinds of materials, including:

- Photographs, drawings, images

- The components of images, for example, colours; fonts; types of material used

Table 9.1   **Example of a Time Log**

Time	Activities	Started task	Finished task	Who did you meet?
8 a.m.	Walked dog	8.05	8.35	Irene
	Newspaper Shop	When walking dog	5 mins	John
9.00	Supermarket Shop	9.00	10.00 back home	No-one
10.00	Put washing on Made beds Cleaned up around house	10.15	11.30	No-one
11.00	Down the gym Workout and lunch with the girls	11.45–2 p.m.	2 p.m. ish	Jill, Dawn, Sandra
12 noon	In gym			
1 p.m.	In gym			
2.00	Left gym			
3.00	And so on...			
4.00				
5.00				
6.00				

- Printed and moving: film, video, digital

- The arrangements of objects

- The visual aspects of words, numbers, diagrams

- Body language and objects

- Ethnographies for example, films and photographs

- The use of space, for example, settings and layouts

- Decorations and adornment

- The meanings of the capture and arrangement of the visual in museums, galleries, archives

Visual researchers look for clues which unlock identities, social structures, rituals, narrative accounts, systems of production and consumption, meanings and social arrangements.

The starting point to recognise the value of the visual, perhaps discarding some of your preconceptions. See Figure 9.2 for Prosser's (2006) overview of the key points, which if you are new to the approach you should bear in mind.

- There is no 'one-way' visual method or perspective that has ascendancy over all other ways of sense-making
- We don't 'see', we 'perceive' since the former is a biological norm and the latter culturally and psychologically informed
- All images are regarded as polysemic (having many possible meanings)
- Word and number based researchers 'skim' imagery, taking it for granted
- Visual researchers give imagery a 'close reading' (in-depth scrutiny and treating the visual as problematic)
- Images can be 'researcher found' (generated by others) or 'researcher generated' (created by the researcher). Both are integral to the visual research process
- The visual, as objects and images, exists materially in the world but gains meaning from humans
- A photograph does not show how things look. It is an image produced by a mechanical device, at a very specific moment, in a particular context by a person working within a set of personal parameters.

Figure 9.2   **Working with Visual Methods: Key Points**
Source: Prosser, J. (2006)

Visual methods have a diverse history, and textbooks and discussions reflect this. They include contributions from Banks (2001) who takes an ethnographic and anthropological view, to the more sociological view adopted by Prosser and Schratz (2006). Some suggested resources which give examples of the various strands of work in the area can be found in Box 9.6.

Box 9.6   Sample Resources: Working Visually

(i) The International Visual Sociological Association.
Provides links to a number of websites of sociologists and social scientists working in the field of the visual, providing access to their projects and image banks, archives etc.
Look for: *links to members and friends*.

Online at:
http://visualsociology.org/links.html

(ii) An example of visual ethnography: Edward Curtis and the Native American project.
Edward Curtis set out to record the lives of the North American Indians in the early twentieth century, producing a spectacular

collection of prints and photographs, and a lantern show. These can be accessed in a number of places, including the Library of Congress and the Peabody Essex Museum (PEM):

Online at:
www.pem.org/exhibitions

(iii) Material Histories at Victoria Museum, Australia.
An example of research using samples of cloth found in an archive box to interpret attitudes of the Board for the Protection of Aborigines over 1910–1920, with informative pages about the politics of such research and representation.

Online at:
http://museumvictoria.com.au/material/material.asp

Task 9.1

Reflection on Qualitative Data Collection

Compare and contrast constructing a family history through:

- A one-to-one interview
- A focus group
- Studying a set of family photograph albums
- Studying the archives of a major institution of relevance (for example the Census)

What methodological issues would you encounter in each case?

Summary

- Qualitative approaches have a long history and were boosted by the so-called biographical turn. They focus upon feelings, meanings, views, and subjective understandings

- The use of life history documents was pursued with great success by Ken Plummer, whose work remains critically important in this field

- Oral and life histories have considerable strengths and weaknesses

- Successful interviews are:

  o Well organised
  o Conducted in a quiet place
  o Conducted with the informed consent of the participant

o Recorded
o Recognised as produced by the interviewer as well as the interviewee

- Interviews can be carried out:

o One-to-one
o By group interviews

Each has their own advantages and limitations

- This chapter has given some tips on running focus groups, including ideal size (6–12), the need to record data, the need for a clear structure possibly including focused exercises and to ensure that all group members participate

- Other qualitative techniques include time studies, such as logs, diaries, time budgets and so on. These allow research participants to participate actively and responsibly, and allow the researcher to collect detailed micro-data which can provide all kinds of useful insights. However, they are prone to human error and performances of, for example, embarrassment, shame and forgetfulness

- Visual methods are a growing area which rests on the idea that there is a difference between seeing (a biological act) and perceiving (a social act). Visual methods are used to trace cultural meanings and indicate shaping structures of the inhabitant's world. The background history of visual methods includes anthropological and sociological uses as well as the study of popular culture and consumption

Further Reading

Banks, M. (2001) *Visual Methods in Social Research* London: Sage.
Darlington, Y. and Scott, D. (2002) *Qualitative Research in Practice: Stories from the Field*. Buckingham: Open University Press.
Dunaway, D. and Baum, W.K. (eds) (1996) *Oral History: An Interdisciplinary Anthology*. London: AltaMira Press.
Jacobs, L. (1979) *The Documentary Tradition*. London: W.W. Norton.
Miller, R. L. (2000) *Researching Life Stories and Family Histories*. London: Sage.
Neilson, J.M. (1990) *Feminist Research Methods: Exemplary Readings in the Social Sciences*. Boulder, Colorado: Westview Press.
Silverman, D. (2000) *Doing Qualitative Research: A Practical Handbook*. London: Sage.
Sontag, S. (1979) *On Photography*. Harmondsworth: Penguin.
Spradley, J.P. (1979) *The Ethnographic Interview*. London: Holt, Rinehart & Winston.

Chapter 10

Carrying Out the Research

Overview

The nuts and bolts of doing research

Accessing different groups

- The snowball method
- Accessing elites

Developing relationships: tips

Hazards: health and safety – clipboard versus reality

Research instruments: using logs, cards and other means of recording

Looking after your data – staying on top of the data collection

Real problems: making adjustments to your research strategy as you go along

This chapter considers the nuts and bolts of doing research, dealing with the various stages of finding hard to reach populations such as the disadvantaged and elites. Following this, how to manage the research relationship is examined with tips on maintaining relationships, dealing with money and other gifts, and what to do about finding yourself cast in the role of expert adviser.

The next section looks at safety and the issues which you possibly face as a researcher with some suggested *Do's and Don'ts*, before moving on to consider how best to manage the research by keeping track of it as a project. Without needing to do anything overly complex, keeping a running log of completed and outstanding tasks is recommended.

Finally, the chapter raises the issue of doing research in real life, and foregrounds the need to stay flexible, go with the flow, and be pragmatic.

Doing It: Carrying Out the Research

The successful development of a research question and shaping a research design is only half the battle, the execution (i.e. carrying it out) is most of the rest. Successful execution can make or break a piece of research. The quality of the decision-making hitherto might have knock-on effects on the quality of the research and the limitations you face in the write-up.

Access: Finding and Accessing the Research Participants

It is one thing to decide on a method and a sample, but it is quite another to find the participants that are needed. Time and tact are required, as well as a certain cheeky, good-natured nosiness which allows you to approach people and ask them for a favour – which is what asking someone to participate in research involves. Trying to find and pin down potential participants, including hard to reach populations, can be difficult, particularly when there is no obvious incentive for them to come forwards.

The Snowball Method

The snowball method relies on research participants referring the researcher on to other potential candidates. One participant gives the researcher the name of another subject, who in turn provides the name of a third, and so on (Vogt, 1999). The researcher may be able to request the participant to facilitate the initial approach or to warm-up the potential candidate, in effect acting as an advocate for you.

This approach is sometimes mistakenly regarded as a cheap and efficient way to find research participants. In fact, the snowball approach is really a method for finding a sample of people who it is otherwise difficult to reach, and often sits alongside other methods. As such it has its own appropriate uses, strengths and weaknesses.

The main use of the snowball method is to access seldom occurring or rare subjects in the population as a whole. What makes a research participant 'rare' may differ, but common reasons are:

- Their minority status, i.e. they are literally a rare occurrence in populations as a whole

- They are hard to reach, i.e. they may be more numerous but difficult to locate for status reasons such as stigma and shame, or because their network of social relations and institutional settings present barriers to access. This applies to elite characters as well as to the disadvantaged

Thus, the snowball strategy can be viewed as a response to overcoming the problems associated with sampling concealed populations such as the criminal and the isolated (Faugier and Sargeant, 1997). Snowball sampling allows researchers to access social networks however loose or vague, since it is based on a system of referrals (Berg, 1988). Accessing the gatekeeper who will refer you on is therefore a critical task. Good gatekeepers might well find you a few referrals. However, you should still expect to do the legwork.

Examples of the use of the snowball method famously include Becker (1963) in his study of marijuana users.

Accessing Elites

Much research in the social sciences has either implicit or explicit aims to ultimately work with, for and on behalf of, socially excluded and disadvantaged groups. However, not all research does, and even that which aims to do so, will sometimes need to engage with the high status and powerful in order to achieve these aims.

Elite interviewing is not as commonly covered in introductory and undergraduate textbooks about doing social and political research, since access to elites has historically been difficult to achieve for most undergraduates and has not been the focus or primary interest of much research, novice or otherwise. However, elites change in their style and composition or definition, and today, new technologies and celebrity cultures have produced the possibilities of travelling shorter social distances than was previously the case, and since many of those in such elite positions are new entrants, they provide a potentially interesting insight into the changing meaning and composition of elites as a line of inquiry in its own right.

Today, there may be increased opportunities to access elites and do genuinely interesting and engaged research at a more junior stage of your career, especially if you are willing to forego the opportunity to attempt to interview the truly famous and settle for a local or regional elite figure, or the 'B' and 'C' celebrity lists.

Discussions of the problem of researching elites show that:

- Researchers are usually at a disadvantage, as they have a lower status and are more expendable by the elite, for example, in terms of actually securing a meeting. We can work from this to see that undergraduate students may be highly disadvantaged

- The elite usually live within shelters. The walls erected by other, sometimes numerous and powerful gatekeepers can be very difficult to breech, and/or may generate substantial costs in terms of time and energy

- Due to difficulties of access, samples are not in the gift of the researcher. Samples are usually unrepresentative and individual interactions (such as interviews) may never be completed and/or their use agreed, making data hard to use

Table 10.1   **Access All Areas? Researching Elites**

Elite	Access Points
House of Lords	Lords of the Blog: Blog set up by Hansard Society and members of the House of Lords, including Lord Clive Soley, Lord Philip Norton of Louth, and Baroness Lola Young of Hackney www.lordsoftheblog.net
House of Commons	Call or go to the local constituency office and ask for the local MP's agent or website
Sports personalities and local elite	Managers, the chairman, long-serving members of staff, coaches, regional officials, and those working in sports, for example, can be accessed via the media officer of the club or website
Actors	Go via their agent, found on Spotlight casting directory's website
Local business owners	Directly, by writing a letter and making a follow-up phone call to their PA. Get the name of the PA first

Therefore, elites do lend themselves to individual case studies, and to snowballing if access can be gained to a receptive part of an elite, i.e. if a good gatekeeper can be found.

Nowadays, many elite members find that they to some extent rely on interaction and publicity with the outside world in order to survive. Thus the social conduct of elites both represents a continuation of past practices and traditions (lived out or conducted within shelters) and an opening out and public construction of accessibility (actual and imagined/presented). The rise of electronic communications has provided new impetus to the behaviour of elites, and suggests opportunities for enterprising young researchers. The main opportunities will be:

- Local and regional elite members

- The out of work/out of favour/the retired: 'Where are they now?'

- Those on the cusp of fame – the 'about to arrive' wannabes or contenders

- Serendipitous opportunities: the lucky break

- Contacts: knowing someone who can introduce you

- Institutionalised elites with formal systems of access (which can work after a fashion)

Developing Research Relationships

As part of conducting your research, you will develop relationships with at least some of:

- Research participants

- Organisations and agencies

- Other researchers

It is important to observe an ethical practice in your relationships so that the integrity of your data and project more generally is beyond question, as well as taking seriously your responsibilities in facilitating public involvement with research – in other words, don't put off the public from agreeing to be involved with a research project ever again!

Permissions and Developing Relationships

Seek permission before embarking on research, unless your chosen method specifically precludes this (for example, participant observation), or it is self-evidently unnecessary (for example, it involves standing at a busy road junction recording traffic usage). Explain that you are a student doing some research, and take some identification with you. Request help, and be 'appropriately' grateful if any is offered. Don't be too surprised if it takes a little nudging to turn offers of help into concrete activity: remain positive and persevere.

Some Do's and Don'ts

- You may find it useful to have a letter from your institution which introduces you and your research, and carry student I.D. with you

- Unless it is useful to your research, try not to take up too much time, especially if the researched are at work and you are not clear if they have permission to spend time out talking to you. You might find it more productive to visit more than once if you need to see several people or want a longer meeting

- Working on the street, square, foyer etc., do keep an eye on your own sampling bias. For example, you will need to approach passers-by, some of whom might feel to you to be counter-intuitive to approach

- Do take some spare cash with you and offer to buy any drinks and snacks etc. which are introduced into the equation. Bear in mind that in offices there may be a kitty system. Check if you are expected to contribute, especially if you are going to be based in an office or shop for any length of time or use it as a base over several visits

- Be open and honest in your research relationships

Working with An Organisation or Agency

Maintaining effective working relationships with organisations can be tricky as the research progresses. Some tips include:

- Be prepared to meet with their representatives more than once in order to get things started

- Consider tactics which will make life easier for them, for example, prepare a note for their staff noticeboard about your role or suggest some wording for a staff email

- If things go wrong, offer to meet people in person to sort things out

- Keep your tutor and supervisor informed of how the research is going

- At the end of the project, close the loop by letting your participants know the outcomes

- Make formal thanks, don't assume that only making informal thanks is okay or that a friend etc. won't want to be formally thanked

Good sources which discuss doing research in real life that involves relationships with clients, organisations, and so on, include Nigel Gilbert (2008) and Catherine Hakim (2008).

Consent

Consent needs to be formally obtained as part of the research process for any research involving human subjects. The purposes of gaining consent from research participants are to ensure that:

- The participants know their rights: for example, their right to withdraw at any stage

- The participants are aware of, and agree to, data being recorded, transcribed and/or coded, and used in publicly available write-ups of the research

- The researcher is covered in case of accusations of their conducting research without consent; using data without consent; or making public the research findings without consent

- The researcher and the participant can demonstrate that the issue of consent was raised, and that both parties agreed to the conduct of the research

This is realised by asking participants to complete a consent form. Most universities will either provide a template or will indicate the contents of the form to be used. Please see Appendix 3 for an example of a template for a consent form.

In addition to the consent form, but as an integral part of the process of obtaining consent, you must ensure that research participants are

- What is expected of the participant: this might cover everything from the kinds of activities which they will be asked to engage with (for example, attending a focus group) to how much time it will take
- Any risks or opportunities which might arise for the research participant
- What the researcher will provide: this might cover transport expenses; refreshments; transcripts; completed write-ups; sundry reimbursements
- What will happen to the data which is collected, specifically:

  o Where it will be stored
  o Who will be able to access it
  o Under what circumstances will they be able to access it
  o Who will have access to personal details relating to the research, if anyone: for example, the participant's contact details

- The research is a voluntary activity and that the participant can withdraw at any point, including the right to step aside from any particular component of it
- The contact information of a third party to whom the participant can appeal in the case of harm or wrongdoing. In the case of students this will normally be a named person at your university, but it might also include professional associations

Figure 10.1   What Should the Covering Notes Tell the Research Participant?

fully aware of what the research is to which they are giving their consent. This is usually achieved by a covering letter or set of notes which clearly indicates information as set out in Figure 10.1, What should the covering notes tell the research participant?

Remember: *Every researcher and every participant involved in the research must complete and keep a set of forms. You must ensure that you get a signed copy of forms for yourself as well as ensuring that everyone else involved in the research does.*

Task 10.1

Approval Procedures in Your University

Please be aware that universities and other bodies which commission research generally set out strict procedures by which approval has to be gained by the researcher *before* any research is carried out.

Check the approvals procedure in your university. Make sure that you follow them, and note in advance if you need to submit completed consent forms with your final dissertation.

Money, Gifts and Advice

It is usually not expected and often inappropriate to give gifts or to pay participants, not least because of the compromise to the integrity of the research which this could suggest.

If you wish to express gratitude you could consider a charitable donation; do ask your subject's views about which one would be a good choice. If you have developed a relationship over time, you may wish to give a small memento, which would not suggest compromise.

An exception to the gift rule is where the exchange of gifts is a necessary step in opening or developing a relationship according to dominant cultural norms. You will almost certainly be aware of this due to being offered gifts, which you should graciously accept and prominently display.

With these kinds of custom and practice, some ideas for reciprocal gifts include:

- Tourist products from home, such as postcards or fancy trinkets

- Flowers (but some are associated with funerals in different cultures)

- Sweets or biscuits for sharing

- If you are likely to be offered business cards: print your own at any machine in shopping malls or a train station, and include the title of your degree programme and your email address and/or website details but not your home address

More than money or things, you might find a different kind of demand or opportunity for exchange arises, around the matter of giving advice. Researchers sometimes find themselves in this position, which tends to raise quite complex and ethical concerns about how this shifts the quality of the research relationship and thus both potentially affects the data collected and the nature of the power relationship between the parties.

As a student researcher this may be a less common hazard, although you may well find yourself quizzed on aspects of being a student, your studies, and your university. How to respond to being asked for advice is generally regarded as a matter of personal judgement and conscience, and if it feels right to you then this could be a positive development. Do be sure that any advice you give is accurate and identify further sources of information. Be clear with the enquirer about the status of your response: clearly distinguish between your personal opinions and experiences and matters of fact.

Hazards: Health and Safety

A further set of issues can arise due to the unregulated nature of research relationships and the speed at which situations can turn and events can occur. The matter of safety in research relationships is a tricky one. It is vital to try to distinguish between feeling challenged and yet obtaining some good data on the one hand and feeling in danger, correctly identifying that you need to get out of the situation which you are in, on the other.

Some Do's and Don'ts

- Evaluate potential hazards early on in your project, preferably at the design and proposal stage. You have a responsibility both to yourself and to others, as discussed in the ethics section at the end of Chapter 5 and should take all necessary steps to minimise your own and your participants' personal danger

- Consider whether you should tell people where you are going and who you are going to meet, and arrange a time for reporting in if that seems like a good idea

- Take a mobile phone with you

- Consider best settings in which to collect your data. It may be unavoidable to collect data in inherently less safe places and settings but give due consideration to this beforehand and evaluate what steps you can take to ensure your safety as far as you can. A rule of thumb is to try not to blunder into situations without thinking it through

- Consider avoiding drink and drugs. If the situation demands your participation, you may wish to limit your intake, particularly if you are generally feeling uneasy

- Be aware of unwelcome sexualised encounters, bearing in mind that doing research with people that you know well changes the nature of your relationship with them, even if temporarily. Meanwhile doing research with people you don't know sets up a range of dynamics which you and other parties might experience quite differently

- At the far end of the spectrum, violent and abusive encounters, including bullying and controlling behaviour of all kinds, is also a dynamic which can and does occur. This can take many forms, not necessarily especially dramatic or awful ones, for example, having your bag or wallet stolen or being dropped off at an especially difficult place to get back from. Again, be aware of your instincts. If you don't see it coming and it happens anyway, extricating yourself and getting help as soon as you can is your first priority

- If you are feeling genuinely uncomfortable seek to leave the situation as soon as you can. If on balance you realise in the movement that it is actually difficult to extricate yourself, this might itself be an indication that all is not well

Remember: Getting the data can incur risks, most of which will be unproblematic. In the heat of the moment it is tempting to go with the flow. Generally, this will be fine and part of life's rich experience, but do take a moment to monitor your comfort levels.

Managing Your Data Collection

Once you have got your research underway, you will find it helpful to do two things:

- Manage your data collection

  Keep an overview of where you have got to and what tasks you have outstanding.

- Keep good records: how, when, were, who, what

  You can return to these when you are writing up.

Keeping Research Logs, Record Cards and Lists of Things 'To Do'

Keeping track of the data which you are collecting in order to maintain a sense of all of the different project tasks which are outstanding can significantly improve your chances of completing everything to your required standard, on time. Furthermore, keeping 'To Do' lists of what you should do next may seem an obvious point, but it does matter when you consider all of the different kinds of tasks which you will do in the preparation of your dissertation.

It is suggested that you keep a (very brief) record of every interview, session in the library, or survey session that you conduct. This research log records all of the empirical and other work which you have done. This will stop you from repeating searches and wasting time looking for references etc. You will also be able to use it to check that you have remembered all the things which you have to add to your 'To Do' list and monitor where you have got to. Its contents will be personal to you. An example is shown in Table 10.2.

Record Card for the Data Which You Collect

You may like to devise a simple record card which can be readily printed from your PC, for each piece of empirical data you collect. It can act as a cover sheet; pin it to the front of each data set (such as an interview transcript or a set of completed questionnaires), so that you can quickly identify it in your filing. See Figure 10.2 for an example of the kinds of things which you might record.

Table 10.2   **Example of a Research Log**

Date	Task	Where filed?	Comments and further actions
1 Oct. 2006	Searches: Google – Youth crime Knife crime Youth Birmingham Youth gangs	List of references to follow up	Youth crime too big a category Youth Birmingham – lots of community organisations to follow up
5 Oct. 2006	Searches: use a database such as Athens to search Youth crime Knife crime Youth Birmingham Youth gangs	List of references to follow up File of articles to read	Google 'Joseph Rowntree' and check recent reports
22 Oct. 2006	Telephoned Chequers Youth Project, spoke to Julie	Contacts database on home PC	Visit fixed for 10 November, 3 p.m.
9 Nov. 2006	Read Jameson on youth in Birmingham and the report on gang crime in the city	Filed notes and entered into bib.	n/a
10 Nov. 2006	Met Julie Recorded interview	Downloaded into folder 'Interviews' in folder 'Dissertation' on home PC	Need to transcribe interview

The Importance of Externalities

In microcosm we see that many problems can be attributed to externalities i.e. factors which lie outside of the actual system but on which the system is dependent. In other words, we do not engage with research in a vacuum but within a social, physical, economic and time context. Working with externalities and recognising interdependencies is one of the key issues doing live research of all kinds in the real world.

Much of the rest of this book, like most books about doing research, being a student, getting a dissertation together and so on, works at the

Item	Interview with Julie from Chequers Youth Project	
Date and Place	10 November at Chequers	
Format	Transcription	**Other Comments:**
No. of pages	25	Consent form is attached
Original	Downloaded on PC in folder 'Interviews' in folder 'Dissertation'	Julie said she wanted me to go and speak to her management committee in January

Figure 10.2　**Example of a Data Record Card**

level of myth, typically a myth of control. But in this chapter we have explored some of the realities of doing live research in the real world and have pointed out the importance of recognising that in social research, we are largely dealing with the messy world of real people with real lives in real places.

Summary

- Getting to grips with the nuts and bolts of doing research is a vital step in doing your dissertation. Conceiving and designing a great research project is not the whole of the task: carrying it off when let loose in the field is an integral part of the process

- Think through how you are going to access your sample. Be prepared to try a few different things, and to be flexible. In terms of accessing particular groups, this chapter reflected upon hard to reach groups:

  o The snowball method
  o Accessing elites

- Once embarked on your data collection, inevitably you will develop relationships, whether short-term or for longer:

  o Permission: it is vital to ensure that your research participants are well informed and give their consent
  o We have covered some do's and don'ts in developing relationships: a checklist of some of the basics. Much of this is common sense and 'good manners', but its significance should not be underestimated.
  o Keep research participants informed as you go along; this is important; if you are working with an organisation, do let them know how it's going

- o Money, gifts, and advice: be wary while remaining human and engaged!
- o Close the loop with organisation or agency that you work with. Make sure that you do let the organisation know when you have finished, how it went, and to thank them

- Hazards: the need for health and safety raises some tricky issues about taking opportunities and minimising risks. A starting point is to be aware of the risks which you take and reflecting on whether you wish to go ahead. Strike a balance between getting good data and staying safe

- Some do's and don'ts: as fully grown adults it is up to you, but bear in mind that students can be vulnerable due to their status. Not everyone loves a student

- Managing your data collection is important. Use logs, cards and other means of recording so that you know where you are, where you have filed things, and what tasks are outstanding

- Look after your data once you have got it. Observe rules of confidentiality and protect this gif

- Deal with real problems: make adjustments to your research strategy as you go along. Bear in mind that sometimes this need isn't anything to do with epistemology or data collection techniques – it might simply be that the grass has grown. When it comes to the contingencies of life, go with the flow and make adjustments as you go along

Further Reading

Bell, J. (2007) (4th edn.) *Doing Your Research Project*. Maidenhead: Open University Press.

Berg, B.L. (2007) Chapter 4, 'A Dramaturlogical Look at Interviewing (Including Tips Such As the Ten Commandments of Interviewing)', in *Qualitative Research Methods for the Social Sciences*. New York: Pearson International.

Hakim, C. (2008) (2nd edn.), *Research Design: Successful Designs for Social Economic Research*. London: Routledge.

Hornsby-Smith, M. (1993) Chapter 4, 'Gaining Access', in N. Gilbert (2008) *Researching Social Life*. London: Sage.

Robson, C. (2005) *Real World Research*. Oxford: Blackwell.

Chapter 11

What Do I Do with All the Data?

Overview

When you have got enough of the right kind of data – stop collecting it!

Coding quantitative data: using statistical techniques to make sense of your quantitative data:

- Univariate and multivariate statistics
- Frequency, distribution and weightings
- Averages: mean, median, and the mode
- Range
- Normal and skewed distribution and calculating the standard deviation; compare standard deviations using Z-scores
- The 3-step process of coding qualitative data

Four examples of working with qualitative data

Using software for coding quantitative and qualitative data

Negative evidence – the importance of noticing what's missing

Qualitative researchers and numbers.

When should we stop collecting data? What happens next? The chapter will briefly cover coding both quantitative and qualitative data starting with a brief overview of the main principles of making sense of quantitative data by bringing variables together using statistical techniques. Examples of working with qualitative data are then given. The next section briefly considers using software for quantitative and qualitative data analysis, before moving on to consider negative evidence, i.e. the significance of the omissions in data, before finally turning to the question of the relationship between qualitative research and numbers. You should note that there are specialised sources of help which can support you in your coding and analysis. The aim of the chapter here is to indicate some of the main areas and to encourage you to delve deeper according to the requirements of your research project.

Time to Stop: Adequacy of Data

An important step in doing your dissertation is to recognise when it is time to stop collecting data. One reason that researchers continue collection is that it can be an enjoyable experience. As you gain confidence, develop experience, and realise that your understanding is improving all the time, the temptation can be to continue with the collection stage. However, a second reason can be that it seems safer and easier to carry on collecting data rather than face the daunting task of making sense of it. In fact, working with data can also be a rewarding experience.

Gathering enough data is essential. Follow your plan, and keep gathering data according to the research design which has been agreed with your tutor. If you are finding a high level of non-responses to surveys or short and thin interviews which seem to be yielding little useful data, then consider whether you should change your research design or whether it is time to stop. In the worst-case scenario, attempting but failing to collect data is itself a form of data, since you will need to reflect upon what it is about your research design and/or the research conditions which has led to this. If you find yourself in a situation where in effect you are leading a failing research project, don't just continue to collect data hoping that things will improve – they might not! Cutting your losses and working with what you have managed to get is a perfectly reasonable response.

An adequate data set is one which allows the researcher to reach a reasoned judgement as to its valid meaning. This doesn't mean the sole interpretation or deduction which is possible, or that the conclusions drawn are infallible. But it does mean that the researcher is relying upon a solid data set to draw conclusions.

In both qualitative and quantitative research, an adequate data set is one which provides sufficient evidence to draw conclusions, i.e. the amount of good quality and relevant data is sufficient. Qualitative research designs might rest upon a close and detailed examination of relatively small numbers of cases, when compared to quantitative studies. Reasoned conclusions are drawn on patterns found in the data made accessible by techniques of interpretation.

For quantitative research, adequacy refers to a large enough number of recurring data which allows the researcher to reach reasoned conclusions based upon patterns within the data, usually made accessible by statistical or mathematical techniques. Quantitative researchers are more likely to use datasets represented in numerical form with relatively closed meanings. They will attend to measuring and counterbalancing variables against one another which prove or disprove hypotheses. Qualitative researchers are more likely to use datasets represented in text, and will attend to establishing patterns and relationships which can be ambiguous in meaning, and which can change in the meanings attributed to them during the course of the research project.

Remember: Health Warning – the Margin of Error

All data, whether qualitative, quantitative or mixed, is prone to fallacious readings. There is scope for human error in the procedures for handling data. Also the data is a product of a sample and will have bias built into it as well. You can take this into account by allowing for a margin of error in both quantitative and qualitative data analyses. You should discuss this problem as part of your discussions of weaknesses and limitations.

You need to decide how big the margin of error was, and whether it was statistically significant. This can be calculated with quantitative data (for example by the chi-square technique using a tab in the SPSS package), but in qualitative data you will need to make reasoned judgements based upon the internal consistency of your data whereby you acknowledge the contingency of the dataset and your own interpretations placed upon it.

In both cases, a margin of error of a small magnitude would be expected to be present in most sound research studies.

Coding: Quantitative Data

Once the researcher has collected the data, the next step is to organise it into a form which can be analysed. This involves translating the data into a condensed form. For example, a selection of 25 vehicle registration plates which were recorded at a crossroads between the hours of ten and eleven o'clock might be re-coded into 25 numbers of one digit each with a time alongside them.

Once condensed, the researcher will want to sort and analyse the data to draw out its significance. For example, recording data which represents the frequency of traffic at different times of day could enable the researcher to work out whether a pedestrian crossing is required. In this instance, further data might also be required, for example the number of pedestrians attempting to cross the road during each time. This feature, the combination of datasets which must be generated and linked in order for reasonable conclusions to be drawn, lies at the heart of quantitative research. Thus research is typically built around a series of variables which are assumed to be at work simultaneously and their interconnections and relationships.

Because of the complications of condensing and sorting data, there are tried and trusted techniques for doing so. See Table 11.1 for an outline of a fairly generic five-step process for coding quantitative data.

Table 11.1   Coding Quantitative Data: The Five-step Process

Step	Task	Description
Step 1	Research design takes into account coding needs	The researcher decides on possible coding early on at the design stage, so that data collection instruments such as questionnaires are designed to make coding easy.
Step 2	Coding method or procedure	The researcher designs a set of rules to be applied to the data. For example, all cars will be labelled (1), whereas all buses will be labelled (2). Every kind of variable needs to have a code allocated to it including miscellaneous and extraordinary ones.
Step 3	Coding book	The researcher puts together a guide to the coding method or procedure to be used. The coding book will indicate how the codes will be presented and read (by human eye, machine-readable media or other means) and specifies the order and layout to be used when transferring the coding from the raw data into a form which can be used for analysis. (NB The wise researcher keeps a spare copy of the coding book in a safe place!)
Step 4	Researcher conducts coding following layout precisely	The researcher carries out coding of each piece of data, entering numerical alue in the right place in the grid, from, or other layout format as set out in the design. This may be entered into the computer by different methods; scanning; direct entry use of bar codes etc.
Step 5	Cleaning the data	The researcher has to establish the margin of error. Margins of error arise from inaccurate coding and layout. While this is difficult to monitor precisely, the researcher can take steps to establish and reduce the margin of error by cleaning data. This means re-coding a random sample of data and seeing if you get the same result. If not, establish the error and correct it accross the whole data set since it may have been incorrectly performed multiple times. This correction is called cleaning the data, and will reduce the margin of error.

Working with Variables

Once the researcher has obtained a good, clean data set and has translated it into a form which can be read and reported upon, they are ready to make sense of it. To do this, researchers bring the various parts of the data set into relation with each other.

This means working out the combination of enquiries which you could make. For example:

- The dependent variable – what you want to explain:

  e.g. unemployment in your neighbourhood; obesity in England

- The independent variable – what you want to explain it with:

  e.g. age, gender, race, level of educational attainment, shopping habits, levels of income

You can bring variables together in order to do two things:

- *Describe* something:

  16% of women in Halifax are unemployed

- *Explain* something:

  60% of all women in Halifax who are unemployed use English as a second language

Statistics: Technical Shorthand for Techniques to Read Data

The technical shorthand for techniques which deal with variables and the data relating to them is easy to understand. Some of the main descriptions and terms are:

- Univariate statistics

  A form of measurement which deals with one variable at a time

- Multivariate statistics

  A form of measurement which deals with two or more variables at a time, working out the relative significance of each to the others

- Frequency distribution

  A chart which shows the distribution of the sample across each category, i.e. how many are in which category

- Normal distribution

  A bell-shaped curve, where the number of cases are at their smallest at either end of the curve, with the maximum volume falling in the middle. This model represents the distribution of cases in most models of distributional norms. Sometimes, data may be distributed in the exact opposite way, as an inverted, i.e. upside down, U-shaped curve

- Skewed distribution

  A curve where more cases lie on one side or the other, i.e. there is a weighting in favour of one direction or the other, where the curve 'leans' to the left or right

- Averages

  Often misused, this category of statistical measurements show the distribution of the data around the central point, for example, how far away from the central point most numbers fall, and so on. The term 'average' isn't that helpful in statistical analyses – specifically choosing between the three kinds of averages is much better:

  (i)   Mode: the most frequent or most fashionable
  (ii) Median: the half-way point, at which half the cases lie above and half the cases lie below
  (iii) Mean: all the scores added together and divided by the number of cases. (NB this is what is generally meant by the term 'average')

- Range

  The gap between the lowest and highest case

- Standard deviation

  The standard deviation is a measurement of the distance between each case and the mean, whereby all the distances of all the cases have been added together and their mean distance, as a class or group, calculated. The number calculated is termed 'the standard deviation'. Standard deviation can sometimes fox students, but it is logical when carefully considered. It is useful for making comparisons between different data sets for a similar phenomenon. The closer to 0.0 the number, the less the deviation. Really high standard deviations are usually interesting to investigate

- Z-scores

  Z-scores are a way of comparing standard deviations which have been calculated for different classes or categories of cases. Take for example the problem, 'How fast can this class run a 10,000 metres race?' In the results, of the group of men aged 40–50 years old, Dan produced a result of 45 minutes. In the class of men aged 20–30 years old, John's result was 35 minutes. Compared to all the other runners aged 40–50, Dan did quite well; although not as fast as the fastest group of runners in his age category, he was ahead of the middle pack. His Z-score is therefore higher than 0.0 but not a great distance away, perhaps 0.4.

  Likewise, in the class of men aged 20–30 years old, John also did quite well, but it has to be said, he was not in the winning group but rather crossed the finishing line in mid-pack position. His Z-score was 0.6. Of the two, Dan performed better than John, even though he took longer to run the race. Thus we can see that Z-scores allow us to make comparisons across different groups in which different means prevail.This example shows how we might use Z-scores to say 'Dan did relatively well.'

Using Software for Quantitative Data Coding

You can use spreadsheets to do at least some coding, and if you have a smallish sample, say less than 30, you might well be able to use spreadsheets for all of your coding and analysis purposes. Spreadsheet packages such as Excel provide tasks such as Counting, Means, and Standard Deviation calculations, and can also be used to express data as charts, diagrams and graphs.

For bigger samples or more complex tasks with lots of variables, you can use Statistical Package for the Social Sciences (SPSS). SPSS has its roots in the big mainframes of the sixties, but it has been adapted over the years and is still very commonly in use. It can be experienced as a little clunky and it takes time to enter data, but it still allows researchers a fair flexibility in setting data against each other and working out some key trends. Having said this, students and professional researchers alike have had some fun over the years with concocting all kinds of nonsense which SPSS will happily produce if you request it to.

The basic process is outlined above, i.e. assigning codes, making a code book, making names for variables and then entering data. Once translated and entered, it is time to run reports on the data, and request charts and diagrams. You can select which sets of data will be expressed in reports, making them easy to decipher. Cleaning the data is quite important, given the scope for human error at different stages of the processes, such as coding and data entry, as well as retrieving good output files you made last time you were working.

Once you have created a range of reports in output files, you are well away. Remember to record the names of the output files and what you have got in each one.

Remember: To save your work – and do keep a codebook so that next time you return to your desk you can pick up where you left off.

Coding: Qualitative Data

Data is first transcribed if in the form of speech, or assembled if in other forms, for example, texts, written or visual. The data is coded by the researcher in an initial sweep. The coding which results from this is generally referred to as Open Coding. Open Coding identifies categories such as those, for example, based upon:

- Particular kinds of interaction, e.g. angry, accusing, identity related, a power struggle etc.

Table 11.2   Coding Qualitative Data: The Three-step Process

Step	Task	Description
Step 1	Open coding	An initial run through the data allocating a code to each piece.
Step 2	Axial coding	Arranging all of the coded segments in relation to each other, using the codes not the underlying data as the point of connection.
Step 3	Selective coding	Revisiting the original dataset and reviewing it, identifying the most useful pieces of data which are selected for further work.
Notes and memos		Qualitative researchers keep notes as they work, sometimes generating quite complex analyses of the data and their coding process and working these into first theories, often in note form. These are a useful archive which the researcher can use to build theory at different stages of analysis and theorising. (See Strauss (1987) data for a discussion of analytic memos.)

- Specific topics which are discussed, e.g. marriage, jobs, a person, an event; or particular discourses used, e.g. growing old, being past it
- The appearance and use of symbols, e.g. personal belongings; the use of texting; identity markers

However, good coding will move beyond being purely descriptive, and will instead be analytical. Thus, while interactions might be coded, they will be coded according to a conceptual view taken of them by the researcher. For example, rather than merely described as 'angry', text might be coded as 'resistive or oppositional', and would form part of a wider theoretical framework, perhaps relating to social movements.

The second stage is Axial coding, and at this stage the researcher will concentrate on making connections between the various coded categories. As the researcher continues to work on the data, they might well find that they move further away from the actual data as they use the codes to work further on the meanings of the data. For this reason, qualitative researchers sometimes return to the raw data before the final stage, of Selective coding. Selective coding allows the researcher to find the pieces of data which deepen the emergent theory as well as identifying anomalous data which contradicts the dominant interpretations.

This approach to coding and its variations provides researchers with a straightforward road map through the mass of data which sits before them. It is usual to number the data entries as you go, so that you can cross refer chunks of data and re-arrange them. See Table 11.2 for a summary of the process.

Coding Visual Data

Coding visual data follows many of the same rules, in the sense of working systematically through the images or records of the visual collected, looking for patterns and groups which can be categorised, and then re-visiting images or their records to fill out the categories. However, since visual data is still less used than written, printed or spoken data, you might have had more limited opportunities to perform visual data collection, coding, and representation to date. However, it can certainly be worth pursuing, and makes a do-able project which is interesting to execute.

The following extract shows the outcomes of Holliday's analysis of film generated by giving Camcorders to participants, and asking them to make recordings about their choices regarding their appearance (for example, what to wear):

> From the material submitted by respondents two important but fundamentally different styles of diary emerged. One style was primarily associated with those respondents who involved partners and friends in the filming process. These tended to be light-hearted pieces incorporating jokes and ironic statements.... these diaries appear to be specifically designed to be 'entertaining'...however, *alone* in front of the camera, these same diarists adopted a different style, as did those diarists who filmed themselves entirely with accomplices. The self-consciousness thus appears to be the result of performing in front of a *known* other. (2004: 51–2)

Examples of Working with Qualitative Data

Developing your skills at coding data and recognising categories is, like so many things, a matter of practice. Practice makes perfect. Here are some examples of data which have been categorised, and which includes examples of how they have been organised, presented, and discussed in the write-up:

- *Skeggs: disidentifications of class*
  The first example is from Beverley Skeggs' work published as *Formations of Class and Gender* (1997). In her chapter which specifically explores class formations, the researcher finds that women talk about social class in ways which locate them in a hierarchical way within class formations. In this example which follows below, Skeggs argues that the respondents are using a social distancing technique, whereby the speakers are at pains to show that they understand and recognise working class people, but don't think of themselves as belonging to that group, which is implicitly beneath

them in class hierarchies. Skeggs calls this category 'disidentification', the opposite of identification. Skeggs opens the section with a subheading, *Disidentifications*, followed by a listing of six pieces of data pulled out and coded as belonging to the category, following this with a discussion of the interpretation of the data. Here is an edited extract:

Disidentifications

To me if you are working class it basically means that you are poor. That you have nothing. You know, nothing. [Sam, 1992]

The ones who batter their kids. [Pam, 1992]

It used to be you were working class if you worked in the railways say and it didn't mean you had no money, but now it's changed. Now it means that you don't work, like it's not those with the good jobs now it's those without jobs, they're the real working class. [Lisa, 1992]

They want to be seen as different ... In their accounts the working class are poor, deprived, depriving, dangerous and degraded. They are well aware of the jokes about 'Sharons and Kevins', about tackiness, about white high heeled shoes. ... The negativity associated with the working class is ubiquitous. (Skeggs, abridged), (1997: 76)

- *Leonard: sectarian stories*

In the following extract Madeleine Leonard presents conversational data to explore teenagers' storytelling in North Belfast, used to construct their identities as part of the Catholic and Protestant communities. The extract here demonstrates a common approach to handling conversations in text. Participants are anonymised and allocated numbers, punctuation is minimal and speech is carefully set out to convey the sense of the interaction to the reader:

The following extract concerns a discussion among a group of Protestant girls in relation to school cross-community events:

Girl 1	Member the time we were at that community thing
Girl 2	Yeah we were at this community thing the other day and there was a wee girl shouting over to her [points to another girl in the group] 'watch yourself'
Girl 3	No she didn't say it to just me, she said it to all of us
Girl 1	Yeah she said 'yous may watch yourself'
Girl 4	Here's me 'what I'll not be watching myself, you may watch yourself'
Girl 1	See anytime we're with them [Catholics] there's always one of them wanting to start something

The extract is one of many whereby groups collectively recalled incidents where as a group they were under attack from the 'other' community. In this extract, Girl 2 attempts to individualize the threat
that the group experienced but this was refuted by Girl 3 as an
attack on the whole group rather than on any individual member of
the group. These events help unify the group by providing a narrative framework which locates the individual within the membership
of the group. (Leonard, 2006: 1125)

• *Murdock et al: marketing blurb*

  In the following example, Murdock et al. (1995) analysed marketing materials to explore the synergy between the official discourse of the 'information age', government policy, and the kinds of messages used to warm up
  market demand for home computers in the 1980s.

  > Their marketing strategy resonated strongly with official discourse
  > about the coming 'information age'…The advertisement for the sec-
  > ond generation of Acorn machines is a good example. Headed
  > 'Think of it as a down payment on your child's future uniform', it
  > featured a girl in her graduation robes, bathed in sunlight, stand-
  > ing in the cloisters of one of the country's ancient universities. The
  > accompanying copy was addressed directly to parental worries:
  >
  > Your child's degree ceremony might seem a long way off. But
  > the BBC Master Compact is equipment to help at every step of
  > the way. Our new micro can provide your child with constant
  > support throughout education, eventually graduating into
  > business and professional use. Put it on your Christmas list. It
  > should help to put a few letters after your child's name.
  >
  > …This vision of the micro as an essential aid to educational and
  > career advancement played a key role in encouraging parents to
  > invest in one. Altogether, three-quarters of all the households in
  > the Midlands survey that had a computer claimed to have pur-
  > chased a machine with children and teenagers in mind. Many had
  > gone out and bought one in much the same spirit as they might
  > earlier have bought a set of encyclopaedias. (1995: 277)

• *Foster: the use of contradictory and historical sources*

  Using historical sources can be equally effective in terms of finding
  rich sources of qualitative data. Working through diaries, letters, and
  other kinds of narrative documents presents all sorts of creative possibilities, even for empirical studies largely set in the present. However,
  a common occurrence in this and with all such data is that of contra-
  diction i.e. conflicting accounts, which presents an issue as to what is
  to be done.
    The following example from *Modern Ireland 1600–1972* neatly combines
  both. Foster first presents an extract from an official polemical account written

in 1610 which demonstrates the thinking of the day in some quarters, following this with an extract from a confession by a leader of an opposition force who was later taken to the Tower of London where he died.

> Afterwards, Protestant attitudes set hard, with Catholicism blamed as the primary motive for the rebellion. Thus Barnaby Rich in 1610:

> It is popery that hath drawn the people from that confidence and trust that they should have in God ... It is popery that hath alienated the hearts of that people from that faith ... It is popery that hath set afoot so many rebellions in Ireland, that hath cost the lives of multitudes, that hath ruined that whole realm and made it subject to the oppression of thieves, robbers, spoilers, murderers, rebels and traitors.

> Others, however, were less certain. The reasons for rebellion given by James, Earl of Desmond, to Carew in 1601 were recorded thus:

> ... he allegeth that the causes that moved the dislike of the Munster men [the rebellion force] against the English government were religion, undertakes encroaching upon gentlemen's lands, the fear of English juries, which passed upon the trial of Irishmen's lives, the receipt of slight evidence upon such arraignment, the general fear conceived of the safety of their lives by the examples of the execution of Redmond Fitzgerald and Connor McCraghe, and the great charge which was yearly exacted...called the composition rent.

> But the order of priority may be Carew's rather than Desmond's; other reasons given under interrogation by Oliver Hussey emphasize taxation and do not mention religion at all... (Foster, 1989: 41)

Using Software for Qualitative Data Coding

Good coding can be done by PC packages which find and link commonly occurring words and phrases or the codes themselves. Specialised packages for qualitative data analysis have advantages over ordinary word processing packages, although the latter are increasing in sophistication. Useful features to look for include:

- Voice recognition and the possibility of rapid or at least less painful transcription

- Finding and matching mis-spelt or mis-pronounced words and incorrectly phrased lines, which better reflects the reality of the spoken word

- Finding substitute words includes allowing for the researcher to search and accommodate dialects and slang

- The ability to stage sophisticated searches using for example Boolean searches, which allow the identification of specific combinations and occurrences to be picked up while excluding others

- The ability to code specific pieces of data, and retrieve and manage the codes not the sections

Commonly available qualitative software packages in use include packages such as Invivio's.

Negative Evidence

In any event, don't forget to study the omissions in data. Omissions arise for different reasons, yet are all valuable to the researcher in their task of making sense of the data. Box 11.1 summarises the reasons for omission given by Lewis and Lewis (1980) who termed it negative evidence.

Box 11.1   Negative Evidence: Noticing What Isn't There

- Missing incidents, events, non-occurrences
  Sometimes something is missing because it did not occur and does not become an issue which is spoken of. The reasons for its non-occurrence may give the most valuable clues as to the power relations, social situation or perception of matters by actors at that point, not least of what is held to be important

- Incidents of which the reporter is unaware
  These are matters of which the actor reporting to the researcher may be unaware. This again might be revealing both of how events are organised in or out of an agenda as well as the power location of the actor in the social network. This may present an ethical dilemma to the researcher who finds that she knows something which the researched does not

- Incidents and actors which are hidden
  This might be for reasons of shame, crime, fear, or other defensive reasons as well as protective reasons, for example to secure the rights of children

- Everyday items are not noticed or assumed to be unimportant
  This might be by the researcher or the reporter, for example, the visit by the postman to the house of an abducted child might not have been noticed by neighbours or recorded by police

---

- Researcher's reluctance to notice contrary evidence
  The researcher consciously or subconsciously looks for evidence which supports their hypothesis, assumptions, or worldviews, and leaves that which contradicts those outside of the frame.

Based on Lewis and Lewis (1980)

Qualitative Research and Numbers: Data Analysis Issues

Finally, a further predictable issue which can arise for new qualitative researchers is that relating to the use of numbers and their representation and uses. For qualitative researchers, numbers are an important source of data, both in their own right when as context setting, for example, allowing the researcher to locate their research within wider trends, but also in their analysis of the use made by numbers collected and organised by others. Those who choose qualitative methods in the belief that they need never look at numbers again, are mistaken, and risk overlooking important sources of data.

1) Documents

Documents which contain numbers and statistical analysis are rich sources of information indicating dominant ideologies, including assumptions made of norms and values, as well as real power relations, which can be seen for example from the level of the commitment of resources and the agenda set. For example, official government statistics, a company's annual report including accounts, and the shopping habits of a household show:

- Decision making over the nature of the data to be collected

- The representation of data and the use to which it is put

- The assumptions about audience reception, which may be grounded in research

- The cultural and aesthetic production values of wider society as well as the producing organisation

2) The use of numbers by the researched

The use of numbers by the researched, for example, during a conversational interview, or in drawing a map or diagram, can also be very revealing, especially if not taken at face value. An example might involve asking a child to draw a map of their recent journeys as part of the data collection. How far away is 'far away'?

As useful are numbers which subjects willingly volunteer. Rather than ignoring numbers and their use, consider coding the use of numbers as an important source of data in its own right. What kinds of objects or which subjects attract quantification and the reasons which lie behind this indicate a rich source of inquiry for qualitative researchers.

3) Using numbers in qualitative research

Finally, in spite of your best efforts to escape numbers, you may find when coding that your code of best fit is in some cases, at least initially, numerical. This may not necessarily tell you why a certain object or subject appears with the frequency that it does or what it means to the user, but a first step might be to accurately record the rates of occurrence or to assign values to them.

Summary

- When you have got enough of the right kind of data – stop collecting it!

- An adequate data set is one which allows the researcher to reach a reasoned judgement as to its valid meaning

- Coding quantitative data involves translating it into a brief form, sortable and usable

- There is a 5-step process for coding quantitative data:

  1) Consider coding early on, at the research design stage
  2) Decide on rules for assigning value/code to each piece of data
  3) Make up a coding book in which it is easy to find and follow the coding rules
  4) Do the coding
  5) Check for accuracy of coding and clean the data. Decide on the margin of error you need to leave

- Use statistical techniques to make sense of your data:

  o Univariate and multivariate statistics
  o Frequency distribution and weightings
  o Averages: mean, median, and the mode
  o Range
  o Normal and skewed distribution and calculating the standard deviation; compare standard deviations using Z-scores

- There is a 3-step process to coding qualitative data:

  1) Open coding: make an initial run through data assigning codes
  2) Axial coding: sort open coded segments in relationships
  3) Selective coding: go back through the dataset looking for the best pieces of data

  Use notes and memos to assist your interpretations

- Examples of working with qualitative data include:

  o Skeggs: disidentifications of class
  o Leonard: sectarian identity stories
  o Murdock et al: marketing blurb
  o Foster: the use of contradictory and historical sources

- Commonly available qualitative software packages in use include Invivio's

- Omissions: notice what's missing. Always look for negative evidence

- The research participants will use numerical concepts including actual numbers in their thinking, talk, drawing, and behaviour

- Even qualitative researchers need numbers. Numbers are themselves an interesting kind of data, they show:

  o Decision-making over the nature of the data to be collected
  o The representation of data and the use to which it is put
  o The assumptions about audience reception, which may be grounded in research
  o The cultural and aesthetic production values of wider society as well as the producing organisation

Further Reading

Bryman, A. and Cramer, D. (2000) *Quantitative Data Analysis with SPSS for Windows – A Guide for Social Scientists*. London: Routledge.
Hinton, P. (2004) (2nd edn.) *Statistics Explained: A Guide for Social Science Students*. London: Routledge.
Parker, T. (1996) *Studs Terkel: A Life in Words*. New York: Henry Holt & Co.
Robson, C. (2002) (2nd edn.) *Real World Research*. Oxford: Blackwell.
Silverman, D. (2000) *Doing Qualitative Research: A Practical Handbook*. London: Sage.
Tabachnick, B.G. and Fidell, L.S. (2001) *Using Multivariate Statistics*. Boston, MA: Allyn & Bacon.
Tacq, J. (1998) *Multivariate Analysis Techniques in Social Science Research: From Problem to Analysis*. London: Sage.
Vogt, W.P. (1999) *Dictionary of Statistics and Methodology: A Nontechnical Guide for the Social Sciences*. London: Sage.

Chapter 12
Drawing Conclusions and Writing Up

Overview

Structuring your work: find out what structure you need to follow and refresh your memory as to regulations

Linking the components of a dissertation

Tips on opening and closing chapters

- o   Use of quotations
- o   Connecting your work to themes
- o   Using and refining concepts

What should a conclusion contain?

Tackling the conclusion: a 3-step thought-process

- o   Step 1 Where the project has come from including the original formulation of the research problem
- o   Step 2 The findings and their limits
- o   Step 3 Future lines of inquiry

Fleshing out the conclusion: the 'Why, what, how, where, when?' questions

Some common challenges

Good drafting

Use of anti-discriminatory language when drafting

Good writing: good reading

What to do if you have too many words – or too few words

Grammar: do you know what you are looking for?

Academic writing: plagiarism

Stopping: drawing things to their end

In this chapter, we finally turn to writing up. A core task is to work towards drawing conclusions which are based on the preceding dissertation. In this chapter we look at what goes where in a dissertation; what a good conclusion looks like; and how to produce a dissertation draft which is interconnected, moves at a pace, and covers all the bases. Specific issues dealt with include managing the process of writing up; good grammar and using English for academic purposes; avoiding plagiarism; and finally, 'knowing when to stop'.

Approaching the Write-up

The write-up is generally the final leg of doing a dissertation. In practice, you will have either already drafted sections of it or will have drafted other documents which you can draw on. Whichever is the case, you need to aim to produce a coherent dissertation which logically leads to reasonable conclusions. This is in contrast to a dissertation which consists of bits and pieces glued together. In writing and shaping your dissertation, try to aim to:

• Show how your research design flows from your research question

• Show how the data you collected leads you to make the interpretations which you make and connect these up to the conclusions. Don't expect the reader to do the joining-up for you

• Make clear how the epistemological and philosophical posistions which you adopted or developed affected your decision-making throughout the process, for example, in your choice and execution of research methods

• Construct a narrative: your dissertation should, to some extent, tell a story. You should show the relevance of each part, and try to demonstrate how completing each stage of the research led you naturally to the next. Include reflections if appropriate, for example, what you learned from one part of the process which informed your approaches and the ideas you developed later on. In other words, tell the story of your discovery, realisation, or developing understanding

• Provide signposts for the reader to follow, so that they can easily navigate the main threads of the disseration, i.e. so they can follow the plot

Structuring the Dissertation

Dissertations generally follow a generic structure. Set up a master folder with a dedicated file for each chapter and section, even though some files will be large and some small. This will save you a great deal of time and trouble the night before the deadline. Do remember that marks can be deducted for getting the basic structure incorrect, for example, laying out the title page incorrectly. Check your department or university's regulations regarding the composition of the dissertation. In Task 12.1 below, complete the table making an assessment of what you need to do in order to finish preparing each chapter or section. Update it from time to time.

Task 12.1

Sections of the Dissertation: Progress Sheet

Guide to likely chapter or sections	How much of this section have you completed? What else do you need to do to?
Title page	
Abstract	
Acknowledgements	
Table of contents	
Tables and figures, and/or perhaps illustrations: numbering them; preparing a listing; check the source of each	
Introduction – including the reasons why the reader should read it	
Literature review, including secondary data sources, recent journal articles, classic texts	
Methodology, including collection, coding, consent, ethics, limitation	
Data findings, discussion	
Conclusion	
Appendix/ces	
Bibliography	

What Goes Where

1) Abstract

A reader should be able to find out from the abstract the what, where, how, why and who of the research:

- What the research set out to achieve – the aims and the main conclusions
- Where it was carried out – the site, location, space
- How it was carried out – the methodology
- Why it was carried out – its importance
- Who was researched, and who did the research

Abstracts typically:

- Are short (250 words or less)
- Are double line-spaced
- Contain a brief statement of the aims of the research
- Summarise the main findings
- Clearly present the conclusions

Abstracts are used by other researchers to establish the relevance of the research to their own work. Judgements about whether or not to obtain and read the full research write-up will be made on the basis of the abstract. Nowadays, abstracts are readily obtainable by accessing electronic, easy to search databases available online. Thus, your fellow researchers and those working in the field may never see the final, bound work, and won't base their choices on their browsing of it. Set aside a little bit of time to get the abstract right; at least allow enough time to sleep on it before submitting it.

2) Acknowledgements

Less common in undergraduate dissertations but sometimes used, this section will acknowledge the help and support of those around you. Those acknowledged may range from family and friends to professionals such as a helpful librarian, along with gatekeeper organisations and your research participants. Alternatively, you may wish to keep things very simple and rather than naming everyone, insert a general word of thanks.

3) Table of contents

The table of contents lists all of the items in the dissertation, including any appendices and the bibliography. It is important that you master your word processing package, setting appropriate heading levels for each and every heading in your dissertation, including the chapter headings. The electronic Table of Contents (ToC) is automatically generated using those heading levels, inserting headings and their page numbers into the correct format. This is very advantageous over the manual method of constructing a table of contents by leafing through the pages of text and making up your own. If you work manually, every time you make a change to any text or heading in the main body of the work, you will need to manually adjust your table of contents, since the page numbers will change. When you are working on the main project, this will lead you to expending much energy trying to find the right section or page to make amendments and keep your documents in order. However, leaving it to the end when you are preparing for final submission will lead you to a frustrating waste of valuable minutes and hours of your time which, at that stage, you may well feel that you don't have.

4) Tables and figures or illustrations
The list of figures should enable the reader to quickly locate any of the graphs, charts, tables, diagrams, and illustrations in the dissertation. Each of these needs to be clearly titled and numbered in the order in which they appear.
Each kind of figure should have its *own* series of numbers. For example:

> Figure 1.1 Demographic structure of the United Kingdom (2006).
> Table 1.1 Labour market activity rates in the United Kingdom (2006).
> Illustration 1.1 Photograph of *Jean Pierre* at Oxford.

Ensure that all such figures are correctly numbered through the work as a whole, and that any new devices, for example a box, chart, graph, etc., all start with number 1.1 irrespective of where they appear in the dissertation. The numbering system is independent of other numbering systems, such as chapters, sections, page numbering and so on.

5) Introduction
The basis of a good introduction is an expanded version of the abstract, in that it contains all of the same elements, such as the what, where, how, why and who of the research:

- What the research set out to achieve – the aims and the main conclusions
- Where it was carried out – the site, location, space
- How it was carried out – the methodology
- Why it was carried out – its importance
- Who was researched, and who did the research
- The contexts of the research

The introduction will also provide the context of the research, giving some background to the research problem and the researcher's reasons for undertaking the research. This should include a brief discussion of the importance of the research, including whom or what it is important to, and why it is a timely study. Usually, these points are made towards the start of the introduction.

6) Literature review

The literature review should show how your research can be located in a wider field of inquiry. Try wherever possible to focus upon making connections between your own work and that of others, by showing how you can link your work to others. You need to develop a narrative in the literature review, showing both the foundation and contexts of your project as well as how you are taking the line of inquiry forwards.

Remember: *Avoid a list-like, descriptive approach to the literature review, and develop a more analytical mode of writing. Be selective, and pick studies or works which develop your argument, rather than including everything. For more information about the literature review, please see Chapter 6.*

7) Methodology

The methodology chapter needs to be closely connected to the research question. You need to show how the research design specifically addresses the research question. You also need to reflect upon how other researchers have carried out research in this area, and what you have learned from this.

The methodology chapter sets out:

- The reasons for your choices of methods

- Your stance in the research: what kind of researcher are you?

- The nuts and bolts of your research: what you actually did, how, when, where and why

- The limitations of the methodology including the margin of error

For further information about the methodology, please see Chapters 4 and 8.

8) Data/findings/discussion

This chapter often causes some of the greatest problems, due to the exciting but daunting issue of being faced with a desk or PC full of data. Work through your data systematically, and be both reasoned and creative with the categories of meanings that you produce in the results of using both quantitative and qualitative methodologies. You need to bring forward issues arising from the methodology, for example, your place in the research process and how this might have shaped interaction or the interpretations which you make on the one hand, and any consequences arising from the coding and the decision-making tree you followed in quantitative studies. For further information about what to do with all the data, please see Chapter 10.

Remember: *the tension between quantitative and qualitative methodology should not present a barrier to you. Go with the flow, and recognise the value and appropriate use of each for different tasks.*

9) Conclusions

Conclusions should flow logically from the text which has been presented so far. Avoid introducing new ideas, new data, or a new direction. Ideally, the conclusion should present conclusions which could be predicted by the reader as they turn to read it. There should be no nasty surprises and wild claims! You can use the conclusion to bring forward some of the other themes of the project alongside the actual methods, data and findings, for example drawing out a personal reflection on what you have learned and whether the project has been what you thought it would be. For more information about conclusions, please see Chapter 11.

Remember: The conclusion should definitely attempt to draw some conclusions about something.

10) Appendix/ces

Each appendix should have its own number and title. Don't cram lots of data into the same appendix, but split data up and make a few different appendices if need be. Make sure that you have inserted the source of the data or figure used in *every* appendix.

Tips on Opening and Closing Chapters

Each chapter should have a clearly identifiable introduction and conclusion. These frame the main body of the chapter, linking the chapter to the dissertation as a whole. From these, the reader should be able to grasp where they have come from, where they are going to, and how far they have got.

Specifically:

- The chapter introduction provides a guide to the contents and layout of the chapter

- The chapter conclusion provides a summary of the journey which we have travelled in that chapter *and* draws a logical conclusion: what does it all add up to?

- Both the introduction and conclusion connect the chapter to the central argument or theme of the dissertation and move the reader along through the various stages of the project

- It can be very useful to remind the reader of your working definitions, terms and the scope of your work

Use of Quotations

The use of quotations at the start of the Introduction or particular chapters can be very powerful. Here, you do not necessarily need to use academic quotations, but can look for something inspirational which speaks of the purpose of your work or the spirit in which you offer it. You could consider using extracts from key documents such as laws or regulations as well as different kinds of texts from speeches to pop songs and other media.

Here is an example:

Xamul aay na, laajtewul a ko raw

Not to know is bad. Not to wish to know is worse.

African Proverb

Commission for Africa (21: 2005), quoted at the start of the section entitled 'The Argument'

Connecting Your Work to the Working Theme and Concept

Reminding your reader of your themes and definition is a way of maintaining the central focus of your work throughout the chapters. Do return to the research problem – don't let it drift away on the wind. Returning to it is a good device to use, for example at the start of chapters, as well as through them, enabling you to connect each chapter back to the research question. For example, draw out the significance of a particularly strong piece of data by specifying how this related to the research question. Remind the readers what the aims and objectives were, for example in your discussion of your choice of methods. Don't shy away from cross-referring to your work in the rest of the dissertation; this is a desirable thing to do.

In the following example drawn from *Education in a Post-welfare Society*, Tomlinson revisits her definition in order to pull forwards the wider argument of the book (that the form that education takes and the role it plays in today's society can be distinguished from that of the postwar era in particular ways). This allows the author to launch into the main theme of her chapter, the connections between education and the economy:

> In the introduction to this book a post-welfare society was defined as one where a work ethic and competition in education and the labour market dominate. It is also a society in which there is a restructuring or removal of welfare benefits on the grounds that excessive welfare provision leads to economic inefficiency. Individuals in post-welfare market societies are instructed to 'learn to compete' (DfEE 1996a) in education and the job market, both for their own economic futures and also to improve the competitiveness of the national economy. (2005: 200)

The introduction to the chapter continues by opening up one of the key debates about such connections, the position of the poor in an increasingly affluent society on the one hand, and whether the 'knowledge poor' are a new class of poor produced in part by the education system's expansion and its increased links with the economy. The chapter has been well framed, and flows logically into a complex debate.

The following extracts from Chapter 3, 'Career Paths: Patterns of Continuity and Change', in, *University Leadership: The Role of the Chief Executive* (Bargh et al. 2000) provide a second example of a chapter introduction.

- Firstly, the authors connect the chapter to the rest of the study, here signposting a link to something which comes up later in the book:

  > ... Over the past few decades, then, both expectations of the role and the processes of selection of vice-chancellors have changed substantially. We explore and assess the actual practice of leadership in the light of the shift towards the chief executive model of leadership in subsequent chapters. (2000: 39)

- Secondly, the reader is introduced to the *specific* problem that this *particular* chapter addresses:

  > In this chapter, however, we are more concerned with changing patterns in the characteristics of the individuals who actually occupy the top posts in university leadership. We focus specifically on vice-chancellors' career paths and ask a series of questions about the attributes of those who become the vice-chancellors. (ibid.)

- Thirdly, the reader is introduced to the layout and specific content of the chapter, clearly telling the reader what is in store for them:

  > To answer these questions we explore extensive data on the educational, career and other related attributes of vice-chancellors appointed to university leadership since the 1960s. Briefly, these comprise 341 separate 'cases' arranged in two separate but linked databases... (2000: 40)

Using Concepts and Refining Their Scope

It is very important that you define the major concepts that you are going to use in your introduction. This is not merely a lexicon or etymological exercise, but defines the scope of your work and locates it within a wider field of study. It also reminds the reader of the approach which you are taking (as opposed to the approach which they might have taken if left to their own devices).

In the following example, the authors need to return to their discussion of the definition of the term 'post-colonial'. They begin by repeating their definition made earlier in the book, on page 2. But immediately following this, the authors outline the alternative meanings of the term – and in this case alternative ways to view history and the present:

Most contentious of all has been the term 'post-colonial' itself. *The Empire Writes Back* uses the term 'post-colonial' to refer to 'all cultures affected by the imperial process from the moment of colonization to the present day' (Ashcroft, Griffiths and Tiffin, 1989: 2). Such a broad-reaching definition has been opposed by those who believe it necessary to limit the term either by selecting only certain periods as genuinely post-colonial (most notably the period after independence), or by suggesting that some groups of peoples affected by the colonizing process are not post-colonial (notably settlers), or finally, by suggesting that some societies are not yet post-colonial (meaning free of the attitudes of colonization). The case of indigenous people in settler societies is an example of this latter argument. (Ashcroft et al., 1989: 194)

The extract demonstrates both how to provide a working definition of a concept, as well as demonstrate your awareness that the term is contested and can be used in different ways, for example as in this case, to refer to clearly delineated periods of history and social experience. In this instance, the author can show their awareness of the political consequences of the use of language, since the variety of uses indicates that it is not merely the concept as a concept which is contested, but the very viewing of history itself. The choice of definition of the term 'post-colonial' then is not made merely on the basis of scientific accuracy or the authors' preferences, but may hint at a much wider social or even political sensibility through which the authors as writers, thinkers, and researchers, locate a field of argument and debate, and take up a stance within it.

Concluding Each Chapter

The conclusion to each chapter is equally important. Firstly, provide a summary of the chapter, as in the following example:

Deleuze and Guattari's (1987) disdain for a culture which is locked into individualistic, possessive concerns is clear, not least in their comments on pets: 'individuated animals, family pets, sentimental, Oedipal animals each with its own petty history, 'my' cat, 'my' dog...' (1987: 240)

Secondly, make sure that you do definitely draw a conclusion, and remind the reader of what you set out to do:

What I have tried to show in this chapter is that the advent of software-driven entities modelled on biological assumptions is a significant event which has the potential to decisively change everyday life by adding in a new range of cohabitees. In particular, it offers a new set of ethical dilemmas which have clearly not been solved in the case of companion animals. (Gaita, 2003)

In this third example, Furlong and Cartmel, in their book *Young People and Social Change* draw conclusions to the chapter 'Crime and Insecurity', demonstrating the importance of doing so *carefully*, providing a nuanced understanding of what claims can be made about crime and society and which are less certain:

> Although many young people engage in criminal activities and while significant numbers will be the victims of crime, it would be wrong to suggest that the patterns of criminality which we have described in this chapter represent a breakdown in the social fabric of society. Young people have always indulged in risky behaviour and in activities which are illegal. The youth of the previous generation engaged in similar types of activities and also found themselves to be the focus of police attention (Pearson, 1983). There is, however, some evidence that the numbers of crimes committed by young people are rising and that criminal careers are becoming longer. However, the increased teenage crime rate is a reflection of an overall rise in crime and there is no evidence to suggest that the trend in youth crime is anomalous. (1997: 93–4)

Fourthly, connect the conclusion to the rest of the text, the main themes, and the research question. Help the reader to keep track of where they are. In this example, Gordon helps us with this by drawing links both to the preceding and subsequent text:

> As noted in Chapter 2, one element in the New Conventional Wisdom (NCW) with substantial support from the academic literature is the proposition that strong local social networks and 'institutional thickness' have become increasingly important for competitiveness. A particular reason is the need for greater collaboration between firms, and the level of trust required for these in a context of high risk and rapid change. A particular version of this argument is developed in relation to innovation and knowledge-intensive activities in Chapter 6. (Gordon, 2005: 91)

Finally, Sugarman rounds off this conclusion to a chapter with a well-chosen quotation, which is another technique you can use:

> As a conceptual tool, narratives provide a vehicle for understanding the life course in the same way as, for example, the notion of stages. Indeed, with the demise during recent decades of set paths through the educational, employment, and personal tasks of adulthood, the life stage model of the life course – and of adulthood in particular – has appeared less tenable...We weave what we select into a narrative and link what is happening now with what has passed, and what might happen in the future: 'If we do not exactly write the plots of our lives, nevertheless it is we alone who create our own stories. Agency lies not in governing what shall happen to us, but in creating

what we make of what happens. We ourselves construct the meaning of our story' (Salmon, 1985: 138–9). Cited by Sugarman (2001: 186)

What Should the Final Conclusions Chapter Contain?

The final conclusions chapter to the dissertation requires the researcher to carefully develop a set of conclusions which are clearly reasoned and based upon the experience and findings of the research project to date. Build up the conclusions chapter by chapter, and build all of them into a wall in the final chapter. This is not the same task as reproducing the findings without connecting them, or of limiting oneself to a summary of the literature review and a few key ideas about the data. Set aside time to work out what the conclusions will contain before commencing writing, and have a few attempts at it. Use Figure 12.1 as a handy guide to the major components of the dissertation.

Remember: The conclusion should be structured in a logical and coherent manner, which leads the reader through the stages of the research project. Thus, not unlike an essay, the structure will follow the project in rough chronological order, beginning with setting out the research problem and reminding readers of its timeliness, importance, and relevance. Even at this late stage, you should once again be sure to make connections between you own work and the wider field of study and to recognise with some accuracy both the importance of your work and its limits.

Task 12.2

Summarising and Describing Versus Concluding and Persuading

How would you describe the differences between the two categories of:

- Summarising and describing

  and

- Concluding and persuading

How do the two categories relate to one another?

Return to the examples of students' dissertations that you have looked at from previous years. Read a few of the conclusions chapters. How successfully do the conclusions conclude?

Step 1

- Provide a summary of the research project, presented in chronological order: always remind the reader of the journey taken so far – but do not spend a lot of space on this
- The original formulation of the research problem should be discussed: strengths and weaknesses? Upon reflection, how could the research problem have been differently formulated and what merits might there have been, if any, in taking that action?
- Consider the effectiveness of the research design. The conclusion should remind us again of the research design and the reasons which lay behind the choices made, which should be both in terms of the actual qualities of specific methods and their connection to your research question, aims and objectives
- Negative choices, i.e., decisions not to take a particular course of action, should be discussed, along with methodological difficulties and actual limitations. These might relate to the appropriateness of the methods used as well as their relative effectiveness in generating an appropriate quantity of the right kinds of data

Step 2

- What are the major findings? A good conclusion will clearly indicate what it is that the dissertation project has actually achieved. Here, you need to synthesise all of your findings, and clearly answer the question 'What does it all add up to?'
- The limits of the study should be clear, and how these have affected the findings should be drawn out
- How does this piece of research add to the pre-existing field of knowledge? The conclusion needs to clearly set out what has been found which you claim is new and specific to your project. Secondly, relate your findings to what had previously been found, for example, does your research confirm or refute aspects of this? Does it provide additional depth to an area? Does it throw up an inconsistency with findings by other researchers?

Step 3

- What future research problems are suggested by this research? These few lines which typically appear at the very end of the conclusion suggest further lines of inquiry

Figure 12.1   **Tackling the Conclusion: A Three-Step Thought-process**

1) Take time to develop and check your conclusions

Having spent time on formulating the research problem and design, further time on the literature review and writing, even more time on data collection and then yet more time on data analysis and developing findings, many students arrive at the conclusion a few days (or even hours) before the dissertation deadline, calm in the erroneous belief that writing it will be much the same as writing the introduction. In fact, a conclusion can be quite difficult to write, and you should try to leave enough time to develop this important part of the project.

2) Negative choices and what went wrong

A common pitfall is to labour under the belief that you should reveal no weaknesses in the dissertation project, either in thought or deed, believing that this will undermine their project findings and will affect the assessment of your personal research skills etc. In fact, the opposite is the case. Reflecting upon choices and working through the issues in what went wrong and what has been learnt, strengthens a piece of work rather than weakens it. If you can see what you would do differently if you were to repeat the exercise, do mention it.

3) The tendency to avoid concluding

The third pitfall found in dissertation conclusions is where the student fails to reach any real conclusions. While some marks can be given for a successful summary of the dissertation's major components, good marks can't be achieved if there is a lack of evidence of a successfully completed dissertation. The evidence which examiners seek are conclusions drawn – and that the conclusions do grow out from everything which has gone before.

Figure 12.2   Drawing the Final Conclusions: Pitfalls and Fixes

Critical Thinking; Fallacies and Weak Conclusions

Fallacies are erroneous reasoning which lead to incorrect conclusions; they may however seem plausible and on first appearances might be easy. Their deceptive nature is a clue about a tell-tale characteristic of fallacies: they are there to be decoded and resisted, but only if the reader is alert, prepared to take apart an argument, and ask difficult questions about the evidence base. See Table 12.1 for a list of examples of fallacies in arguments.

Table 12.1   Examples of Fallacies in Arguments

Fallacy	Definition
Emotional language	Using heavily loaded language
Selected instances	Only some cases are selected, and these 'prove' the case. If a different set were selected, the evidence would stack up the other way
Similarity	Passing off cases or instances as the same or similar enough, when there are grounds for indicating their extensive differences
Appealing to authoritative sources	Citing authoritative sources in order to legitimate your argument
Claims against the counter position	Discrediting those who put forward other arguments; smears; undermining claims
Extremities	Avoiding the centre ground: using the polar extremes to prove against, or otherwise discredit

Source: Hart (2000: 98) (abridged)

The Importance of Being Robust

Having said all of the above, we now turn to the most important point of all: the importance of being robust.

By being robust is meant:

• Being clear and confident about your work

• Taking pride in your work

• Knowing the value of your work, warts and all

Good Drafting

A good draft is one which, as well as fulfilling the intellectual demands of a research write-up, is well presented, with clean, error-free text. A good draft is characterised by the sense that the author:

• Is in control of the words, not the other way around!

• Has got something to say and knows how to say it

• Has spent time proofreading, structuring and laying out

You need to set aside time to achieve this. Be patient, work systematically, and expect to go back over what you have written several times.

- For readability, refresh your memory with Appendix 2
- Remember that proofreaders may routinely read a manuscript of a book anything between 6–10 times before it is sent to print
- When editing, work with a hard copy of your work as well as on screen
- Treat checking your referencing and bibliography construction as a discrete task which needs a special, dedicated, read-through
- Delete surplus words in sentences: use one word to do the job of two or three
- Once you have identified a pattern (for example, you have spelt a word wrong) use search and replace
- Never rely on the spell checker or grammar checker or automatic search and replace – look at each instance before making corrections
- Make one pass through the document ignoring the meaning of the sentences: concentrate on spelling, grammatical issues such as noun-verb-adjective, surplus words, use of punctuation, spacing, heading levels etc.
- Don't guess the right answer – have a dictionary, thesaurus and a good grammar guide to hand
- Fix the key terms which you will be using and stick to them, i.e. use the same word or phrase to refer to the same thing throughout your text. Common choices include choosing just one term from the following:

    o   The researched; the subject; the participant; the interviewee
    o   The research project; the dissertation; the final year research
    o   The patient, the client, the user
    o   The voter, the citizen, the supporter
    o   With acronyms, once you start using, one carry on using it throughout the remainder of the text

- Give the script (or a part of it) to someone else to read. Accept their feedback with good grace – but carefully consider each of their suggested corrections before you make amendments (are they right?)
- Read your work aloud: you will soon find sentences which are too long; jargon which does not make sense; the wrong kind of punctuation in the wrong place

Figure 12.3   **Good Editing**

Use of Language When Drafting

It is important to reflect upon the use of language which you use during writing up with regard to sexist, racist or other offensive uses. There are some excellent sources of help available to assist you with this matter as well as with writing for academic purposes more generally. See Box 12.1.

The British Sociological Association website has guidelines for language use on the themes of:

- Sex and gender

- Ethnicity and race

- Non-disablist

Look under the Equality pages at www.britsoc.co.uk/equality

Box 12.1   Sources for Writing: Academic and Otherwise

The Academic Writing in English (AWE) site from the Virtual University of Finland, which looks at cohesion, grammar, punctuation, and style
http://kiepc10.cc.tut.fi/~english/kirjoittamo/awe

The BBC Get Writing website, which has lots of ideas, mini-courses with simple exercises, tips etc. to improve your writing and unlock your creativity
www.bbc.co.uk/getwriting

Bogazici University's online writing lab has exercises, tips and links
www.buowl.boun.edu.tr/

The Royal Literary Fund website, under the 'Fellows' section, has a sub-section on writing which contains some interesting materials on writing essays and dissertations
www.rlf.org.uk/fellowshipscheme/writing

See Using English for Academic Purposes UEfAP (www.uefap.com/writing/writfram.htm). This is an excellent website designed to support students in writing for academic purposes, with an excellent section on plagiarism.

What to Do if You Have Too Many Words – or Too Few Words

A common battle is when there are too many or too few words. (See Table 12.2 for some tips.) You also need to make sure that your chapters are approximately the same length each.

Grammar: Do You Know What You Are Looking For?

Subjects, verbs, adjectives, the active and passive, singular and plurals, compounds and conjunctives... if such concepts feel a little rusty or alien, swallow your pride and purchase the grammar book to which

Table 12.2   Too Many Words: Too Few Words

Too Many Words	Too Few Words
Aim to make most of your paragraphs of a roughly even length – and thus reduce all the ones which are much longer.	Make sure that you have introduced and then discussed each diagram, chart, table and graph.
Reduce long sentences by using punctuation effectively, especially full stops, colons and semi-colons.	Similarly, make sure that you have included quotes – and then discussed them.
Keep quotations brief and to the point. Use three dots (like this: …) to indicate small pieces of text which have been deleted.	Make sure that you have discussed all of the different kinds of literature, for example, both methods literature and literature of the substantive area of inquiry.
Represent complicated data and relationships in diagrams, charts, tables and graphs.	Identify sections which are overly descriptive. Reduce the description and add some analysis as a starting point.
Use sub-sections, reduce the length of overly long sections, consider whether you can combine any sections.	Make sure that each chapter has got its own introduction and conclusion.

so very many writers, journalists, diarists and researchers have succumbed – *The Elements of Style* by William J. Strunk. It may have been first published in 1918, but the rules haven't changed that much! Strunk's book can be purchased or found online at Bartleby (www.bartleby.com).

There are other books which are equally useful, see Further Reading at the end of this chapter for some suggestions.

Task 12.3

Grammar Check: The *Blade Runner* Exercise

Complete the punctuation for the following text. A clue: *Blade Runner* is the name of a science fiction film made from the novel by Philip K. Dick, *Do Androids Dream of Electric Sheep*? The correct text can be found on page 222 at the end of this chapter.

the city in Blade Runner with its rain soaked los angeles streets faux-forties fashions private eye plot and world weary narration derives plenty from noir this is a dark city of mean streets moral ambiguities and an air of irresolution Blade Runners Los Angeles exemplifies the failure of the rational city envisioned by urban planners and science fiction creators and it also recalls by implication the air of masculine crisis that undergirded film noir – witness Dekard's struggle to retain or regain his humanity if the metropolis in noir was a dystopian purgatory then in Blade Runner with its flame belching towers it has become an almost literal inferno

Task 12.4

Academic Writing Check

- Firstly, correct the grammar and referencing in the following example
- Secondly, correct the bibliographical details using Harvard style

Collaboration itself is a complex phenomenon hennermann et al. 1995 and different models have been explored hudson 1999 different philosophies of team working can present difficulties for multi-professional teamwork freeman et al. 2000 indicators for positive inter–professional team working appear to be the personal qualities and commitment of staff communicaton within the team and the opportunity to develop creative working methods within the team molyneux 2001 issues of 'personhood' cannot be ignored as professional and disciplinary differences are manifested in terms of who professional persons consider themselves to be in relation to what is expected of them dombeck 1997.

Malin, Wilmot & Manthorpe (2002: 101)

- Thirdly, here are some references to assist you – which also need to be corrected:

(1995) E. Hennermann et al. *Collaboration: a concept analysis*, Journal of Advanced Nursing, 21; pages 103-9.

Hudson, B. 1999, *Primary Health Care and social care: working across professional boundaries, Managing Community Care* 7, (1) 15-22 Pt.1: The changing context of inter-professional relationships.

M. Freeman, C. Miller, & N. Ross, (2000) The impact of individual philosophies of teamwork on multi-professional practice and the implications for education, 14 number 3: (237-47) *Journal of Interpersonal Care,* London: Sage.

Molyneux (2001) *Journal of Interprofessional Care* Interprofessional team working: what makes teams work well? Volume 15 29-35 (1):

Dombeck, M. (1997) Professional personhood: training, territoriality and tolerance, *Journal of Interpersonal Care* 11, 1, pps 9-21-14.

- See page 223 for the revised version

Academic Writing: Plagiarism

Plagiarism is a deliberate attempt to use other people's words and ideas as though they were your own, i.e. without referencing and due acknowledgement (see Figure 12.4). The lack of recognition implied and the attempt to steal the reputation and ideas of others make this an intellectual breach, tantamount to a breach of copyright or theft. For these reasons, academic integrity is always taken very seriously, and plagiarised work, whether intentional or unintentional, opens its author to criticisms of various kinds including stealing, breaking a contract, and incompetence.

As you can see, plagiarism as a category can be used to describe what you might rather see as poor study skills and unintentional error as well as act of theft such as using work taken from the internet. The price of plagiarism is very high – you can be kicked out of university and may find that explaining this to future organisations puts you in a difficult position. It can affect an individual's ability to go forwards in some occupations such as law and medicine. You must exercise great care over your references: be scrupulous. If in doubt, put the reference in and ask your tutor.

- Claiming the work of others' as your own, for example, by failing to clearly indicate by referencing that it is not your own
- Where text is cut, pasted, copied, and edited so that a cunning mixture of texts laced together give the appearance of a consecutive run of text of the author's own (at least, to the student)
- Work which is so poorly punctuated and referenced that it is impossible to tell where the author's work starts and their mysterious contributor's begins
- Purchased and free texts, for example, from internet sites or freelance students or ex-tutors, which are presented for assessment
- Paraphrasing but not acknowledging the base source of the claims, ideas, data, findings, or conclusions found in the work

---

Figure 12.4   Definitions of Plagiarism

Why Do People Plagiarise?

Common reasons are to do with lack of confidence and/or poor study skills. Many students resort to plagiarism as a pragmatic solution to an increased workload which they are having trouble coping with. Other students simply get it wrong – this is unfortunate but it is not considered a viable excuse. A small minority of students deliberately plagiarise due to a lack of commitment to their programme of study and themselves as students.

Academic Integrity: Pride in Your Work

By far a better alternative to plagiarism is to have confidence in your work and enjoy your increased self-esteem by achieving recognition for the work that you do. You are a real student on a real programme of study who is really at university. There is no need to resort to plagiarism. It is quite difficult to do and hard to get away with in any case – you would be surprised how poor bought essays from the internet etc. actually are – you would be better off doing the job yourself.

Checking for Plagiarism

Students often underestimate how easy it is to sense that a piece has been plagiarised. There are several ways in which the naked eye can tell:

- There are abrupt changes of style and tone
  This feels like listening to a compilation CD or download. The switches of tone and style between different bands and singers are instantly recognisable to the most unfamiliar audience, let alone anyone who is keen on the music and knows any of the bands well

- Idiosyncratic use of grammar and other conventions
  When people write they develop their own writing conventions, including what are strictly speaking erroneous ones, such as the incorrect use of punctuation, or a particular way of phrasing. Generally, an author will repeat their approach throughout a piece because they are unaware of it. A tell-tale sign of a plagiarised piece is, for example, where the author suddenly and inexplicably displays a mastery of advanced punctuation, but only in the second paragraph of page three, and the fourth paragraph of page nine

- The use of concepts and theories particular to their originator: *leitmotifs*
  For example, an essay which largely explores the relationship between Weber and democracy may suddenly switch to an in-depth, intense, and irrelevant discussion of assemblages and lines of flight (à la Deleuze and Guattari), before un-smoothly switching back to the known world of ideal types and the iron cage

- Use of instantly recognisable ideas and extracts
  Students will often use work in the belief that they have found something obscure – unbeknown to them, the tutor will in fact recognise it.
    Likewise, dissertations from previous years are recalled. Tutors remember their students and their work to a much greater extent than students sometimes realise. The elephantine quality of the collective memory of academic departments should never be underestimated

e-Plagiarism

Nowadays, neither students nor tutors rely on the naked eye. The advent of software and the internet has raised the game. It has become increasingly easy to obtain text – but increasingly difficult to successfully get away with presenting it as your own.

- The sources of purchased and downloadable e-coursework are well-known and can be accessed by the tutors: what the student can buy, so can the tutor

- Using the internet to find sources and cut and paste them can be carried out by the student – and repeated by the tutor a little later

- Using databases for searches can be carried out by students and tutors alike

- Many universities are using software such as Turnitin (see Box 12.2)

**Box 12.2   Turnitin and other Plagiarism
Detection Software**

Turnitin is an internet-based, text detection software programme which will alert users to plagiarised text. This kind of software works at two levels:

1) As a deterrent – you might be asked to submit the Turnitin report with your coursework.
2) Learning and skills development – students submit their text in private, and no-one need know the first results. This is extremely useful since it provides instant, accurate feedback which allows the user to go back through the coursework carefully and make amendments as needed. Doing this allows you to develop a greater, more specific understanding of the level of referencing which is required – and how best to do it.

This is especially useful where students are plagiarising for unintentional reasons, and rather for reasons of poor study skills or carelessness etc.

Remember: Using Turnitin and other packages and self-tuition systems on the web could dramatically improve your referencing and acknowledgements.

Stopping: Drawing Things to Their End

And finally:

> Know when to stop! A dissertation is finite. Marks are not awarded according to the weight in kilograms. Marks are awarded for quality rather than quantity (provided of course that the quantity is reasonable). A dissertation is rather like a non-fiction book – it is never actually finished. There will always be more things you can add to it...There will always be some things that are wrong in it! There will still be some typos or grammatical glitches in it. Spending too long on all the minor details invokes the law of diminishing returns. You may only get a fraction of a mark more for that last two weeks' worth of editorial overhaul. (Race, 2003: 121)

Task 12.5

Stopping: Paraphrase the Concept of 'The Law of Diminishing Returns'

Rewrite the above quotation from Phil Race, in particular highlighting what is meant in this context by the expression 'the law of diminishing returns.'

Box 12.3   Answers to the Exercises

Grammar Check: Spot the Difference

The city in *Blade Runner,* with its rain-slicked Los Angeles streets, *faux*-forties fashions, private-eye plot and world-weary narration, derives plenty from noir. This is a *dark city* of mean streets, moral ambiguities and air of irresolution. *Blade Runner*'s Los Angeles exemplifies the failure of the rational city envisioned by urban planners and science fiction creators, and it also recalls, by implication, the air of masculine crisis that undergirded film noir – witness Dekard's struggle to retain, or regain, his humanity. If the metropolis in noir was a dystopian purgatory, then in *Blade Runner*, with its flame-belching towers, it has become an almost literal inferno. (Bukatman, 2005: 50)

Academic Writing Check: Spot the Difference

Collaboration itself is a complex phenomenon (Hennermann et al., 1995) and different models have been explored (Hudson, 1999). Different philosophies of teamworking can present difficulties for multi-professional teamwork (Freeman et al., 2000). Indicators for positive inter-professional team working appear to be the personal qualities and commitment of staff, communication within the team and the opportunity to develop creative working methods within the team (Molyneux, 2001). Issues of 'personhood' cannot be ignored, as professional and disciplinary differences are manifested in terms of who professional persons consider themselves to be in relation to what is expected of them (Dombeck, 1997). (Malin, Wilmot and Manthorpe, 2002: 101)

Bibliography

Dombeck, M. (1997) 'Professional personhood: training, territoriality and tolerance', *Journal of Interpersonal Care,* 11 (1): 9–21.
Freeman, M., Miller, C. and Ross, N. (2000) 'The impact of individual philosophies of teamwork on multi-professional practice and the implications for education', *Journal of Interpersonal Care,* 14 (3): 237–47.
Hennermann, E., Lee, J. and Cohen, J. (1995) 'Collaboration: a concept analysis', *Journal of Advanced Nursing,* 21: 103–9.
Hudson, B. (1999) 'Primary health care and social care: working across professional boundaries, pt.1: The changing context of inter-professional relationships', *Managing Community Care* 7 (1): 15–22.
Molyneux, J. (2001) 'Interprofessional teamworking: what makes teams work well?', *Journal of Interprofessional Care,* 15 (1): 29–35.

Summary

- The aim of writing up is to shape a persuasive narrative which shows each stage of the project logically unfolding from the one before. The dissertation needs to be synthesised, knitted together to show how decision making about methods addresses the research question, how ethical issues arise as a result and so on

- The literature review needs to show the work in the wider field, and needs to directly link your piece of research with everyone else's

- Conclusions need to be developed throughout the dissertation, building up to a logical and what seems natural sets of conclusions to the reader

- Refresh your memory as to regulations and make sure that you know the final structure of the dissertation including all of its constituent parts

- What goes where: the components of a dissertation:

  o Abstract
  o Acknowledgements
  o Table of contents
  o Tables and figures or illustrations
  o Introduction
  o Literature review
  o Methodology
  o Data/findings/discussion
  o Conclusions
  o Appendix/ces

- Tips on opening and closing chapters:

  o Use of quotations
  o Connecting your work to themes
  o Using and refining concepts

- Tackling the conclusion: a three-step thought-process:

  o Step 1: where the project has come from including the original for-mulation of the research problem
  o Step 2: the findings and their limits
  o Step 3: future lines of inquiry

- Fleshing out the conclusion: the 'Why, what, how, where, when?' questions need to be addressed, and a nod to the future is expected

- Challenges:

  o Leaving enough time to develop and check the conclusions reached
  o Explaining negative choices and talking through what went wrong
  o The tendency to avoid concluding: clinging to summarising and describing rather than doing that *as well as* synthesising, concluding and persuading

- Good drafting: a good draft is one where the author:

  o Is in control of the words, not the other way around
  o Has got something to say and knows how to say it
  o Has spent time proofreading, structuring, and laying out

- Use of anti-discriminatory language when drafting: it is important to ensure that your use of language does not discriminate in terms of race, class, gender, disability, sexual orientation and so on. Use guidelines if in doubt

- Too many words?

  o Even up the length of your paragraphs
  o Split up long sentences
  o Reduce the length of quotations using three dots (...) to indicate that something is missing

- o Turn data into charts and consider putting data into appendices
- o Reduce long sections

- Too few words?

  - o Introduce and discuss each chart and quotation
  - o Make sure that you have included a full set of literature:
    - – Methods and substantive topic
    - – Journal articles as well as books
    - – Recent reports
  - o Increase the amount of analysis which accompanies the description
  - o Frame each chapter with introductions and conclusions

- Grammar: do you know what you are looking for? If not, buy a decent grammar guide – and then follow it!

- Academic writing: plagiarism

  - o Definitions of plagiarism
  - o Why do people plagiarise?
  - o Academic integrity: pride in your work
  - o Checking for plagiarism
  - o e-Plagiarism
  - o Turnitin

- Know when to stop! You run into the law of diminishing returns the longer you hang on to your words and the greater the level of microscopic detail that you insist on developing

Further Reading

Becker, H.S. (2008) *Writing for Social Scientists: How to Start and Finish Your Thesis, Book or Article.* Chicago: Chicago University Press.

Cook, C.K. (2006) *Line By Line: How to Edit Your Own Writing.* Amsterdam: Elsevier Science.

Creme, P. and Lea, M.R. (2003) (2nd edn) *Writing at University: A Guide for Students.* Maidenhead: Open University Press.

King, G. (2005) *Collins Good Writing Guide.* Oxford: Collins.

Seely, J. (2005) *Oxford Guide to Effective Writing and Speaking.* Oxford: Oxford University Press.

Wolcott, H.F. (2001) *Writing Up Qualitative Research.* London: Sage.

Chapter 13

Troubleshooting

I found some participants and they gave their consent; but when I got home X's mother contacted me explaining that her daughter no longer wants to take part.

This is tricky in the sense that a different adult is informing you of the research participant's decision not to participate. It is reasonable to ask to speak with the participant, if only to see what the problem is. You will need to accept the decision with good grace. Note that they are not obliged to provide an explanation.

I am not sure how much data to collect or how long to collect it for.

This is a common issue. It is easier to judge with quantitative datasets and sample sizes than with qualitative sets. You should aim for around 80+ surveys in the first instance and a few good interviews in the second. If they are life history interviews then literally a very small sample is fine. If however you are interviewing to collect data for other purposes, for example, from different nodes of a social network, then you should go for more, anything up to 12 to 15. You might want to do more interviews if you have time – but bear in mind that the transcription of interview data and the coding and analysis stages of both kinds of data are time-consuming. You should definitely check with your supervisor before stopping your data collection.

I've run out of time!

Firstly, write up what you can. Make sure that what you hand in is at least as good as you can get it at that point.

Secondly, consider whether you can submit any other materials to support your unfinished dissertation. You should aim to get agreement from your department or faculty before doing that. If you do take this course of action, make sure that you include a guide to the paperwork, so that your tutors can make sense of it.

I tried to find research participants and did make some plans with some: but several didn't turn up.

Firstly, try again. You could go back to the same people or seek some new faces. In future, always over-recruit, since people often drop out at the last minute.

If you don't have time to try again, write up what you have got. Acknowledge the data collection problem in your write-up and evaluate how it has affected your project and the findings.

The manuscript is too short or long.
See Chapter 12 on writing up for suggestions to length and shorten your dissertation text.

The project as I originally conceived it was too large. At my current rate of progress, I will still be collecting data or writing it a year after I (fail to) graduate?
See a useful discussion of reshaping research, 'Choices and Combinations' (Chapter 10) in Catherine Hakim's book *Research Design: Successful Designs for Social Economic Research,* which contains a useful discussion of both what she calls 'trading down' and 'trading up' to smaller and cheaper or larger and more complex research studies while mid-stream.

I've got writer's block!
In the first place, strictly speaking there is no such thing as writer's block. A useful first step is to think through what the problem is. If it is about procrastination, look at Chapter 1. But if it is rather that you don't know where to start, then a good next step is to make a writing plan, working out a series of tasks and allocating specific days or times of day to completing each task. Make sure that you attempt each task. Don't worry if they are less than perfect. You can go back over your writing when you have reached the end of the draft – not before! Make sure that when you do start writing, you pick a task that you feel more confident about. Leave the more difficult parts to another day.

The research participants asked me for my advice. What should I do?
Anticipate participants' questions as far as you can. Develop appropriate responses, but, it is suggested, simple and limited referrals if needed. Stick to things that you know about, for example sources of further information and helplines, useful organisations to contact and so on. It is important to refer on to other more expert sources wherever possible.

I need to analyse some statistics but I am hopeless with this.
The key here is working out what it is that you want to know. Then clearly identify a strategy to develop and work out how best to acquire the know-how you need. Remember: it is not necessarily the case that you are really hopeless with statistics – it is much more likely that you have never really learnt how to handle them. There are some suggestions in the skill set booster section of Chapter 1 for dealing with statistics. Secondly, find a friendly colleague who can help you, and do consider talking to your supervisor about it, they might have some ideas.

I want to do a comparative study of political systems across three states.
This might be manageable, although at first appearances it seems quite large. It isn't immediately clear how you would be able to handle the

workload given your situation as an undergraduate student were you to be contemplating jetting off to various countries to do it. A key here is to work out what studies have already been done, and what data sets there are available. This might allow you to do a library-based project, in which case three countries might be manageable, or to have a wider and more general literature review than involved in taking one country as a case study.

I don't know anything about the philosophy of science: does it matter?

It is better that you have some sense of it, although you don't need to be able to write the whole dissertation about it. Start with one of the introductory or survey texts found under Further Reading in Chapter 4. Ask your colleagues if they have taken any courses which covered this area: they might also be able to fill you in.

Appendix 1

Compendium of Online Sources

Academic Writing in English at the Virtual University of Finland
http://kiepc10.cc.tut.fi/~english/kirjoittamo/awe

Alerts
www.google.com/alerts

American Indian Resource Directory
www.indians.org

American Psychological Association
www.apa.org

Animal Procedures Committee
www.apc.gov.uk

Artcyclopedia
www.artcyclopedia.com

Ask an expert
www.allexperts.com

Bartleby
www.bartleby.com

Birmingham City University
www.bcu.ac.uk

British Broadcasting Corporation (BBC)
www.bbc.co.uk

British Library Sound Archive
www.bl.uk/nsa

British Polling Council
www.britishpollingcouncil.org

British Politics Links
www.ukpolitics.org.uk

British Psychological Society (BPS)
www.bps.org.uk

British Sociological Association (BSA)
www.britsoc.co.uk

Bogazici University online writing lab
www.buowl.boun.edu.tr

Centre for Longitudinal Studies
www.cls.ioe.ac.uk

Centre d'Etudes de Populations, de Pauvreté et de Politiques Socio-Economiques + International Networks (CEPS/INSTEAD)
www.ceps.lu

Center for Social and Economic Research, Poland (CASE)
www.case.com.pl

The Child Centre, Baltic Sea region
www.childcentre.info

Classified: access to formerly classified documents (USA)
www.paperlessarchives.com

Commonwealth Writers' Annual Prize
www.commonwealthfoundation.com

Companion for Undergraduate Dissertations at the Learning Centre for Sociology, Anthropology, and Politics (C-SAP)
www.socscidiss.bham.ac.uk/s2.html

COPAC (Consortium of University Research Libraries Public Access Catalogue)
http://copac.ac.uk/copac

Council of European Social Science Data Archives (CESSDA)
www.nsd.uib.no/cessda

Country codes for Google
www.iana.org/cctld/cctld-whois.htm

Dictionary and thesaurus
www.dictionary.com

Documents of the American Revolution 1774–1776
http://dig.lib.niu.edu

Dun & Bradstreet
www.dnb.com/us

Economic and Social Research Council (ESRC)
www.esrc.ac.uk

Equality and Human Rights Commission
www.equalityhumanrights.com

Eurostat – the European Union statistics agency
http://epp.eurostat.ec.europa.eu

Federal state statistics (USA)
www.fedstats.gov

Gallup polling company
www.gallup.com

General Social Survey (GSS) (USA)
www.gss.norc.org

***Geoverse* – journal of undergraduate research for geography at Oxford Brookes University**
www.brookes.ac.uk/schools/social/geoverse

Getty Photographic Images
www.gettyimages.co.uk

Project Gutenberg
www.gutenberg.org

The history of photography
www.bjphoto.co.uk

The Imperial War Museum
www.iwm.org.uk

Interdisciplinary Centre for Comparative Research in the Social Sciences (ICCR)
www.ICCR-international.org

International Social Survey Programme
www.issp.org

International Visual Sociological Association (IVSA)
http://visualsociology.org

Internet Movie Database
www.imdb.com

Internet Public Library
www.ipl.org

Inter-University Consortium for Political and Social Research based at the University of Michigan (ICPSR)
www.icpsr.umich.edu

Library of Congress
www.loc.gov

Lords of the Blog
www.lordsoftheblog.net

The Man Booker Prize
www.themanbookerprize.com

Mass Observation Archive (Sussex University)
www.massobs.org.uk

Medical Research Council (MRC)
www.mrc.ac.uk

MORI polling company
www.mori.com

The Museum and Galleries of Manchester and the North West
www.manchestergalleries.org

Museum Victoria
http://museumvictoria.com.au/material/material.asp

National Archives of Australia
www.naa.gov.au

National Centre for Research
www.natcen.ac.uk

National Children's Bureau
www.ncb.org.uk

National Health Service: National Patient Safety Agency
www.nres.npsa.nhs.uk

Nobel Prize for Literature
http://nobelprize.org/nobel_prizes/literature

Nordic and East/Central Eastern Network for Qualitative Social Research (NECEN)
www.necen.org

Northern Ireland Statistics and Research Agency
www.nisra.gov.uk

Nuffield Council on Bioethics
www.nuffieldbioethics.org

Office of National Statistics (UK)
www.statistics.gov.uk

Oral History Society
www.ohs.org.uk

Orange Prize for Fiction
www.orangeprize.co.uk

Oxford Brookes University
www.brookes.ac.uk

Peabody Essex Museum
www.pem.org

Political protest portal
www.protest.net

Political Resources (USA)
www.politicalresources.com

Prime Minister's website (UK)
www.pm.gov.uk

Private Eye Online
www.private-eye.co.uk

Publications from Parliament in UK
www.publications.parliament.uk

Quality Assurance Agency for Higher Education
www.QAA.ac.uk

Question Bank: questions for questionnaires
http://qb.soc.surrey.ac.uk

Quotations, quick reference
www.quotationspage.com

Reinvention Centre at the University of Warwick
www.warwick.ac.uk

Robert Niles' website: Statistics Every Writer Should Know: a simple guide to understanding statistics, for journalists and other writers who might not know math
www.robertniles.com/stats

Royal Literary Fund
www.rlf.org.uk

Scotland Executive Central Research Unit
www.scotland.gov.uk/topics/research

Social Research Association (SRA)
www.the-sra.org

The Social Sciences Data Collection based at the University of California at San Diego (SSDC)
www.ssdc.ucsd.edu/ssdc/conf.html

StatSoft Glossary
www.statsoft.com/textbook/stathome.html

The Statue of Liberty and the Ellis Island Foundation
www.ellisisland.org

STILE questionnaire database
www.stile.be/surveydb

TIME Magazine Best 100 English Language Novels Since 1923
www.time.com/time/2005/100books/the_complete_list.html

United Nations Educational, Scientific, and Cultural Organisation (UNESCO)
www.unesco.org/en/about

Universitas 21, international universities network
www.universitas21.com

University of Lancashire undergraduate research journal, *Diffusion*
www.uclan.ac.uk

University of Pennsylvania
www.psu.edu

University of Texas
www.utexas.edu

Using English for Academic Purposes
www.uefap.com

Welcome Institute
www.wellcome.ac.uk

Welsh Assembly and Government
www.wales.gov.uk

Which?Book
www.whichbook.ne

The White House (USA)
www.whitehouse.org

World Health Organisation
www.who.int

Appendix 2

Readability: Reading Age Scales

Readability scales came from the USA in the early twentieth century. They are used today, for example:

- To work out the reading ages of children and young people

- As a rule of thumb guide for producers of media, such as newspapers and websites, who gear their output, for example to the most common literacy levels found in their audiences

The FOG Index

There are several different readability scales available; the Fog Index is a commonly used one.

How to calculate the FOG:

1) Select a chunk of text between 100 and 250 words.

2) Calculate: The average number of words per sentence. The total number of words divided by the total number of complete sentences = the average number of words per sentence (call this W)

3) Calculate: The percentage of words with lots of syllables. The total number of words divided by the total number of words which consist of three or more syllables = the percentage of words with lots of syllables (call this S)

4) W + S divided by 0.4 = the FOG Index. (i.e. adding the answers to 2) and 3) and dividing the total by 0.4 = FOG Index.)

FOG Index	Resources
6	TV guides, the Bible, Mark Twain
8	*Reader's Digest*
8–10	Most popular novels
10	*Time, Newsweek*
11	*Wall Street Journal*
14	*The Times*, The *Guardian*
15–20	Academic papers
Over 20	Only government sites can get away with this, because you can't ignore them
Over 30	The government is covering something up

Source: http://juicystudio.com/services/readability.php

How Does the Number Relate to Different Kinds of Media?

The table below provides a good indication of this:

Typical FOG Index Scores

Using Reading Scales

It is suggested that you check the readability of your research instruments, for example, the wording of your questionnaires, information sheets and covering letters etc., before giving them out. You should aim for a relatively low FOG Index in order to facilitate speedy and accurate responses. You might find it illuminating to check the FOG Index of books you've read as well as an example of your coursework essay.

Health Warning

It is not advisable to use these scales to practise on your friends, parents, children and so on, without talking it over with them first. It should not be assumed that the results mean that people literally have 'young' reading ages etc., since the scales are a crude measure of years of education and amounts of reading time etc., i.e. they are a measure of the impact of social factors on reading rather than actual reading ages as such. On the other hand, they are not a crude measure of deprivation either. Misinforming your unsuspecting compatriots of the 'results' may aggrieve them unnecessarily: so do be careful of how you discuss the results

Appendix 3
Example of a Consent Form

Title of Project:	
Researcher's Contact Details:	
I have read and understood the information sheet attached	
I agree to participate in this research	
I understand and agree that the research may be recorded	
I understand that the research may be used in future books, journals, reports, websites, and conference presentations and that what I say may be quoted	
I agree that the research may be used in future books, journals, reports, websites, and conference presentations and that what I say may be quoted as long as what I say is anonymised	

I understand that I can withdraw my consent and participation from the research at any time; and from any specific aspect of the research at any time; and that I don't need to provide a reason	

Name of research participant   **Signature**   **Date**

Name of researcher   **Signature**   **Date**

Glossary

Abstract   A summary, usually of one side of A4 or less, setting out the research question, methods used, main findings, and conclusions. Used by other researchers to decide whether or not to read the whole research paper.

Action research   The focus of action research is to make interventions which are informed by that research. It aims to develop a line of inquiry; make investigations; arrive at recommendations for action; and will seek to facilitate those actions as part of the research project.

Adequacy of data   An adequate data set is one which allows the researcher to reach a reasoned judgement as to its valid meaning. This doesn't mean the sole interpretation or deduction which is possible, or that the conclusions drawn are infallible. But it does mean that the researcher is relying upon their data set to draw conclusions.

All-nighter   Staying up late to finish a piece of work – 'just in time', student style!

Benchmark statements   Documents, one per subject, which describe the attributes, skills and capabilities that a graduate with an honours degree in a specific subject might be expected to have. Produced by the QAA.

Bibliography   All works referenced in the dissertation, and all works consulted but not referenced.

Bibliographic index   A system of record-keeping which typically includes all bibliographic information as well as brief notes, for example, on the use and location of items.

Case study   An in-depth study of one particular instance, which could be an organisation, a social setting, institution, person or group and so on. Can be used with other methods, for example an individual respondent may be selected from a survey sample to be interviewed in depth.

Comparative studies The aim is to compare cases (for example, area studies, historical studies and so on), and to arrive at insights specific to those cases as well as more generalised conclusions about the category of cases as a whole.

Coding Assigning categories to data using a system of numbers.

Coding book Sets out a code and how to use it, i.e. the procedures to be followed in order to assign the right code to each piece of data.

Constructivism/ Constructionism The view that reality is socially constructed through social, cultural, economic, and political systems, processes, and interactions. This means that the interplay of researcher and the researched raises epistemological and ethical issues for research.

CREAM A mnemonic of a study strategy coined by Cottrell (1999: 49), meaning Creative (C), Reflective (R), Effective (E), Active (A), Motivated (M).

Deductive Deductive approaches start from the top, from theory. Gaps and problems in theories lead to the identification of a hypothesis, which is then tested at ground level, i.e. empirical level. Testing is generally carried out by scientific methods such as testing, experimentation, and observation.

Dissertation team The dissertation team is your group or network, individuals who are essential to your study success. The team might include friends and family, as well as your bank manager and landlord.

Documents of life A concept coined by Plummer (2001, for example) to conceptualise a methodological approach using objects including texts to tell life histories, and an epistemological stance described as critical humanism.

Empirical A style of research which rests upon the collection and analysis of data: visual, spoken, textual, behavioural, physical, from the 'real' world, informed by a diversity of philosophical assumptions about the nature of the world.

Epistemology	The philosophy of knowing. This explores ways of knowing and the difficulty of knowing; questions such as with what certainty and contingency might we know; knowing versus understanding; and how we might go about finding out or similar.
Ethics	The problematisation of research processes and issues on the basis of values, beliefs, and norms. Standards of behaviour based on beliefs about what is right and wrong.
Ethnography	Working within a selected site or field, researchers will observe and possibly participate in the social life of a community in order to learn from the actors' perspectives the basis and operation of the systems which govern them, for example, discourses, rituals, the basis and operation of systems of stratification and rule, etc.
Frequency distribution	Plotting the distribution of the population across the range.

- Normal distribution – a U-shaped curve
- Skewed distribution – the data is clustered in one direction or the other

Grounded theory	An approach to research: qualitative data is collected and analysed. During this process theory is generated and checked against further data collected. (See Glaser and Strauss, 1967.)
Hypothesis	A proposition in theory; i.e., the proposition is literally hypothetical, and the researcher's task will be to test it empirically.
Inductive approach	Research is approached from the ground level. Data is obtained and its sense inferred upwards to create theory. Data is collected from the specific, local case, and generalised upwards and outwards.
Interpretive research	A broad approach to research which assumes that reality can only be under stood by the interpretations which we make of it, typically for example through using language and exploring meanings.

Interviews

Purposeful interactions, typically conversations, which generate data.

- Semi-structured interviews: these have planned and common components or frameworks with fluid spaces which allow improvisation and spontaneity.

- Structured interviews: these are entirely planned, with wholly common components and frameworks from which an entirely consistent data set is generated.

- Group interviews: more than one participant is interviewed simultaneously; sometimes they use techniques of focusing, in which instance they are more likely to be known and organised as focus groups.

Literature review

A critically engaged discussion of the state of research in a field incorporating landmark studies and the most recent research. Good reviews are ones where students place their own research in the field, making connections between it and the field.

Litmus test

The litmus test, or acid test, is a definitive test used to ascertain the degree of acid in a substance by using litmus paper. The 'litmus' test of research involves asking: Does this method produce the kind of data which the researcher claims it does? Did this method produce the kind of data needed in order for the researcher to arrive at the conclusions that they do? Was this research conducted in both an ethical and timely manner? Is the researcher aware of the imperfections and problems in the research – and has she taken them into account? Does this research tell us something which we didn't know before?

Longitudinal research

Longitudinal research refers to research carried out over a period of time. Typically, data is collected at intervals either from the same people or from different people with the same characteristics. Depending on how the study is set up (as a trend study; a cohort study or as a panel study), different kinds of readings can be achieved, for example, of cause and effect versus underlying trends.

Mind map	A diagram showing connections between different concepts; it is sometimes demarcated into segments, for example with coloured pens
Mixed methods	Generally, this refers to the use of more than one method in a research project; specifically, it often means combining both quantitative and qualitative approaches.
Multivariate set analysis	Working with more than one variable in one ting, to see their inter-relationships, for example their cause and effects and their relative importance or impact.
Narrative research	Seeks to work out the narratives used by research participants to structure their experience in ways meaningful to them.
Negative evidence	Identifying what isn't there and using it as a source of data in its own right.
Plagiarism	Using the work of others as your own. Includes copying; cutting and pasting to assemble work as though it were your own; referencing work poorly; using work purchased or free of charge; using sources unacknowledged.
	• Plagiarism detection software: this is software used to identify copied text; it can be used to improve referencing technique
Positivism	The belief that the truth is out there: that external reality can be studied objectively using scientific methods. The social sciences are viewed as akin to the natural sciences. Positivism is often exemplified by quantitative methods and deductive approaches which set out to measure variables which are independent of the researcher.
Procrastination	Putting something off, even when it is essential that it is done.
QAA	The Quality Assurance Agency for Higher Education (QAA) provides quality assurance regulation to the higher education sector in the UK.
Qualitative methods	These methods aim to develop understandings of meanings. They often rely on interpretation

and typically work with 'soft' data: words, images, sounds, feelings and so on.

Quantitative methods   Aim to identify and make sense of patterns in data, for example by attempting to establish cause and effect between different variables. Data is generally 'hard' in the form of numbers, and reliant on quantification for its analysis.

Reliable   This means that if the research was done again using the same design, under similar circumstances, we would get the same or close enough results.

Research problem and or research question   The problem formulation. A closely defined circumscribed research question which is narrower than a topic, theme, or line of inquiry. Good questions are: Clear, Specific, Answerable, Interconnected, Substantially Relevant (Punch, 2005).

Samples   A sub-group of the population selected for research.

- Convenience sample: a readily available sample

- Purposive sample: a deliberately selected sample believed to be representative

- Stratified sample: a sample that represents the sub-groups (or strata) to the same extent that the sub-group is represented within the whole group

- Random sample: here, all objects/subjects have an equal chance of selection

Scales   A scale is a system of arranging data in order.

- Ordinal scales: a scale of quantity – measures the degree to which each object possess a certain characteristic

- Nominal scales: categorises objects into groups

- Interval scales: objects are presented in periodic intervals where each object is the same distance apart as all the others

Scientific method   An approach which intrinsically includes collecting data, evaluating its parts in relation to each other; or interpreting the data's meaning, with testing theory or constructing theory as an aim. Scientific methods lend themselves to characterisations, such as rational, objective, analytical and so on, much debated by natural as well as social scientists.

SMART and SMARTER
SMART is an mnemonic based on the work of management guru Drucker (1954), who coined the phrase 'Management By Objectives' (MBO), and constructed SMART objectives: Specific (S), Measurable (M), Achievable (A), Realistic (R), Time-bound (T). It has been more recently extended to include Evaluated, Exciting (E) and Recorded and Reviewed (R).

Sources (good)
Good sources are authoritative, up-to-date, accurate. You can have confidence in them.

Standard deviation
The standard deviation is a measurement of the distance between each case and the mean, whereby all the distances of all the cases have been added together and their mean distance, as a class or group, calculated. The number calculated is termed 'the standard deviation'.

Surveys
Surveys ask the same questions of members of a selected population, and their answers are compared. The data generated in this way will reveal social patterns, and will carry some explanatory power.

Tally sheets
Record sheets for use in the field.

Theoretical exploration
An approach to research which aims to compare, debate and critically take forward theories in terms of other abstract theories: this may not involve empirical research.

Triangulation
Using more than one method, object or subject in order to obtain a few different data sets. Triangulation is a tactic whereby the researcher compares the data sets and identifies a position broadly lying in the middle. This amounts to a 'most representative' position, and prevents the researcher from being (mis)led by outliers or other kinds of unique cases or sources of bias which skew the data.

Univariate analysis Working with only one variable to ascertain its direction and importance.

Validity The extent to which you evaluate or measure what you claim to evaluate or measure.

Variables Items which you can bring together to see how they affect each other, i.e. to see the relationship between them.

- The dependent variable – what you want to explain them with

- The independent variable – what you want to explain them with

Verstehen Understanding based upon interpretation

WHITTLE Whittle down your research proposal.

- What: What is the research question?

- How: Which methodologies have you selected and why have you rejected others?

- Importance: Why is the proposed research important?

- Timely: Why do you think that this research should be carried out now?

- Title: Does the reader know what the project is about from the proposed title?

- Literature: Have you identified the key *academic* research which has been carried out in this field so far?

- End result: When you have completed this piece of research, what will the end result be?

Z-scores A way of calculating the standard deviation between different categories or classes. Z-scores are a way of enabling alternative comparisons such as between the absolute best (the winner of the London Marathon), and the best in each class (the fastest U19-year-old; the fastest octogenarian).

Bibliography

Angell, R. (1945) 'A Critical Review of the Development of the Personal Document Method in Sociology 1920–1940', in L. Gottschalk, C. Kluckhohn, and R. Angell, (eds), *The Use of Personal Documents in History, Anthropology, Sociology*. Prepared for the Committee on Appraisal of Research. New York: Social Science Research Council.

Ashcroft, B., Griffiths, G. and Tiffin, H. (1989) *The Empire Writes Back*. London: Routledge.

Aveyard, H. (2007) *Doing a Literature Review in Health and Social Care*. Maidenhead: Open University Press.

Bailey, S. (2006) *Academic Writing: A Handbook for International Students*. London: Routledge.

Banks, M. (2001) *Visual Methods in Social Research*. London: Sage Publications.

Bargh, C., Bocock, J., Scott, P. and Smith, D. (2000) Chapter 3, 'Career Paths: Patterns of Continuity and Change', in *University Leadership: The Role of the Chief Executive*. Buckingham: The Society for Research into Higher Education (SRHE) and Open University Press.

Barnes, R. (1992) *Successful Study for Degrees*. London: Routledge.

BBC Newsnight Discussion of Andrew Keen's book *The Cult of the Amateur*, www.bbc.co.uk/blogs/newsnight/2007/06/the_cult_of_the_amateur_by_andrew_keen_1.html.

Becker, H.S. (1963) *Outsiders: Studies in the Sociology of Deviance*. New York: Free Press.

Becker, H.S. (1998) *Tricks of the Trade: How To Think About Your Research While You Are Doing It*. Chicago: Chicago University Press.

Becker, S. and Bryman, A. (2004) *Understanding Research for Social Policy and Practice: Themes, Methods and Approaches*. Bristol: Policy Press.

Bell, J. (2007) *Doing Your Research Project*. Maidenhead: Open University Press.

Beresford, P. and Croft, S. (2001) 'Service Users' Knowledges and the Social Construction of Social Work', *Journal of Social Work* (1) 3: 295–316.

Berg, B.L. (2007) *Qualitative Research Methods for the Social Sciences*. New York: Pearson International.

Berg, S. (1988) 'Snowball Sampling', in S. Kotz and N.L. Johnson (eds), *Encyclopaedia of Statistical Sciences*, (8) 528–32. New York: John Wiley.

Bertaux, D. and Delcroix, C. (2000) 'Case Histories and Social Processes: Enriching Sociology', Chapter 3, in P. Chamberlayne, J. Bornat and T. Wengraft, *Biography and Society: The Life History Approach in the Social Sciences*. Beverly Hills: Sage Publications.

Bianchi, S.M., Milkie, M.A., Robinson, J.P. and Sayer, L.C. (2000) 'Is Anyone Doing the Housework? Trends in the Gender Divison of Labour', *Social Forces* (79) 1: 191–229.

Blackburn, S. (2001) *Think! A Compelling Introduction to Philosophy*. Oxford: Oxford Paperbacks.

Bloor, M., Frankland, J., Thomas, M. and Robson, K. (2001) *Focus Groups in Social Research*. London: Sage.

Bochel, H.M. and Duncan, S. (2007) *Making Policy in Theory and Practice*. Cambridge: Policy Press.

Bogdan, R. (1974) *Being Different: The Autobiography of Jane Fry*. London: Wiley.

Bowell, T. and Kemp, G. (2005) (2nd edn) *Critical Thinking: A Concise Guide*. London: Routledge.

Brafield, H. and Eckersly, T. (2008) *Service User Involvement: Reaching the Hard to Reach in Supported Housing*. London and Philadelphia: Jessica Kingsley Publishers.

Brodkin, K. (2004) *How Jews Became White Folks and What That Says About Race in America*. New Brunswick, New Jersey, and London: Rutgers University Press.

Bryman, A. (1992) 'Quantitative and Qualitative Research: Further Reflections On Their Integration', in J. Brannen (ed.), *Mixing Methods: Qualitative and Quantitative Research*. Aldershot: Avebury.

Bryman, A. (2001) *Social Research Methods* Oxford: Oxford University Press.

Bryman, A. (2008) (3rd edn) *Social Research Methods*. Oxford: Oxford University Press.

Bryman, A. and Cramer, D. (2000) *Quantitative Data Analysis with SPSS for Windows – A Guide for Social Scientists*. London: Routledge.

Bukatman, S. (2005) *Blade Runner*. London: British Film Institute.

Burke, A. (2000) *A Social History of Knowledge: From Gutenberg to Diderot*. Cambridge: Polity Press.

Callinicos, A. (2005) *Social Theory: An Historical Introduction*. Cambridge: Polity Press.

Calvocoressi, P. (1997) *Fall Out: World War II and the Shaping of Postwar Europe*. London and New York: Longman.

Campbell, A. (2003) *Iraq's Weapons of Mass Destruction: The Assessment of the British Government*. London: HMSO.

Chamberlayne, P., Bornat, J. and Wengraf, T. (2000) *The Turn to Biographical Methods in Social Science: Comparative Issues and Examples*. London: Routledge.

Clark, A. and Kjorholt, A. T, and Moss, P. (eds) (2005) *Beyond Listening. Children's Perspectives on Early Childhood Services*. Cambridge: Policy Press.

Clear, T.R. and Frost, N.A. (2007) 'Informing Public Policy', *Criminology and Public Policy* 6 (4): 633–40.

Clegg, B. and Birch, P. (2007) *Instant Creativity: Simple Techniques to Ignite Innovation and Problem Solving*. London: Kegan Paul.

Collins, P.H. (1990) *Black Feminist Thought: Knowledge, Consciousness; and the Politics of Empowerment*. London: Routledge.

Commission for Africa (2005) 'The Argument', *Our Common Interest: Report of the Commission for Africa*. Penguin Books.

Consumers in NHS Research Support Unit (2000) *Involving Consumers in Research and Development in the NHS: Briefing Notes for Researchers*. Winchester: Help for Health Trust.

Cook, C.K. (2006) *Line By Line: How to Edit Your Own Writing*. Amsterdam: Elsevier Science.

Cornwell, J. (1984) *Hard Earned Lives: Accounts of Health and Illness from East London*. London: Tavistock.

Cottrell, S. (1999) *The Study Skills Handbook*. Basingstoke: Palgrave Macmillan.

Coverley, M. (2006) *Psychogeography*. Harpenden: Pocket Essentials.

Crapanzano, V. (1985) *Tuhami: Portrait of a Moroccan*. Chicago: University of Chicago Press.

Crawford, K. and Walker, J. (2004) *Social Work with Older People*. Exeter: Learning Matters Ltd.

Creme, P. and Lea, M.R. (2003) (2nd edn) *Writing at University: A Guide for Students*. Maidenhead: Open University Press.

Cresswell, J.W. (2002) (2nd edn) *Research Design: Qualitative, Quantitative, and Mixed Methods Approaches*. London: Sage.

Cudd, A. and Andreasen, R. (2004) *Feminist Theory: A Philosophical Anthology*. Oxford: Wiley-Blackwell.

Czaja, R. and Blair, J. (2005) (2nd edn) *Designing Surveys: A Guide to Decisions and Procedures*. Thousand Oaks, California: Pine Forge Press.

Darlington, Y. and Scott, D. (2002) *Qualitative Research in Practice: Stories from the Field*, Buckingham: Open University Press.

Darwin, C., (1987) in J. Laurent, 'More Sex Please, We're Vicarious', *New Scientist*, 22 January cited in D. Heater (2004) *Citizenship: The Civic Ideal in World History, Politics and Education,* Manchester: Manchester University Press.

Darwin, C. (2000) *The Descent of Man*, the Project Gutenberg e-text, www.gutenberg. org/dirs/etext00/dscmn10.txt

Deleuze, G. and Guattari, F. (1987) *A Thousand Plateaus: Capitalism and Schizophrenia*, trans. B. Massumi. Minneapolis: University of Minnesota Press.

Denscombe, M. (2003) *The Good Research Guide: For Small-scale Social Research Projects*. Maidenhead: Open University.

Descartes, R. (2007) *Discourse on Method and the Meditations*. London: Penguin.

Dick, P.K. [1966] (1968) *Do Androids Dream of Electric Sheep?* New York: Del Rey Books.

Dickens, C. [1868] (2007) *Hard Times*. London: Penguin Books.

Dombeck, M. (1997) 'Professional Personhood: Training, Territoriality and Tolerance', *Journal of Interpersonal Care,* 11 (1): 9–21.

Drucker, P. [1954] (2007) *The Practice of Management*. New York: Butterworth-Heinemann Ltd.

Dunaway, D. and Baum, W.K. (eds) (1996) *Oral History: An Interdisciplinary Anthology*. London: AltaMira Press.

Emmison, M. and Smith, P. (2001) *Researching the Visual*. London: Sage.

Eriksen, T.H. (2001) *Small Places, Large Issues: An Introduction to Social and Cultural Anthropology*. London: Pluto Press.

Faugier, J. and Sargeant, M. (1997) 'Sampling Hard to Reach Populations', *Journal of Advanced Nursing*, vol. 26, 790–7.

Finch, J. (1987) 'The Vignette Technique in Survey Research', *Sociology*, 21, 105–14.

Fink, A. (2005) *Conducting Research Literature Reviews: From the Internet to Paper*. London: Sage.

Foster, R. (1989) *Modern Ireland 1600–1972*. London: Penguin.

Foucault, M. (2001) *Madness and Civilization*. London: Routledge.

Fowler, F.J. (1995) *Improving Survey Questions: Design and Evaluation*. London: Sage.

Fowler, F.J., Jr. (2002) *Survey Research Methods* (3rd edn), London: Sage.

Freeman, M., Miller, C. and Ross, N. (2000) 'The Impact of Individual Philosophies of Teamwork on Multi-professional Practice and the Implications for Education', *Journal of Interpersonal Care*, 14 (3): 237–47.

Friday, N. (1976) *My Secret Garden*. New York: Pocket Books.

Fromm, E. [1979] (2005) *To Have or To Be?* London: Continuum Books.

Furlong, A. and Cartmel, F. (1997) *Young People and Social Change: Individualization and Risk in Late Modernity*. Maidenhead: Open University.

Gaita, R. (2003) *The Philospher's Dog*. London; Routledge.

Geertz, C. [1973] (1993) *The Interpretation of Cultures*. London: Fontana.

Gilbert, N. (1993) *Researching Social Life*. London: Sage.

Gilbert, N. (2008) (3rd edn) *Researching Social Life*. London: Sage.

Glaser, B. (1992) *Basics of Grounded Theory Analysis: Emergence versus Forcing*. Mill Valley, California: Sociology Press.

Glaser, B. and Strauss, A. (1967) *The Discovery of Grounded Theory: Strategies for Qualitative Research*. Chicago: Aldine.

Goldblatt, D. (2004) *Knowledge and the Social Sciences: Theory, Method and Practice*. London: Routledge.

Gomm, R. and Davies, C. (eds) (2000) *Using Evidence in Health and Social Care*. London: Sage.

Gordon, I. (2005) 'Integrating Cities', in *Changing Cities: Rethinking Urban Competitiveness, Cohesion and Governance*, ed. N. Buck, I. Gordon, A. Harding and I. Turok. Basingstoke: Palgrave Macmillan.

Gramsci, A. (1988) *Gramsci's Prison Letters*. Translated by H. Henderson. London: Zwan.

Gregory, J. (1990) 'The Adult Dietary Survey', *Survey Methodology Bulletin*, The National Food Survey OPCS. London: HMSO.

Gubrium, J.E. and Holstein, J.A. (1995) 'Biographical Work and New Ethnography', in R.E. Josselon and A. Lieblich (eds), *Interpreting Experience: The Narrative Study of Lives*. Thousand Oaks, CA: Sage.

Hakim, C. (2008) (2nd edn) *Research Design: Successful Designs for Social Economic Research*. London: Routledge.

Harding, S. (2003) *The Feminist Standpoint Theory Reader*. London: Routledge.

Hart, C. (2000) *Doing a Literature Review: Releasing the Social Science Imagination*. London: Sage.

Heater, D. (2006) *Citizenship: The Civic Ideal in World History, Politics and Education*. Manchester: Manchester University Press.

Heath, S. (2008) *Dissertation Handbook, for Current Second Year SSP Students: Spring 2008*. Division of Sociology and Social Policy, School of Social Sciences, University of Southampton.

Hennermann, E., Lee, J. and Cohen, J. (1995), 'Collaboration: A Concept Analysis', *Journal of Advanced Nursing*, 21: 103–9.

Hinton, P. (2004) *Statistics Explained: A Guide for Social Science Students*, (2nd edn), London: Routledge.

Holliday, R. (2004) 'Reflecting the Self', in *Picturing the Social Landscape: Visual Methods and the Sociological Imagination*, ed. C. Knowles and P. Sweetman. London: Routledge.

Hoskins, J. (1998) *Biographical Objects: How Things Tell The Stories of People's Lives*. London: Routledge.

Huberman, A.M. and Miles, M.B. (1994) 'Data Management and Analysis Methods', in N.K. Denzin and Y.S. Lincoln (eds), *Handbook of Qualitative Research*. Thousand Oaks, California: Sage.

Hudson, B. (1999) 'Primary Health Care and Social Care: Working Across Professional Boundaries, Pt.1: The changing context of inter-professional relationships', *Managing Community Care* 7 (1): 15–22.

Jacobs, L. (1979) *The Documentary Tradition*. London: W.W. Norton.

Jones-Devitt, S. and Smith, L. (2007) *Critical Thinking in Health and Social Care*. London: Sage.

Keen, A. (2007) *The Cult of the Amateur: How Today's Internet is Killing Our Culture and Assaulting Our Economy*. London and Boston: Nicholas Brealey Publishing.

Kennett, P. (2001) *Comparative Social Policy: Theory and Research*. Buckingham: Open University Press.

Kenyon, E. and Hawker, S. (2000) '"Once Would be Enough": Some Reflections on the Issue of Safety for Lone Researchers', *International Journal of Social Research Methodology* (2)4: 313–327.

Kern, S. (1983) *The Culture of Time and Space 1880–1918*. Cambridge, MA: Harvard University Press.

King, G. (2005) *Collins Good Writing Guide*, Oxford: Collins.

Kuhn, T.S. (1996) *The Structure of Scientific Revolutions*. Chicago: Chicago University Press.

Ledwith, M. (2007) *Community Development: A Critical Approach*. Bristol: Policy Press.

Leftwich, A. (2004) *What is Politics? The Activity and its Study*. Cambridge: Polity Press.

Letherby, G. (2003) *Feminist Research in Theory and Practice*. Maidenhead: Open University Press.

Levin, P. (2005) *Excellent Dissertations!* Maidenhead: Open University.

Leonard, M. (2006) 'Teenagers Telling Sectarian Stories'. *Sociology* 40 (6): 1117–1133.

Lewis, G.H. and Lewis, J.F. (1980) 'The Dog in the Night-time: Negative Evidence in Social Research'. *British Journal of Sociology*, 31: 544–58.

Lewis, O. (1961) *Children of Sanchez: Autobiography of a Mexican Family*. New York: Random House.

Lim, H-C. 'Towards a More Democratic and Just Society: An Experience of a Sociologist from Korea', in M. Deflem (ed.), *Sociologists in a Global Age: Biographical Perspectives*. Aldershot: Ashgate.

Malin, N., Wilmot, S. and Manthorpe, J. (2002) *Key Concepts and Debates in Health and Social Policy*. Maidenhead: Open University Press.

Marsh, D. and Stoker, G. (2002) *Theories and Methods in Political Science*. London: Palgrave Macmillan.

Merton, R.K., Fiske, M. and Kendall, P.L. (1956/1990) (2nd edn) *The Focused Interview: A Manual of Problems and Procedures*. New York: The Free Press.

Milgram, S. and Bruner, J. (2005) *Obedience to Authority: An Experimental View*. Pinter & Martin.

Miller, R. (2000) *Researching Life Stories and Family Histories*. London: Sage.

Mills, C.W. [1959] (1970) *The Sociological Imagination*. Harmondsworth: Penguin.

Molyneux, J. (2001) 'Interprofessional Teamworking: What Makes Teams Work Well?', *Journal of Interprofessional Care,* 15 (1): 29–35.

Murdock, G., Hartmann, P. and Gray, P. (1995) 'Contextualizing Home Computing: Resources and Practices', in *Information Technology and Society: A Reader*. London: Sage.

Neilson, J.M. (1990) *Feminist Research Methods: Exemplary Readings in the Social Sciences*. Boulder, Colorado: Westview Press.

Okasha, S. (2002) *Philosophy of Science: A Very Short Introduction*. Oxford: Oxford University Press.

Oshima, A. and Hoque, A. (2005) *Writing Academic English*. London: Pearson.

Pampel, F.C. (2000) *Sociological Lives and Ideas: An Introduction to the Classical Theorists*. London: Palgrave Macmillan.

Parker, T. (1996) *Studs Terkel: A Life in Words*. New York: Henry Holt & Co.

Pember-Reeves, M. (1990) *Round About A Pound A Week*. London: Virago Press.

Phelan, P. and Reynolds, P. (1995) *Argument and Evidence: Critical Thinking for the Social Sciences*. London: Routledge.

Pirsig, R.M. (1999) *Zen and the Art of Motorcycle Maintenance* (25th anniversary edn). London: Vintage.

Plummer, K. (2001) *Documents of Life: An Invitation to Critical Humanism*. London: Sage.

Popper, K. R. (2002) *The Open Society and Its Enemies*. London: Routledge.

Prosser, J. (2006) 'Researching with Visual Images: Some Guidance Notes and a Glossary for Beginners', ESRC National Centre for Research Methods (NCRM) Working Paper Series 06/06 NCRM: Leeds University.

Prosser, J. with Schratz, D. (2006) 'Photographs within the Sociological Research Process', in D. Hamilton (ed.), *Visual Research Methods*. Sage: London.

Punch, K.F. (2005) (2nd edn) *Introduction to Social Research: Quantitative and Qualitative Approaches*. London: Sage.

Question Bank, University of Surrey (http://qb.soc.surrey.ac.uk/)

Race, P. (2003) *How To Get A Good Degree: Making the Most of Your Time at University*. Buckingham: Open University.

Ramazanoglu, V. and Holland, J. (2002) *Feminist Methodology: Challenges and Choices*. London: Sage.

Roberts, H. [1971] (1997) *Doing Feminist Research*. London: Routledge.

Robson, C. (2002) *Real World Research*. Oxford: Blackwell.

Rose, G. (2001) *Visual Methodologies*. London: Sage.

Rudestam, K.E. and Newton, R.R. (2001) *Surviving Your Dissertation: A Comprehensive Guide to Content and Process*. London: Sage.

Sayer, A. (2000) *Realism and Social Science*. London: Sage.

Sedgwick, E.K. (2007) *The Epistemology of the Closet*. University of California Press.

Seely, J. (2005) *Oxford Guide to Effective Writing and Speaking*. Oxford: Oxford University Press.

Shaw, C.R. (1966) *The Jack-Roller: A Delinquent Boy's Own Story*. Chicago: University of Chicago.

Silbergh, D.M. (2001) *Doing a Dissertation in Politics: A Student's Guide*. London: Routledge.

Silverman, D. (2000) *Doing Qualitative Research: A Practical Handbook*. London: Sage.

Skeggs, B. (1997) *Formations of Class and Gender*. London: Sage.

ONS (2008) *Social Trends 38*, London: HMSO.

Sontag, S. (1979) *On Photography*. Harmondsworth: Penguin.

Sorokin, P.A. and Berger, C.Q. (1938) *Time Budgets of Human Behaviour*. Cambridge, MA: Harvard University Press.

Spradley, J.P. (1979) *The Ethnographic Interview*. London: Holt, Rinehart & Winston.

Stanley, L. (1992) *The Auto/Biographical I: Theory and Practice of Feminist Auto/Biography*. Manchester: Manchester University Press.

Steedman, C. (1986) *Landscape for a Good Woman: A Story of Two Lives*. London: Virago.

Strauss, A. (1987) *Qualitative Analysis For Social Scientists*. New York: Cambridge University Press.

Sugarman, L. (2001) *Life-Span Development: Frameworks, Accounts and Strategies*. Hove: Psychology Press Ltd.

Tabachnick, B.G. and Fidell, L.S. (2001) *Using Multivariable Statistics* (4th edn) Boston, MA: Allyn & Bacon.

Tacq, J. (1998) *Multivariate Analysis Techniques in Social Science Research: From Problem to Analysis*. London: Sage.

Tashakkori, A. and Teddlie, C. (1998) *Mixed Methodology: Combining Qualitative and Quantitative Approaches*. London: Sage.

Taylor, D. (2008) *Module EDUC3805*, School Of Education, Faculty of Education, Social Sciences, and Law, Leeds: University of Leeds

Templeton, J.F. (1985) *Focus Groups: A Guide for Marketing and Advertising Professionals*. Chicago: Probus Publishing Co.

Terkel, S. (1970) *Hard Times: An Oral History of the Great Depression*. London: Allen Lane.

Thomas, V. *Real Problems? Real Research* (www.cse.psu.edu/~hurson/percom2007/PerCom07_Panel/VIC_PerCom07-panel.ppt March 2008).

Thomas, W.I. and Znaniecki, F. [1918–21] (1958) *The Polish Peasant in Europe and America*. New York: Dover Publications.

Thompson, P. (1978) *The Voice of the Past: Oral History*. Oxford: Oxford University Press.

Thrift, N. (2005) *Knowing Capitalism*. London: Sage.

Titmuss, R.M. (1950) *Problems of Social Policy*. London: HMSO.

Tomlinson, S. (2005) *Education in a Post-Welfare Society*. Maidenhead: McGraw Hill Education and Open University Press.

Tracy, B. (2004) *Eat That Frog! Get More of the Important Things Done, Today!* San Francisco: Berrett-Koehler Publications.

Vogt, W.P. (1999) *Dictionary of Statistics and Methodology: A Nontechnical Guide for the Social Sciences*. London: Sage.

Walliman, N. (2004) *Your Undergraduate Dissertation: The Essential Guide for Success*. London: Sage.

Welland, T. and Pugsley, L. (2002) *Ethical Dilemmas in Qualitative Research*. Aldershot: Ashgate.

Wengraf, T. and Chamberlayne, P. (2006) *Interviewing for Life Histories, Lived Situations and Personal Experience: The Biographic-Narrative-Interpretive Method (BNIM). Short Guide to BNIM Interviewing and Interpretation*. Available from tom@tomwengraf.com

Wilkinson, S. (1998) 'Focus Group Methodology: A Review', *International Journal of Social Research Methodology*. 1: 181–203.

Wilkinson, S. (1999) 'Focus Groups: A Feminist Methodology'. *Psychology of Women Quarterly* 23: 221–44.

White, A. (ed.) (2002) *Ethnicity*. London: Office for National Statistics.

Williams, M. (2000) *Science and Social Science: An Introduction*. London: Routledge.

Williams, J.P. (1947) 'The Present Status of Religion in Research', *The Journal Of Bible and Religion* XV (1): 3.

Wolcott, H.F. (2001) *Writing Up Qualitative Research*. London: Sage.

Index

Note: the letter 'b' after a page number refers to a box in the text; 'f' refers to a figure; 'tb' refers to a table; 'tk' refers to a task.